The

A L Y S O N

ALMANAC

A treasury of information for the gay and lesbian community

$t. Petersburg
Junior College

BOSTON • ALYSON PUBLICATIONS, INC.

Portraits of Elizabeth Cady Stanton and Bayard Taylor
reproduced from *The Dictionary of American Portraits*,
published by Dover Publications, Inc., in 1967.

Published as a trade paperback original by
Alyson Publications
40 Plympton Street
Boston, Massachusetts 02118.

Distributed in the U.K. by GMP Publishers,
PO Box 247, London, N17 9QR, England.

First U.S. edition: June, 1989

ISBN 0-932870-19-8

CONTENTS

ACKNOWLEDGMENTS

The Alyson Almanac is compiled by the staff of Alyson Publications. Past and present staff contributors to this edition were: Sasha Alyson, Joe Chapple, Wayne Curtis, Doug Dittman, Lori Freedman, Darryl Pilcher, and Tina Portillo.

Many other individuals and organizations provided advice, information, photographs, and help. In addition to those credited in specific chapters, we'd like to thank the following: David J. Coynik, M.D.; Eric Garber; Barbara Grier; Terry Helbing; Richard Labonte; Jim Morrow; ONE, Inc.; Jeff Pike; Peri Jude Radicic and the National Gay and Lesbian Task Force; Leigh Rutledge; and Vito Russo.

In preparing this book, we often referred to back issues of *The Advocate* and *The Washington Blade*. We benefited from their reporting, and recommend them to readers.

INTRODUCTION

The Alyson Almanac represents a new step for the gay and lesbian community. It's a reference book that's fun to read. You'll find these pages packed with facts about our past, as well as where we stand now.

The *Almanac* can be read in several different ways. Sometimes you'll refer to it for specific facts or advice. Is election day approaching? You can look up the voting record of the men and women who currently represent you. Are you looking for something to do tonight? Some experts on gay films, books, plays, and music have suggestions about the best and worst that those fields have to offer. Is it time you finally joined the National Gay and Lesbian Task Force? Their address and phone number are here — along with those of other national organizations and publications.

You'll also enjoy just browsing through the *Almanac*. At a time when AIDS, the Supreme Court, and anti-gay violence have many of us discouraged, it's important to keep a perspective on the overall progress that we're making. The chronology in the first chapter provides that perspective. It also calls attention to the deep roots of the modern gay movement.

As you browse, you may especially enjoy the short biographies at the end of the book. It's interesting to realize just how many of the people we learned about in school were involved in gay relationships — but that fact was left out of the curriculum.

• • •

This is the first edition of *The Alyson Almanac*. We plan for it to be a continually growing record of our community. Every year or two, we'll revise and expand it. Your suggestions, corrections, and additions are welcome; please enclose documentation (clippings or source references) when relevant and send to: The Alyson Almanac, Alyson Publications, 40 Plympton St., Boston, Mass. 02118. If you're the first person to send material that we incorporate into the next edition, we'll send you a free copy as soon as it's published.

HIGHLIGHTS OF OUR HISTORY

There's more to gay and lesbian history than you'll find in the history books. Here are a few highlights from the past that involved lesbians and gay men — or have affected us.

About 1900 B.C.: The cities of Sodom and Gomorrah, according to Chapter 19 of the Book of Genesis, are destroyed with fire and brimstone. Centuries later, this was interpreted by Philo of Alexandria, and then by religious writers, to have been an angry God's punishment for the homosexuality of the inhabitants.

That interpretation, although common, hinges on an unlikely translation of the ambiguous Hebrew word meaning "to know." The term is used 943 times in the Old Testament; only 15 of those times is it a euphemism for sexual activity. It seems probable that the story of Sodom and Gomorrah did not involve homosexuality at all.

594 B.C.: Solon is elected ruler of Athens, and is empowered to write a new code of law. He declared the death penalty for any unauthorized adult male who mingled in a schoolyard with boys below the age of puberty. Yet he apparently had no problem with relationships between adult men and post-pubescent youths; his own poetry includes such unmistakeably homoerotic lines as "Boys in the flower of their youth are loved."

580s B.C.: Sappho's famed girls' school flourishes on the isle of Lesbos. The exquisite love poems she wrote to her students are the earliest known lesbian writings.

About 393-387 B.C. Plato writes *The Symposium*, *Phaedrus*, and other works celebrating homosexual love.

About 371 B.C.: The Sacred Band of Thebes forms in Greece. This military unit, consisting of 150 male couples, was based on the belief that men fighting alongside their lovers would die together rather than shame one another. The Sacred Band was annihilated thirty-three years later by Phillip of Macedon and his son, Alexander the Great, at the Battle of Chaeronea.

About A.D. 60: Saint Paul writes several Biblical passages (especially Romans 1:26-27 and I Cor. 6-9) which have been used to support homophobia. However, as scholar John Boswell points out, the translations which lead to this interpretation probably do not reflect the real intent of the writer.

533: Byzantine emperor Justinian I, combining Roman law and Christian morality, decrees that homosexuality and blasphemy are equally to blame for famines, earthquakes, and pestilences; he orders castration for offenders.

About 650: The Cummean Penitential, a manual used by priests, provides them with guidelines for homosexual sin. The nature of the offense, and the age of the offender, were taken into account. "Simple kissing" by two males under the age of twenty called for six special fasts; kissing "with emission or embrace" called for ten special fasts. Mutual masturbation by men over twenty made the offenders liable to twenty days penance; for anal intercourse, the period jumped to seven years.

1073: All known copies of Sappho's lesbian love poems are burned by ecclesiastical authorities in Constantinople and Rome. As a consequence, today we have only one-twentieth of Sappho's total output, and even that exists only because of a freak archeological discovery in 1897.

1210-15: The Council of Paris declares sodomy to be a capital offense.

1252: St. Thomas Aquinas begins his theological teaching. Aquinas declared that God created the sex organs specifically and exclusively for reproduction; homosexual acts were thus "unnatural" and heretical. He was not the first to take such a stand, but because of his enormous influence within the church — continuing even today — Aquinas's statements did much to increase intolerance.

about 1260: The legal school of Orleans orders that women found guilty of lesbian acts have their clitoris removed for the first offense; that they be further mutilated for a second offense; and burned at the stake for a third.

1310: On October 12, King Philip the Fair of France orders the arrest of all French members of the Order of Templars. They were charged with heresy, sodomy, and being in league with the Moslems; many were tortured and executed. Philip benefited enormously from property confiscated as part of the arrests, and modern-day scholars still disagree about the accuracy of the allegations.

1450-53: Pope Nicholas empowers the Spanish Inquisition to investigate and punish homosexuality.

1513: Balboa, on his explorations of present-day Panama, reports that "the most abominal and unnatural lechery is practiced by the King's brother and many other younger men in women's apparel." He threw forty of the offenders to his dogs.

Balboa's observation of homosexuality was echoed by others throughout the rest of the century. In 1519 an anonymous conquistador reported that he found the Mayan people of Mexico to be "great sodomites"; a later European wrote back that everyone in the New World seemed to practice sodomy.

In reality, it appears that homosexuality was accepted by the Mayan civilization (centered chiefly in the Yucatan peninsula), which often portrayed anal intercourse between men in its art. Both male homosexuality and lesbianism were practiced, but not as accepted, by the more authoritarian cultures of the Aztecs and Incas. On occasion, these two civilizations are known to have punished such acts by death.

1553: The "buggery" law is passed in England, decreeing a penalty of death for "the detestable and abominable Vice of Buggery committed with mankind or beast." This marked the first time that the crime was covered under civil law in England; previously, it had been considered a church matter.

1583: The Third Provincial Council of Lima, in Peru, in promulgating Christianity to the native Indians there, tells them that "sodomy, whether with another man, or with a boy, or a beast . . . carries the death penalty, . . . and the reason God has allowed that you, the Indians, should be so afflicted and vexed by other nations is because of this vice that your ancestors had, and many of you still have."

1585: In one of the earliest recorded cases of masochism, Sister Mary Magdalene de Pazzi begs other nuns to tie her up and hurl hot wax at her. She also made a novice at the convent thrash her.

1610: The Virginia colony passes the New World's first anti-sodomy law, with a penalty of death for offenders.

In 1553, "buggery" became a capital offense in England. This illustration is from *The Life and Death of John Atherton,* published shortly after Bishop Atherton's execution for buggery in 1640.

1624: Richard Cornish is tried and, despite flimsy evidence, hanged for sodomy. He thus became the first known person in America to be convicted of this offense.

1641-42: The Massachusetts Bay Colony incorporated the language of Leviticus 20:13 into its laws: "If a man lyeth with mankinde, as he lyeth with a woman, both of them have committed abomination, they both shall be surely put to death." Other New England colonies soon followed suit.

1649: Mary Hammon and Goodwife Norman are charged with "lude behavior uppon a bed" in Plymouth, Massachusetts. The charges against Hammon were dropped, but Norman was convicted and had to make a public confession. She was the first woman in America known to be convicted of lesbian activity.

1655: The colony of New Haven expands its definition of sodomy — a capital offense — to include sexual relations between women.

1682: *Venus in the Cloister, or the Nun in her Smock,* is published in France, and created a scandal — it was about lesbian nuns. Unfortunately, the work seems to have been written to titillate male readers rather than to portray real life.

1730-31: Authorities announce that a major homosexual network has been discovered in Amsterdam. Three hundred prosecutions and seventy executions resulted.

1810: The mother of a schoolgirl accuses Marianne Woods and Jane Pirie, mistresses of a boarding school for girls, of "improper and criminal conduct" with each other. The British courts debated whether a sexual relationship between women was even possible. Lillian Hellman used this plot 120 years later as the basis for her play *The Children's Hour*.

1828: The English Parliament closes a loophole in the definition of the capital crime of buggery. It would no longer be necessary to demonstrate "the actual Emission of Seed" to convict someone of buggery or rape; "carnal Knowledge shall be deemed complete upon Proof of Penetration only."

Courtesy Tamiment Institute Library

Elizabeth Cady Stanton promulgated the idea that women could live independently of men.

1848: The first Women's Rights Convention, organized by Elizabeth Cady Stanton, passes a "Declaration of Sentiments and Resolutions," based on the Declaration of Independence. This convention is generally seen as the precursor of the modern feminist movement, and provided support and communication for many lesbian and bisexual women.

1860: Walt Whitman brings out the second edition of his *Leaves of Grass*, in which the homoeroticism of his poems is more evident than in the first edition, published several years earlier. The book provoked much public debate about Whitman's possible homosexuality, and inspired other gay poets in the years to come.

1861: England eliminates the death penalty for male homosexual acts; offenders are now subject to imprisonment for ten years to life. This change, however, reflected a rethinking of capital punishment more than a change of attitude about homosexuality. Since 1826, the British Parliament had reduced the number of capital crimes from some two hundred to only four.

1863: Karl Ulrichs writes two short pamphlets in German — *Vindex* and *Inclusa* — in which he attempts to present an unbiased and scientific explanation of homosexuality. He estimated that one German in 500 was homosexual. The pamphlets were published early in 1864.

1867: Karl Ulrichs, speaking to a conference of jurists in Munich, becomes the first known person in modern times to publicly declare himself a homosexual (although he used the term "Urning") and to speak out in favor of gay rights.

1869: In an anonymous pamphlet, Karl Maria Kertbeny urges the repeal of anti-gay laws. In this pamphlet, Kertbeny first introduced the term *homosexual*.

1870: The first American gay novel, *Joseph and His Friend*, is published. Written by the prominent poet Bayard Taylor, it is dedicated "to those who believe in the truth and tenderness of man's love for man, as of man's love for woman."

1891: John Addington Symonds's book *A Problem in Modern Ethics* is published, providing a systematic review of scholarly literature on homosexuality.

1895: Oscar Wilde is put on trial for "unnatural acts" committed with the young Lord Alfred Douglas. His trial caused a public sensation, and the playwright was condemned to two years'

Karl Heinrich Ulrichs, in 1867, became the first person in modern times to publicly declare himself homosexual.

hard labor. The ensuing anti-gay hysteria proved a serious setback for the nascent gay movement in England.

1896: The first known gay periodical, *Der Eigene,* is published in Germany.

— For the first time, two actresses on an American stage are seen to kiss one another. Immediately afterward, writes historian Kaier Curtin, ushers rushed down the aisles to offer ice water to any patron on the verge of fainting. The play, however, had nothing to do with lesbians; the plot focused around a young woman who magically changes into a young man.

1897: The Wissenschaftlich-humanitre Komitee (Scientific-Humanitarian Committee) is formed in Berlin by Dr. Magnus Hirschfeld and others. The Committee's main purpose was to decriminalize homosexuality by working for the removal of Paragraph 175, the infamous anti-gay statute of the German Penal Code of 1871. The effort was not successful, but the Committee did a

great deal of important work until the Nazis forced it to disband in 1933.

1906: Maximilian Harden, publisher of Berlin's *Die Zukunft*, publishes an editorial warning of the danger presented by the homosexual conspiracy. Homosexuals, he wrote, form "a comradeship . . . which brings together men of all creeds, states, and classes. These men are to be found everywhere, in the army and navy, in newspaper offices, behind teachers' desks, even in courtrooms." His editorial gives support to a public reaction against the growing gay movement.

1908: Edward Carpenter's *The Intermediate Sex* is published in England. In it, Carpenter idealizes the concepts of friendship, "comrade attachment," and homosexuality.

1909: Two black men are accused of oral sex with one another in Kentucky. They were not convicted because the judge couldn't find any law on the books under which to find them guilty. He urged that lawmakers remedy this problem, and soon many states had outlawed oral sex.

1912: The Scientific-Humanitarian Committee, which has been gaining influence since it was founded in 1897, polls candidates for the forthcoming Reichstag election to learn their views on gay issues. *Ninety-one out of ninety-six who respond indicate that they favor gay rights.*

1913: Alfred Redl, head of Austrian Intelligence, is exposed as a Russian double agent and as a homosexual. Redl shot himself after being arrested, and his widely-publicized case gave prominence to the idea that homosexuals are security risks.

1917: The new revolutionary government of the Soviet Union abolishes the anti-gay laws of the tsarist regime.

1919: Magnus Hirschfeld founds the Institute for Sexology in Berlin. In a huge palace in Berlin, which Hirschfeld had purchased, the Institute combined the world's first sex counseling center, a museum, and an ongoing series of educational events. The Institute devoted its work to the fields of civil rights for women and gay people, legalization of contraception and abortion, sex education, and confidential treatment of sexually-transmitted diseases. In the same year, Hirschfeld co-starred with Konrad Veidt in *Anders als die Andern (Different from the Others)*, the first known film to offer viewers a gay-positive perspective.

1920: Natalie Barney's *Pensées d'une amazone* is published. It was a collection of thoughts on homosexuality including references to Whitman, Ulrichs, Symonds, and Wilde.

1921: Marcel Proust's *Sodome et Gomorrhe* is published in France. Despite the book's stereotyped ideas, it contributed greatly to the demystification of homosexuality in France and elsewhere. The book was especially notable for its depiction of homosexuality as a social world, rather than just a few isolated individuals.

— The Theater des Eros, the first known gay theater company, is founded in Berlin.

1922: Despite protest from many, the Soviet Union re-introduces the concept of "crimes against nature" and begins the process (finished by Stalin in 1933) of recriminalizing homosexual acts.

— *The God of Vengeance*, a play by Sholom Asch which features a lesbian relationship, is produced in Provincetown. It was the first play on an American stage to depict gay or lesbian characters, and created an outcry the next year when it reached Broadway.

1924: Henry Gerber forms the Society for Human Rights, and incorporates it as a nonprofit corporation in the state of Illinois. This was the first known homosexual organization in the United

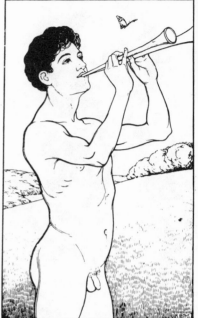

"Springtime," a drawing by Karl Konrad Poths, appeared in *Der Eigene* in 1905. *Der Eigene* began publishing in 1896, and for three decades it was the leading publication of the early gay movement.

States. It lasted only a few months before police forced it to dissolve.

— André Gide, in *If It Die,* makes his homosexuality public. He was the first major public figure in modern times to do so.

1928: Radclyffe Hall's *The Well of Loneliness* is published. Calling for the "merciful toleration" of "inverts," it became the best-known book in English with a lesbian theme. By breaking the silence surrounding the subject, it gave hope to many simply by depicting a relationship between two women.

1933: On January 30, the new Hitler regime bans the gay press in Germany. Five gay papers had their offices raided.

— On May 10, four days after Nazis raid Magnus Hirschfeld's Institute for Sexology in Berlin, an estimated twelve

Reproduced from *Eldorado*

In the late 1920s and early 1930, the German magazine *Die Freundin (The Girlfriend)* openly discussed lesbian issues. This drawing appeared in a 1932 issue.

thousand books, periodicals, and other documents from the Institute library are burned. Many irreplaceable items were lost, including unpublished manuscripts by Karl Heinrich Ulrichs and Krafft-Ebing. This burning marked the death of the early gay rights movement in Germany.

— The gay group Der Kreis, which would last for thirty-five years, is founded in Switzerland.

1934: Ernst Röhm and other Nazi leaders known or believed to be homosexual are murdered. Throughout the year, the anti-gay holocaust in Germany grew in intensity and the Nazis began rounding up gay people from German-occupied countries and sending them to concentration camps. In these camps, each persecuted minority was identified with a particular symbol.

For gay people, that symbol was an inverted pink triangle.

1935: The Nazis expand their anti-gay laws; kissing and embraces between men, and even gay fantasies, are criminalized.

1941-1945: The American involvement in World War II brings together millions of young men and young women in sex-segregated environments; many of them discover their gay feelings during the war. The dramatic growth of a gay consciousness in the decade following the war is a direct consequence.

1945: Bob Mizer founds the Athletic Model Guild in Los Angeles, which will become a leading source of erotic male photography — published, however, under the guise of "physique" and "physical culture" magazines.

1947: Lisa Ben (the pseudonym was an anagram of "lesbian") begins publishing *Vice-Versa*, the first U.S. lesbian magazine.

1948: The Kinsey Report is published. Sex researcher Alfred Kinsey found that 4% of the adult men he interviewed identified themselves as exclusively homosexual, another 13% were more than incidentally homosexual for at least three years after the age of sixteen, and 37% had had a homosexual experience in their adult lives. The fact that gay people were so numerous surprised nearly everyone, and offered hope to millions of closeted gays.

— Gore Vidal's novel *The City and the Pillar* is published. Although hardly the first American gay novel, it received more widespread attention than its predecessors, and marked the beginning of a post-war surge in gay writings.

1950: Androgynes Anonymous, which soon changes its name to The Mattachine Society, forms in Los Angeles in November. (The name Mattachine came from medieval French history, when it referred to jesters who always wore masks in public.) Its earliest organizers, Harry Hay, Chuck Rowland, and Bob Hull, had all been members of the Communist Party. They combined the politics and strategies of that group with the elaborate initiation rites and secrecy of the Masons. Although gay organizations existed in the U.S. as early as 1924, the Mattachines represent the beginning of today's organized gay movement.

— The McCarthy witch-hunt begins. A subcommittee of the U.S. House Committee on Un-American Activities reported that homosexuals are particularly subject to blackmail, emotionally unstable, and of weak "moral fiber." A purge of lesbians and gay men from the government and military followed.

1951: The group Arcadie is created in France. The goal of the group was to be a ministry to homosexuals suffering from oppression.

— In Los Angeles, Dorr Legg and others start Knights of the Clocks, an interracial gay social group.

1952: The founders of ONE, Inc., an early gay organization, hold their first meeting.

1953: ONE begins publishing the first openly gay magazine in the U.S.

— The Mattachine Society is split by political differences. At a conference held in May, newer members of the organization demand (and get) the resignation of the founders, and any other members who are affiliated with the Communist Party, threatening to turn their names over to the FBI otherwise. The de-politicized group virtually disappeared in the Los Angeles area, but gained new members elsewhere, especially in San Francisco.

1955: In January, the first issue of *The Mattachine Review* is published by the Mattachine Society.

— The Daughters of Bilitis is formed in San Francisco by Del Martin and Phyllis Lyon. It was the first national lesbian organization, combining educational and social goals; chapters of the DOB are still active today.

— In Boise, Idaho, a major anti-gay witch-hunt stirs up homophobia on a dramatic scale. Over a thousand men were questioned (in a city of only forty thousand); ultimately, nine were sentenced to prison terms of up to fifteen years each.

1956: The Church of ONE Brotherhood is founded in Los Angeles by Chuck Rowland. This was the first documented gay church; it lasted only a year.

— In San Francisco, the Daughters of Bilitis begins publishing *The Ladder*, a lesbian magazine.

1957: The British government publishes the Wolfenden Report, recommending the legalization of homosexual acts between consenting adults. The British Medical Association endorsed

The Ladder, which began publishing in 1956, promptly established itself as the leading lesbian publication in the U.S.

UNDER NO CIRCUMSTANCES DO THE EDITORS FORWARD LETTERS FROM READERS TO OTHER PERSONS NOR DO THEY ANSWER CORRESPONDENCE MAKING SUCH REQUESTS.

Dear ONE:
I did not like the story "A Place to Go" (December, 1958). It reads too much like too many of my own experiences. In the letters you print I note that every now and again some reader refers to ONE Confidential. What is it? I'd like to know more about it. (ONE Confidential is a monthly newsletter sent to the "Friends of ONE," or voting and non-voting Members of the Corporation—those who support the Corporation's work financially and in other ways. EDITOR.)

Have been interested in your comments about Police Chief Cleon Skousen. I heard that one of his "boys" had a very torrid date with a fellow in a bath house. Then donned his clothes and left. His partner did not know he was a policeman until he got dressed. The sad part is that this policeman would not hesitate to arrest his bed partner under different conditions, calling it "his duty."

Mr. W.
SALT LAKE CITY, UTAH

Dear Sir:
I have not forgotten ONE but I have been in jail. I had been arrested for attempting a "pick-up." When arrested I was threatened with bodily harm by the police, not allowed to contact a lawyer or to notify my parents. The judge was "lenient" however. As there had been no sexual contact I was sentenced to **only** 364 days. I had to agree to surrender my driver's license, agree not to even own a car, have psychiatrist's treatment for a "cure," and be on five year's probation. Even after I agreed to all that the judge backed down and wouldn't release me.

An interesting sidelight was that while in jail I was in solitary confinement. One of the prisoners who brought me food was a "voodoo murderer" who cut off a thirteen-year-old boy's head to make a love potion. Being homosexual I was, naturally, more dangerous. So, to protect the other prisoners I was kept in solitary for damn near four months.

You can bet that from now on I'll be one of your staunchest supporters. The "dark age" witch hunters scream loudly, but you have shown great courage in standing up for our rights. As soon as I can get back on my feet you can count on me.

Mr. H.
TRENTON, NEW JERSEY

Dear Sir:
I think that you are doing a terrific job of educating the public as to homosexuality. The colored people in the face of prejudice have gotten together to form a union (just as the United States itself once did) to fight this prejudice and they are defeating their enemies by getting laws passed. Why cannot all of the homosexuals do the same thing, form a union, collect funds and fight for legalization of this way of life—**so long as they do not use violence and both parties are willing participants?** All that it would take would be a few, good strong leaders to approach **the** Senators and Congressmen in Washington to sponsor such a bill. There is no reason to consider sex a crime, except our narrow-minded upbringing and training.

The only reason that I can see for homosexuality being scorned by the people is that the homosexual will not get up and fight for his ideas and beliefs. Until the colored people fought for their rights they got nowhere. The world is ready for a change but it will take funds and strong leadership to put it across. The great psychiatrists all agree that the sex laws are inadequate, having been written in olden times by superstitious, ill-informed people.

Another thing that I think should be done is to stop the harrassment of homosexuals by the police. If a policeman knows of a homosexual, or one who has been arrested for a homosexual act, what is to stop him from blackmailing him for life? You should also fight to have all previous arrest records for homosexual acts removed from the records and destroyed so that a man will not have to be exposed to public ridicule when he goes to apply for a job. I believe the questionnaires for jobs which ask, "Have you ever been arrested?" are against a man's civil rights, and leave him wide open for blackmail. It would be at least better to change the question to, "Were you ever **convicted** of a crime?"

Nothing is gained without fighting for it. You will run into prejudice, but follow the example of various unions, such as the labor unions. With a union you can get the voting power and by showing the homosexuals who have done great things, and by using the writings of modern psychiatrists I don't see how you can lose.

Mr. A.
UPPER DARBY,
PENNSYLVANIA

This page of letters from *One* magazine (May, 1959) gives a sense of the concerns and perspectives of that era.

the recommendation. Even the Catholic church, while emphasizing that it believed homosexuality to be a sin, recommended its decriminalization. A nationwide debate ensued. Three years later, a proposal to adopt these recommendations was defeated by a two-to-one margin in the House of Commons.

— In the U.S., the American Civil Liberties Union expresses disinterest in pursuing gay rights cases. The government was correct, the ACLU said, in classifying gays as security risks.

1961: Illinois becomes the first state to repeal its sodomy laws, effective January 1962.

— The first television special on homosexuality, titled "The Rejected," is aired by station KQED in San Francisco. Margaret Mead was among the guests.

— Jose Sarria runs for the position of San Francisco city supervisor. He is believed to be the first openly gay person to run for public office in the United States.

1962: A well-publicized study by Dr. Irving Bieber claims to analyze homosexuality scientifically, and concludes that it is caused in large part by seductive mothers and hostile fathers. This theory had been heard before, but only with Bieber's study did it gain widespread currency.

1964: The Society for Individual Rights (SIR) is founded by disgruntled members of an earlier gay organization, the League for Civil Education. By the end of the year, SIR had brought out the first issue of its magazine, *Vector*, and it soon became the leading gay advocacy group on the west coast.

1965: The State Department is picketed by the Daughters of Bilitis, the Mattachine Society, and other gay organizations, protesting its security policies. One of these organizations, ECHO, also held public demonstrations at the Civil Service Commission, the Penta-

gon, the White House, and at Independence Hall in Philadelphia calling for homosexual rights.

1966: Forty delegates from various local and regional groups meet in Kansas City to form a national organization, the North American Conference of Homophile Organizations (NACHO). NACHO was dissolved in 1970.

— Dick Leitsch, president of the Mattachine Society of New York, decides to challenge a New York state liquor regulation stating that any meeting of three or more homosexuals in a bar would be considered grounds for suspending the bar's license. Although Leitsch was ready to go to court over the issue, he never got a chance; as soon as the test case began, the New York Liquor Authority changed its policy, realizing that it would never hold up in court. Gay bars, at least in New York state, were legal.

— In San Francisco, radical street people form Vanguard, a new kind of gay-liberation group which brings anarcho-communist politics into the movement.

1967: Britain legalizes homosexual activity between consenting adults, except for those in the military and police forces.

— Robert A. Martin, a student at Columbia College in New York City, obtains a charter from the school for a Student Homophile League. It was the first such organization to appear on a college campus.

— In its first episode, on September 5, the television show *N.Y.P.D.* features a story about a blackmail ring that preys on gay people. According to gay activist and media historian Vito Russo, this was the first network program to portray gay characters.

— A CBS Special Report on "The Homosexual" also appears. Mike Wallace, as commentator, reported that "the average homosexual, if there be such, is promiscuous. He is not interested in,

HOMOSEXUALS (ARE) DIFFERENT...

but...

we believe they have the right to be. We believe that the civil rights and human dignity of homosexuals are as precious as those of any other citizen . . . we believe that the homosexual has the right to live, work and participate in a free society.

Mattachine defends the rights of homosexuals and tries to create a climate of understanding and acceptance.

WRITE OR CALL:
MATTACHINE SOCIETY INC.
OF NEW YORK

1133 Broadway, New York, N.Y. 10010   212 WA4-7743

A Mattachine Society ad from the early sixties. . . .

nor capable of, a lasting relationship, like that of a heterosexual marriage. His sex life, his love life, consists of a series of chance encounters at the clubs and bars he inhabits, and even on the streets."

— The American Civil Liberties Union, which had previously been unsympathetic to gay rights cases, calls for an end to anti-gay laws. In security cases, said the ACLU, the burden of proof should be on the government to prove that a gay employee was a security risk.

1968: Der Kreis, the Swiss group founded thirty-five years earlier, folds, and is replaced by the Swiss Organization of Homosexuals (also known as Club 68), with younger leaders. Many gay organizations, in the U.S. as well as Europe, were experiencing a shift toward a more radical leadership.

— The Metropolitan Community Church is founded. It soon became the leading gay church throughout the country.

1969: The Stonewall Rebellion reshapes the gay movement.

Early in the morning of June 28, a routine police raid on the Stonewall Bar at 53 Christopher Street, in New York City, turned into a riot when the patrons put up unexpected resistance. A group of uniformed policemen arrived at the bar about 3:00 a.m. They ordered customers to leave, then began arresting employees, as well as several drag queens. Although such arrests had often taken place without protest, this time the crowd began to react. They began chanting "Pigs!" at the police, then threw bottles. The police barricaded themselves inside the bar, which itself came under attack from the crowd. According to one observer, the riot was escalating and the trapped police were about to begin firing on the crowd when reinforcements arrived, and the group dispersed. Further riots continued, for the next several evenings.

The Stonewall Rebellion marks the beginning of the modern lesbian and gay movement. The homophile movement of the 1950s and 1960s, with its emphasis on social respectability, gave way to groups such as the Gay Liberation Front (a militant leftist organization begun in July) and the Gay Activists Alliance (a less militant group formed by activists who were put off by the GLF's alliance with often-homophobic leftist groups.)

1970: Rita Mae Brown and other lesbians are purged from the National Organization for Women. The following year, however, NOW acknowledged the "oppression of lesbians as a legitimate concern of feminism."

— In July, the Gay Liberation Front of the Tri-Cities (Albany, New York area) obtain what is believed to be the first telephone listing to contain the word "Gay."

— The country's first legislative hearing on gay rights is held in November at the New York Bar Association in New York. It was called by Assemblymen Franz Lichter, Tony Olivieri, and Steve Solarz.

1971: The first gay march on the Canadian Parliament takes place in Ottawa.

— The first statewide gay rights march in the U.S. is held in Albany, New York. Some 3,500 people marched on the state capitol.

1972: Jim Foster, of San Francisco, addresses the Democratic National Convention. He is the first openly gay person to address a national convention of a major political party.

— "That Certain Summer" airs on network television. This made-for-TV movie, about a boy who learns that his divorced father is gay, was the first television drama to focus on gay issues.

1974: The National Gay Task Force is formed in New York by Dr. Bruce Voeller. It soon became a leading force within the gay movement.

— Homosexuality is removed from the American Psychiatric Association's official diagnostic manual of mental disorders.

— The United States gets its first openly gay elected officials:

The first of them was Kathy Kozachenko. Running as a member of the Human Rights Party, she was elected in the spring to the Ann Arbor (Michigan) city council.

In November, Elaine Noble was elected to the Massachusetts state legislature, becoming the first openly gay person to win election to a state office. However, she was not the first such person to *hold* a state office; on December 9, encouraged by Noble's victory, Minnesota state senator Allan Spear publicly declared his homosexuality.

Leonard Matlovich's battle with the Air Force in 1975, which put him on the cover of *Time* magazine, shattered many popular stereotypes about gay men.

— An episode of *Marcus Welby, M.D.*, titled "The Outrage," portrays a high school teacher who sexually assaults and beats one of his students. Hearing in advance of the plot, the Gay Media Task Force in New York and Hollywood coordinated a major nationwide protest. ABC ran the show anyway, but some of its local affiliates refused to air it, and others allowed time for rebuttals by gay advocates. It was the first time the lesbian and gay community had exercised such power in responding to prejudicial coverage.

1975: Leonard Matlovich, discharged from the Air Force after he came out, appears on the cover of *Time* magazine. The cover story in that issue, combined with this image of a conservative flag-waving gay man, shattered many popular stereotypes of gay people.

— Ernest O. Reaugh is appointed by New York state senator Manfred Ohrenstein to act as liaison to the gay community. Reaugh, who still serves in that position, is believed to have been the first gay liaison appointed by any public official in the U.S. Today, hundreds of mayors, governors, and legislators have such positions.

1976: The San Francisco police department officially urges gay officers to come out. It was the first to do so.

1977: Midge Costanza, acting as community liaison in the new Jimmy Carter administration, receives the first official lesbian and gay delegation to the White House.

— Anti-gay singer Anita Bryant starts a highly emotional campaign to repeal a gay rights ordinance in Dade County, Florida. The campaign took on massive proportions, mobilizing both the gay community and anti-gay forces nationwide. The ordinance was repealed by a two-to-one margin.

— In New York, Ellen Barrett is ordained, becoming the first openly gay Episcopalian priest.

— Harvey Milk is elected to the San Francisco Board of Supervisors, the first openly gay city official in a major city. Milk was endorsed by the mainstream San Francisco *Chronicle*, but not by many local gay activists.

1978: The Civil Service Reform Act bars discrimination against gay people in the federal government's civilian positions.

— San Francisco mayor George Moscone and openly gay city supervisor Harvey Milk are assassinated by homophobic ex-cop Dan White. Milk thus became the first modern-day gay martyr.

1979: Stephen Lachs becomes the country's first openly gay judge when California governor Jerry Brown appoints him to to the State Superior Court. The next three openly gay judges appointed in the U.S. were also Brown's appointees.

— On October 14, an estimated 50,000 to 100,000 lesbians, gay men, and supporters show up for the first National March on Washington for Gay and Lesbian Rights. It was, up to that time, the largest such march ever held.

1980: The government of Holland, in an unusually strong official statement, informs the governments of Ireland and New Zealand that it considers their anti-gay laws to be unacceptable.

Aaron Fricke went to court in 1980 to be able to take a man to his high school prom.

— Rhode Island high school student takes a gay date to his high school prom. The school administration tried to stop him, but a court order forced the school to back down. The nationwide publicity that ensued provided moral support and a positive role model for hundreds of thousands of gay teenagers.

— Mel Boozer's name is put in nomination for the vice-presidency at the Democratic National Convention. He told the convention, "I know what it means to be called a nigger, and to be

called a faggot. The difference is none."
That convention also included some seventy-five openly gay delegates, the most of any such convention to date.

1981: On June 5, the Centers for Disease Control announces that five previously healthy gay men in Los Angeles have been diagnosed with pneumocystis carinii pneumonia (PCP), a rare disease that was previously unknown in people with healthy immune systems. This was the first official warning of what would become the AIDS epidemic. At first, the disease was known as GRID — Gay-Related Immunity Disorder.

— Mary Morgan, an appointee of California governor Jerry Brown, becomes the first openly lesbian judge in the U.S.

— In Strasbourg, after lobbying by the International Gay Association, the Council of Europe votes overwhelmingly to encourage member countries to pass gay civil rights legislation. Among their recommendations: Abolish laws against homosexual acts; ban job discrimination against gay people; eliminate discriminatory child-custody laws; and destroy police files on gays.

1982: Following a lengthy effort by Rep. David Clarenbach, Wisconsin becomes the first state to pass a wide-reaching gay rights law. Republican governor Lee S. Dreyfus, as he signed the bill into law on Feb. 25, expressed his belief in the "fundamental Republican principle" of restricted governmental involvement in the lives of citizens.

— The first international Gay Games are held in Kezar Stadium in San Francisco, with 1300 gay and lesbian athletes from 22 countries competing. The Games had originally been called the Gay Olympics, but a court suit brought by the U.S. Olympic Committee against the organizer, Dr. Tom Waddell, forced the change of name.

1983: Openly gay mayors take office in both Santa Cruz and Laguna Beach, California.

— Congressman Gerry Studds becomes the first politician elected to national office to openly and unapologetically state that he is gay. Studds had been charged by the House with making improper advances to a male page ten years earlier. Instead of blaming it on alcohol or calling it a temporary error, as politicians in similar situations had done in the past, he decided not to contest the charge. Instead, he talked openly about the difficulties of combining a closeted gay identity with a public life, and expressed relief at finally being out.

1984: Robert Ebersole, the town clerk of Lunenberg, Mass., comes out, and is easily re-elected. He was the country's first openly gay Republican elected official. Barney Frank, the congressman from Massachusetts who came out three years later, cited Ebersole's experience as a factor in his own coming out.

1985: The U.S. Supreme Court strikes down an Oklahoma law banning the favorable mention of homosexuality in schools as an unconstitutional interference with free speech.

1986: In June, the U.S. Supreme Court upholds the right of states to legislate against gay sex between consenting adults.

— A settlement is announced between the Pacific Bell and the National Gay Rights Advocates, in which Pacific Bell agrees to compensate individuals against whom it discriminated because they were gay. This closed a lawsuit which had begun eleven years earlier, when several gay job applicants had learned that they were turned down because the company policy discriminated against anyone who was openly gay. The settlement was expected to cost Pacific Bell some five million dollars, and was the largest single finan-

Between 200,000 and 600,000 marchers crowded into the national capital for the 1987 March on Washington.

cial settlement to date in the history of gay rights litigation.

1987: On January 14, station KRON in San Francisco becomes the first television station to agree to run condom ads. The major networks continued to refuse such advertising, explaining that such ads would be "intrusive to the moral and religious beliefs of many of our viewers," explained a CBS spokesman.

— In March, the AIDS Coalition to Unleash Power (ACT-UP) forms in New York. ACT-UP advocated a more confrontational style than what many AIDS activists had taken, and similar groups soon formed in other cities.

— In May, the Danish Parliament votes to ban discrimination against lesbians and gay men.

— Threatened with a gay boycott, Delta Airlines apologizes for past homophobia and announces that it will not discriminate against passengers with AIDS. The airline had come under fire in 1986 after its attorneys argued that the life of a gay passenger, who had been killed in a Delta crash, was worth less money than that of a heterosexual passenger, because the gay passenger might have had AIDS.

— On May 30, U.S. congressman Barney Frank comes out in an interview published in the Boston *Globe*. He explained that he did not feel his gayness was really relevant, but that to continue to skirt the issue would suggest that he felt it was something to hide. He was the first person elected to national office to come out strictly of his own choice.

Doug Hinckle/The Washington Blade

The Names Project Quilt displayed on The Mall was one of the most memorable aspects of the 1987 March on Washington.

— The New York *Times* finally decides the word "gay" is acceptable to use, as an adjective. Previous policy had forbidden use of the term except as part of an organization's name. "We're inching into the twentieth century," commented one *Times* employee.

— A U.S. Court of Appeals orders the Army to reinstate Miriam ben-Shalom. Eleven years earlier she had been discharged after stating that she was a lesbian. The verdict was legally binding only in the Eastern District of Wisconsin.

— On October 10 and 11, the largest gay and lesbian gathering of all time assembles in Washington, DC, to march for gay civil rights and to push for more action against AIDS. The crowd was variously estimated at 200,000 to 600,000 people.

The same weekend, the Names Project unveiled a giant quilt containing nearly two thousand panels, each commemorating a person who had died of AIDS.

Two days later, the largest civil disobedience action since the Vietnam war took place as six hundred demonstrators allowed themselves to be arrested on the steps of the Supreme Court, protesting the Court's upholding of state sodomy laws.

1988: The National Black Gay and Lesbian Conference in Los Angeles draws over four hundred participants, making it the largest such gathering ever. Organizers were successful in including mainstream black organizations, such as the Urban League and the National Association for the Advancement of

Colored People, in conference activities.

— Nearly two hundred gay and lesbian leaders meet at a first-of-its-kind "War Conference" to plan goals and strategies for the movement.

— The nation's first lesbian sorority makes the news. On February 24, the Los Angeles *Times* ran a prominent story about Lambda Delta Lambda, a lesbian sorority at UCLA. Soon the new sorority was getting attention on national network news, as well as *Saturday Night Live.* The goals of Lambda Delta Lambda, as stated in its constitution, are to "promote awareness of women's, minorities' and gay issues on campus and in the community."

A month later, the country's first gay fraternity received official recognition at the same school.

— On February 29, Svend Robinson becomes the first member of the Canadian Parliament to come out.

— In June, the president's commission on AIDS surprises observers with the tone of its final report. A year earlier, most AIDS activists had expected the commission to merely serve as a mouthpiece of administration policy. Instead, it urged the federal government to ban discrimination against people who are HIV positive, and to protect the confidentiality of HIV status information. But on August 2, when President Reagan announced his new strategies for fighting AIDS, he ignored most of the commission's recommendations.

— During the summer, the U.S. Public Health Service brochure *Understanding AIDS* is mailed to every household in the country. It was the first time the government had done such a massive mailing on a health issue. Most AIDS activists felt the brochure, while long overdue, proved useful in reducing AIDS hysteria.

— On September 12, 1988, the U.S. Army finally re-enlists Sergeant Miriam ben-Shalom after being held in contempt of court for refusing to do so earlier. She was the first openly gay person ever re-enlisted by the U.S. military.

For more reading:
We especially wish to acknowledge the following books, from which much of this chronology has been drawn:

Boswell, John. *Christianity, Social Tolerance, and Homosexuality.* Chicago: University of Chicago Press, 1980.

Bray, Alan. *Homosexuality in Renaissance England.* London: Gay Men's Press, 1982.

Curtin, Kaier. *"We Can Always Call Them Bulgarians".* Boston: Alyson Publications, 1987.

D'Emilio, John. *Sexual Politics, Sexual Communities.* Chicago: University of Chicago Press, 1983.

Faderman, Lillian. *Surpassing the Love of Men.* New York: William Morrow and Company, 1981.

Katz, Jonathan. *Gay American History.* New York: Avon, 1976.

Katz, Jonathan. *Gay/Lesbian Almanac.* New York: Harper & Row, 1983.

Kennedy, Hubert. *Ulrichs: The Life and Works of Karl Heinrich Ulrichs.* Boston: Alyson Publications, 1988.

Kepner, Jim. *Becoming a People.* Hollywood: The National Gay Archives, 1983.

Lauritsen, John, and David Thorstad. *The Early Homosexual Rights Movement (1864-1935).* New York: Times Change Press, 1974.

Martin, Del, and Phyllis Lyon. *Lesbian/Woman.* New York: Bantam Books, 1972.

Tannahill, Reay. *Sex in History.* New York: Stein and Day, 1980.

Weiss, Andrea, and Greta Schiller. *Before Stonewall.* Tallahassee: The Naiad Press, 1988.

LIFE BEFORE STONEWALL

The Stonewall Riots of 1969 are often seen as marking the start of the modern gay movement, and the decade that followed saw a dramatic rise in the number of gay books being published. But gay literature existed long before that, and some of the leading examples of it are briefly described here.

JOSEPH AND HIS FRIEND, by Bayard Taylor, 1870. Taylor was an eminent poet and leading writer of his time. In the 1850s, he wrote several poems with subtle gay themes, including "To a Persian Boy." His novel *Joseph and His Friend* tells the story of Joseph Asten, a young blue-eyed Pennsylvania farmer who feels different from those around him, and who worries that love must be "hidden as if it were a reproach; friendship watched, lest it express its warmth too frankly." But never is he clearly shown to engage in homosexual activity, and the occasional hints of Joseph's gay feelings are counterbalanced by a marriage and other heterosexual musing on Joseph's part. Like most other gay-themed novels published for the next hundred years, *Joseph and His Friend* has an unsatisfying ending, as Joseph marries the sister of the man with whom he has fallen in love. Nevertheless, it was a breakthrough as the first American novel known to portray gay characters.

NORMA TRIST, OR PURE CARBON: A Story of the Inversion of the Sexes, by Dr. John Wesley Carhart, 1895. This early novel featured a heroine, Norma Trist, who was physically and emotionally attracted to other women. The story, based on an actual event, is not a cheerful one — in a fit of anger, Norma murders a former female

Poet and author Bayard Taylor wrote the first American novel known to portray gay characters.

lover who is about to be married. The lesbian theme, however, is treated in a relatively positive light. Norma's lesbianism is presented as normal for her, and on the witness stand, she says that "My love for and relations with Marie afforded the highest and profoundest satisfaction of which the entire human being is capable in the realm of human love." This, says gay historian Jonathan Katz, is "probably the most explicit, unequivocating defense of genital-orgasmic relations between women published in English in the nineteenth century."

IMRE: A Memorandum, by Xavier Mayne, 1906. For its time, *Imre* presented a remarkably positive portrayal of homosexuality. Presented as a true memoir, it describes the narrator's love affair with a handsome, virile Hungarian lieutenant named Imre. Mayne (a pseudonym for Edward I. Stevenson) identified with the philosophy of Edward Carpenter, the British socialist who saw homosexuality as the supreme form of friendship, and his novel ends with the two protagonists living happily together. It did little good for the average gay person, however; the book was published in English, in Italy, in a limited edition of 125 copies.

BERTRAM COPE'S YEAR, by Henry Blake Fuller, 1919. Set in the 1870s and told through the eyes of narrator Basil Randolph, *Bertram Cope's Year* portrays three characters who seem to be homosexual. Basil himself is a middle-aged bachelor with clearly repressed homosexual feelings. He becomes attracted to Bertram Cope, a likeable young professor at the local college, and makes thinly veiled passes at Bertram. Bertram is also being pursued by Arthur Lemoyne, a more overtly gay character with "dark, limpid eyes," and fingers that "displayed certain graceful, slightly affected movements." Arthur is run out of town after trying to seduce another male student, and as the book draws to a close, Bertram also leaves town to join him. *Bertram Cope's Year* was turned down by the major publishers, and never achieved wide distribution.

DER PUPPENJUNGE, by John Henry Mackay, 1926. Mackay, a Scottish-born anarchist who lived in Berlin most of his life, was primarily attracted to teenaged boys. During the early 1900s, he devoted much of his energy to expounding the merits of man/boy love. In *Der Puppenjunge,* he depicted a young closeted gay man who finds himself irresistibly enamored with a street hustler he encounters in Berlin. The novel combines a poignant love story with a colorful portrayal of the gay subculture that thrived in Berlin during the 1920s. Mackay's depiction of the life

of a Berlin hustler is especially illuminating. In 1985, Hubert Kennedy translated the novel into English, and it was published for the first time in the United States under the title *The Hustler.*

THE WELL OF LONELINESS, by Radclyffe Hall, 1928. The best known novel before World War II to depict either a lesbian or gay male protagonist was certainly this one, brought out by a reputable publisher in London. The protagonist, Stephen Gordon, is a woman who was born to parents who fervently wanted a boy; everything from her name to her upbringing reflects that desire. By the age of eight she has already developed a passion for an adult woman. Further infatuations follow, eventually culminating in a love affair that might last except for the pressures of straight society. Hall was clearly familiar with the work of Ulrichs, who believed that both lesbians and gay men represented the soul of one sex trapped in the body of another. Her book, although depressing, served to tell lesbians of the time that they were not alone. For today's reader, however, Hall's characterization of a lesbian seems stale.

BETTER ANGEL, by Richard Meeker, 1933. The first American novel to combine a positive gay character and a happy ending was probably *Better Angel,* in which a young man struggles successfully to find love and contentment in the years between the wars.

The story behind *Better Angel* has an ending as happy as the novel itself. It was republished in 1987, with an introduction by Hubert Kennedy stating that the author had probably used a pseudonym and that "over a half century after the novel's original publication, we are unlikely to discover what became of Richard Meeker." But soon thereafter, an elderly man in Los Angeles came forth and identified himself as the

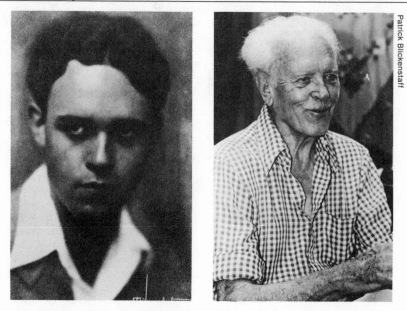

Patrick Blickenstaff

In 1933, Forman Brown (left) wrote the groundbreaking gay novel, *Better Angel*, and published it under the name Richard Meeker. Fifty-four years later (right), Brown saw a new edition of the book and identified himself as the author.

author of the pseudonymously-published novel. He and his lover and another gay friend — all of whom had provided the basis for characters in the book — had lived and traveled together for over sixty years. At the age of eighty-seven, Forman Brown finally received public credit for a pioneering work of gay fiction.

WE TOO ARE DRIFTING, by Gale Wilhelm, first English publication in 1935. Although better written than *The Well of Loneliness,* Gale Wilhelm's work never received the public attention shown to Hall's earlier novel. *We Too Are Drifting* tells the story of Jan Morale, a young artist with decidedly masculine traits. Morale becomes sexually involved with an older married woman, while falling in love with another: the young and innocent Victoria. She is reluctant, however, to initiate Victoria into a world that for her has caused so much pain, and the pressure for Vic-

toria to conform to her family's expectations prove too much for the relationship.

DIANA: A Strange Autobiography, by Diana Frederics, 1939. Published under a pseudonym, *Diana* purported to be a true autobiography and may actually have been so, but its often melodramatic tone suggests that the author took occasional liberties with the facts. The title character grows up surrounded by brothers and a father whom she loves. At the age of sixteen she falls in love with another schoolgirl, and is thoroughly frightened as she comes to realize the different nature of her sexuality. An older brother tries to help by introducing her to works of Havelock Ellis and Sigmund Freud, which portrayed homosexuality in a less judgmental light, but Diana is still troubled. The road to self-acceptance is not easy, but by the end of the novel Diana has met a woman with whom she can live in happiness, and the author has presented a strong case for the validity of lesbian love. This upbeat ending, unusual for its time, and the widespread distribution of *Diana,* made the book a godsend for thousands of women.

THE CITY AND THE PILLAR, by Gore Vidal, 1948. The first gay American novel to get wide public circulation was unexceptional as far as its content. While in high school, Jim Willard and Bob Ford go on a camping trip together, where an evening swim and wrestling match by a campfire lead to sex. The incident becomes etched into Jim's mind as a perfect moment, which he seeks throughout his life to recreate. Years later he re-encounters and tries to seduce Bob, who is now married; when Bob refuses his advances, Jim rapes him. In the 1940s, however, this ending wasn't sufficiently gloomy for the book's New York publisher, who had Vidal write a new ending in which Jim strangles Bob to death. Only in the 1965 edition was the original ending restored.

QUATREFOIL, by James Barr, 1950. The decade following World War II saw a dramatic increase in both the quality, and quantity, of gay novels. Among the best-written and most positive was James Barr's story of Phillip Froelich, a brash young naval officer who is just realizing his homosexuality, and the more experienced man who becomes his mentor and lover. An unwritten code dictated that gay novels written in this period should nearly always end with a death, and *Quatrefoil* is no exception, but

Barr went as far as he could within the constraints of his time. The death is an accident rather than a suicide or murder, and the overall tone of the book is positive and uplifting. Many men who grew up in the 1950s remember *Quatrefoil* as one of the two books (Fritz Peters's *Finistere* is the other) that provided their most positive early role models.

For more reading:

Two excellent sources of information about early gay literature are:

Austen, Roger, *Playing the Game.* New York: The Bobbs-Merrill Company, Inc., 1977.

Foster, Jeannette H., *Sex Variant Women in Literature.* Tallahassee: The Naiad Press, Inc., 1985.

THE BEST AND THE WORST

KATHERINE FORREST'S TEN BEST AND MANY WORST LESBIAN NOVELS

Katherine V. Forrest's novels include *Curious Wine, An Emergence of Green,* and *Daughters of a Coral Dawn.* Her articles and book reviews have appeared in a number of journals and newspapers. She is the fiction editor for Naiad Press.

THE BEST

OTHER WOMEN by Lisa Alther. Richly detailed portraits of a suicidal woman in desperate search of personal and sexual identity and the therapist determined to help her.

RUBYFRUIT JUNGLE by Rita Mae Brown. The joyful, irrepressible novel by the irrepressible Rita Mae, who showed us the meaning of gay pride before we had the words.

SINKING, STEALING by Jan Clausen. A strong and beautifully textured novel about a lesbian parent who defies the law to keep the child of her dead lover.

CHAMBER MUSIC by Doris Grumbach. A moving tone poem of a novel about a woman married to a famous composer, and her unfolding love for the tender, giving woman who nurses her dying husband.

PATIENCE AND SARAH by Isabel Miller. Everyone who reads this splendid, classic story of two country women in the nineteenth century forevermore lists it among her best loved novels.

THE PRICE OF SALT by Claire Morgan. The celebrated story of Carol and Therese, first published in 1952. This famous and literate novel was the first to endow our love with dignity.

MEMORY BOARD by Jane Rule. If a definition of true art is a work that alters the perception of the viewer, then *Memory Board* is true art. Tender and beautiful, it permanently alters the reader's perceptions of the nature of loving and commitment.

CONTRACT WITH THE WORLD by Jane Rule. A deeply intelligent, often stunning portrayal of seven people, four of them gay men and women, against the panorama of the larger world. A fireworks display of Rule's talent — the depth and range and power of the finest writer we have working today.

WE TOO ARE DRIFTING by Gale Wilhelm. **TORCHLIGHT TO VAL-HALLA** by Gale Wilhelm. The portrait of Jan Morale in *We Too Are Drifting* is indelible. These two luminous novels, published in the 1930s, tragically small oeuvre that they are, establish this writer's claim to greatness.

Editor's note: Had this list been compiled by anyone but Katherine Forrest, at least one of her own excellent novels would have been included here. We especially recommend the ever-popular *Curious Wine* and, perhaps her best book to date, *Murder at the Nightwood Bar.*

THE WORST

THE WELL OF LONELINESS by Radclyffe Hall. In its day an invaluable

Joe Doherty

Three of the best women's writers: Jane Rule (left), Isabel Miller (center), and Katherine V. Forrest (right).

contribution to our historical struggle for tolerance. But, unfortunately, the first novel that many, if not most, lesbians continue to discover as they grapple with emerging sexual identity. The despairing self-pity of this novel does nothing to ameliorate that initial sense of differentness and alienation.

Every lesbian novel ever written by a heterosexual man (such as *A Crown of Wild Myrtle* by H.E. Bates), most of them written in the fifties and sixties, many of them under female pseudonyms — novels which were male fantasies of lesbianism, murky imaginings of our lives and a sick indulgence in heterosexual male supremacy when lesbian characters inevitably turned heterosexual or committed suicide.

RICHARD LABONTE'S TEN BEST AND FIVE WORST GAY BOOKS

Richard Labonte is a former Canadian journalist. He became a bookseller in 1979 when he helped start A Different Light bookstore in Los Angeles. He writes about books and publishing for *The Advocate, In Touch,* and other periodicals.

THE BEST

A BOY'S OWN STORY by Edmund White. The coming-out novel will always be a staple of gay fiction: *Better Angel* by Richard Meeker (Forman Brown) was published in 1933, and is among the best of the genre. But White's 1982 work sets the standard with its sexy meditation on the yearnings, confusions, and satisfactions of reconciling the emotional, physical, and intellectual selves — and all before the young narrator heads to college.

THE CELLULOID CLOSET by Vito Russo. Most of the books listed here are fiction. Film scholar Russo's accomplishment, however, is different. He has taken film, the American art form with the most appeal, and has detailed with saucy insight the undeniable presence of gay life both on the screen and behind the scenes. No community survives long without a sense of its history: Russo's 1981 survey (revised in 1987) is an invaluable exposition of one more aspect of a too-often-hidden gay past.

CITY OF NIGHT by John Rechy. Back before there were gay bookstores, gay bestseller lists, or gay publishers, there were of course gay writers writing books about gay life. None seized America's shocked, astounded, or secretly thrilled imaginations as much as Rechy's 1963 first novel. A resonant depiction of pre-Stonewall sexual style, this book is part history and part sociology, and it is completely compelling in its raw honesty and unabashed lack of inhibition. There were youngmen then, there are youngmen now. Fiction is history, too.

FADEOUT by Joseph Hansen. Hansen, arguably one of the finest writers to consistently hit the top of gay bookstore bestseller lists, has done more than give good mystery in his ten-book (as of late 1988) Dave Brandstetter insurance-sleuth series; he's also satisfied the lust of readers for easy genre entertainment, with dry wit, intelligent style and, since the first book (1970), occasional attention to community politics. Better yet, he opened the way for the likes of Richard Stevenson, "Nathan Aldyne," and Michael Nava.

GAY SPIRIT, edited by Mark Thompson. Not many books kick-start the collective conscious of a community: this 1987 collection of many essays (Harry Hay, Edward Carpenter, Malcolm Boyd, Dennis Altman, Gerald Heard, Christopher Isherwood, Mitch Walker, et al.), their theme of spiritual essence linked by Thompson's elegant introductions, ranks as the major anthology of the 1980s, charting a future while exploring our past and confronting the present. It's a book from which many others will be spun.

IN HEAT by Larry Mitchell. Not all best books are obvious and some are too diffident for their own good. It's time, then, to spotlight a tale of falling in love and of growing old with grace, set in a New York of hypnotic hues, peopled with men honest enough to fret and chat about the fearsome gulf between sex and love. Mitchell's 1985 novel quietly captures the post-Stonewall, pre-AIDS world of pretty common gay guys, neither closeted nor, ahem, flamboyant, and does so with gracious, gorgeous writing.

THE MALE MUSE, edited by Ian Young. Culture is presence, culture is essence, culture is survival, and poetry is culture distilled. That's why Canadian poet Young's landmark 1973 anthology (see also *Son of the Male Muse*), while not the first and certainly not the last such collection, is a definite must on any discerning gay booklover's bookshelf. And, like any good pile of poetry, Young's choices have it all: coming out, falling in love, challenging norms, telling fictional tales, and exploring biographical fact.

ONE TEENAGER IN TEN, edited by Ann Heron. Honesty about self is the only way to fight homophobia; the first thing that haters deny is that children, if left to learn and grow without hate and prejudice and fear stunting them, may be gay women- and men-in-waiting. That's why this slim collection of young voices, a simple idea in itself, is among the most powerful political books of the decade. It gives form to the reality of gay generations and hope to every new generation of teenagers. Role models are rare, and they do make a difference.

A SINGLE MAN by Christopher Isherwood. Before the elegant snapshot of Andrew Holleran's *Dancer From the Dance,* or the slit-eyed reportage of Larry Kramer's *Faggots,* or the cultured romance of Mary Renault's *The Charioteers,* or the soap-opera aura of Marion Zimmer Bradley's *The Catch Trap,* there was this eloquent 1964 novel of the singular life of a gay man who had loved in his time. Each generation of gay writers crafts a masterpiece defined by its era. This one transcends.

Stephen Stewart

Lee Snider

Editor Ann Heron (left) and authors Mark Thompson (center) and Vito Russo (right) appear on Richard Labonte's list of the best gay books.

TALES OF THE CITY by Armistead Maupin. Five, eventually six, books in one — a sneaky way of inflating a ten best list, no? Maupin's decade-spanning account of life, friendship, laughter, love, and death started in the San Francisco of 1978 but has a generous universality to it, as characters deal with growing up and growing older. Best of all, they do so with wit through *Tales, More Tales, Further Tales, Babycakes, Significant Others,* and, says the author, one more volume to close off the decade.

THE WORST

THE CLOSET HANGING by Tony Fennelly. There is a danger in even the most well-meaning of straight women portraying the gay life. In this mystery set in New Orleans, the absorbing atmosphere and readable banter don't mask the fact that Fennelly's main character can't help but think he'd be better off if he were, well, more of a man. Who needs self-hatred masking as light entertainment? Not us.

THE FRONT RUNNER by Patricia Nell Warren. It's an eternal bestseller, nurturing the fevers and the fancies of thousands and thousands of pubescent boys and men. It's a book about a young homo athlete, hence a useful role model for the teen jock yearning to be himself. Why, then, is it one of my five worst? Because. Just because. It's the idiosyncratic flip side to my choice of *In Heat* as one of the best.

THE GREAT URGE DOWNWARD by Gordon Merrick. Only the self-loathing symbolism of the title makes this particular one of Merrick's too-many sucky romances stand out. Merrick's heroes, from *The Lord Won't Mind* to *Measure of Madness,* teach none too subtly that being gay is a horrible way to live a life. Warning: reading Merrick will be hazardous to your development as a well-rounded gay person.

THE SMILE OF EROS by John Coriolan. Because many men define themselves only by sex, a lot of gay writing is about sex. Some (for example, the work of Samuel Steward, aka Phil Andros, or the sexy collections of Boyd McDonald) is raunchy fun. Most is a feckless bore. And Coriolan sets a sad standard here, with too many dozens of references to "dangling manthings" and no apparent self-parody in sight.

Helen Shaver (left) and Patricia Charbonneau in the 1986 film, *Desert Hearts*, which Andrea Weiss calls "uncompromised in its representation of lesbians."

THE WORLD CAN BREAK YOUR HEART by Daniel Curzon. A boy is picked on by his snot-nosed peers, suffers miserable teen years, is ashamed of his sexual feelings, marries desperately, abandons his wife and kids, heads for Hollywood, finds no fame, fails again and again at love, rails against the world (it can break your heart, you know), and dies alone of AIDS. The author says it's reality, but it reads like a fundamentalist bigot's wet dream.

ANDREA WEISS'S TEN BEST AND FIVE WORST LESBIAN MOVIES

Andrea Weiss won an Emmy Award for her research for the television documentary *Before Stonewall*. With Greta Schiller, she produced and directed the films *International Sweethearts* and *Tiny and Ruby: Hell Divin' Women*. Her articles have appeared in *Ms., The Advocate, Cineaste,* and other journals.

THE BEST

MÄDCHEN IN UNIFORM (1931), directed by Leontine Sagan. West Germany. Distributed by Films, Inc. The recent emergence of lesbian independent cinema doesn't offer anything that can hold a candle to this classic story of a sensitive, defiant schoolgirl's passion for her teacher.

ENTRE NOUS (1984), directed by Diane Kurys. France. Although the jury is still out on whether this is a "lesbian film," the relationship between Madeleine (Miou-Miou) and Lena (Isabelle Huppert) is passionate, intellectual, dependable, and sensual, and provides the crucial tension which propels the film.

DAMNED IF YOU DON'T (1987), directed by Su Friedrich. United States. An experimental exploration of a nun's sexual desire which has been awakened by a beautiful stranger from outside of the convent.

I'VE HEARD THE MERMAIDS SINGING (1987), directed by Patricia Rozema. Canada. A funny, absurdist comedy about a "person Friday" in an art gallery who falls in love with her curator; weak on plot line but more than compensates by its resourcefulness and ingenuity.

QUEEN CHRISTINA (1933), directed by Rouben Mamoulian. Screenplay by Salka Viertal. United States. Never mind that Queen Christina falls in love with the Spanish ambassador in the snow. Greta Garbo as Queen Christina will always be remembered by lesbian viewers for her masculine attire, her refusal to marry, and her love for Countess Ebba.

DESERT HEARTS (1986), directed by Donna Deitch. United States. A great lesbian Western, this independently produced feature is conventional Hollywood in style but uncompromised in its representation of lesbians.

THE VIRGIN MACHINE (1988), directed by Monika Treut. West Germany. An ironic initiation of a young, naive West German researcher into the lesbian sexual underground of San Francisco, beautifully shot by cinematographer Elfi Mikesch.

DAUGHTERS OF DARKNESS (1970), directed by Harry Kumel. Belgium. Providing a feminist twist on the lesbian vampire genre, this film makes heterosexuality abnormal and violent, and offers a lesbian vampire (played by Delphine Seyrig) as its most sympathetic and likeable character. A "campy" lesbian classic.

17 ROOMS, OR WHAT DO LESBIANS DO IN BED? (1984), directed by Carolyn Sheldon. Great Britain. This ten-minute gem was banned from English television because the question it poses was considered too shocking, but it is the film's humorous answers which provide ironic commentary on voyeurism and lesbian sexuality.

THE GROUP (1966), directed by Sidney Lumet. United States. Based on the novel by Mary McCarthy. Perhaps the first Hollywood film to include an obviously lesbian character without exploitation and sensationalism. Candace Bergen plays the sophisticated, well-tailored Lakey who, when gay-baited, coolly and proudly proclaims her "Sapphism."

THE WORST

WAITING FOR THE MOON (1987), directed by Jill Godmillow. United States. Although this film is a portrait of the world's most famous lesbian couple, Gertrude Stein and Alice B. Toklas, it carefully avoids giving any sexual dimension to their lives or any intimacy to their interactions.

THE FOX (1968), directed by Mark Rydell. United States. The archetypal lesbian film in that it follows the bisexual triangle formula (man rescues woman from lesbian lover) and ends with the obligatory death of the lover as well. A straight man's wet dream.

MY TWO LOVES (1986), directed by Noel Black. ABC made-for-TV movie. United States. Written by Reginald Rose and Rita Mae Brown. Lynn Redgrave plays an aggressive, predatory lesbian, a la *The Killing of Sister George,* making her moves when her "prey," Mariette Hartley, is most vulnerable.

PERSONAL BEST (1982), directed by Robert Towne. United States. Lesbianism is an adolescent phase that Chris (Mariel Hemingway) passes through en route to a more mature relationship with a man. Three quotes: New York *Times*, "Undisguised voyeurism." New York *Daily News,* "According to this movie, lesbianism is something they catch in the locker room, like athlete's foot." Director's statement, "I like looking at [the athletes'] thighs. I adore them. I want to fuck the daylights out of them."

THE COLOR PURPLE (1985), directed by Steven Spielberg. United States. Spielberg isn't afraid of creatures from outer space, but a lesbian relationship is simply too threatening. His adaptation of Alice Walker's novel is classic Hollywood erasure of lesbian characters and themes (not to mention its objectionable treatment of race).

VITO RUSSO'S TEN BEST AND FIVE WORST GAY MOVIES

Vito Russo is the author of *The Celluloid Closet: Homosexuality in the Movies*. As a freelance journalist, he has had articles published in *Rolling Stone*, *The Advocate*, *The Village Voice*, and other national publications. He is a native New Yorker, and a co-founder of ACT-UP (AIDS Coalition to Unleash Power).

When listing the "best" of anything it is advisable to cite one's criteria for selection. Are we judging art or politics? Must the best gay films qualify as good cinema as well as good politics? Are the worst gay films those which are homophobic regardless of their value as art? As a rule I have chosen to list those films which I think have illuminated diverse aspects of the gay and lesbian experience in an exciting, personal, or unusual way. In doing so, I found that those listed among the best were generally good films and those on the worst list were usually not.

I have avoided obscure or inaccessible titles. Most of the films listed are available on videotape. Because of space limitations, I was forced to omit several worthy titles which came to mind or were suggested to me by friends. What remains is, I think, a valid primer for anyone wishing to sample the best and

the worst ways in which the twentieth century's most popular art form has reflected lesbians and gay men.

THE BEST

ABUSE (1983), directed by Arthur J. Bressan, Jr. The story of a gay independent filmmaker and his relationship with a battered teenager. A daring and powerful exploration of the issues of child abuse and intergenerational sex.

UN CHANT D'AMOUR (1947), directed by Jean Genet. An early homoerotic classic dealing with the repressed yearnings of an incarcerated passion.

MAURICE (1987), directed by James Ivory. A little too "Masterpiece Theatre" for some tastes, but an effective adaptation of the Forster novel which explores, perhaps for the first time onscreen, the fact that homosexuality is not a choice but a state of being.

MY BEAUTIFUL LAUNDRETTE (1986), directed by Stephen Frears. Pakistani playwright Hanif Kureishi's screenplay explores class, race, and sex in Thatcher's Britain. The central romantic relationship is quite incidentally — and charmingly — between two men.

PARTING GLANCES (1986), directed by Bill Sherwood. Superbly written, directed, and acted independent film about twenty-four hours in the lives of some gay New Yorkers in the age of AIDS.

SCORPIO RISING (1963), directed by Kenneth Anger. A dazzling array of images celebrating camp culture, homosexuality, and Little Peggy March.

SUNDAY BLOODY SUNDAY (1971), directed by John Schlesinger. Witty and literate original drama featuring a triangular relationship between Peter Finch, Murray Head, and Glenda Jackson. The first major film in which two men kissed onscreen.

Daniel Day-Lewis (left) and Gordon Warnecke (right) provided the romance in Stephen Frears' *My Beautiful Laundrette.*

TAXI ZUM KLO (1980), directed by Frank Ripploh. Intensely personal, funny, and controversial independent German film about the sexually promiscuous lifestyle of a high school teacher.

THE TIMES OF HARVEY MILK (1985), directed by Robert Epstein. Powerful, Oscar-winning documentary about the life of the San Francisco city supervisor who was assassinated along with Mayor George Moscone in 1977. Also won five Emmys and The New York Film Critics Award for best documentary.

VICTIM (1961), directed by Basil Dearden. Landmark blackmail thriller starring Dirk Bogarde as a London barrister who risks his marriage and career to change the laws which made homosexuality a criminal offense.

THE WORST

BUSTING (1974), directed by Peter Hyams. A slezoid look at the world of the vice squad with an emphasis on homosexual life in the ghetto.

CRUISING (1980), directed by William Friedkin. This murder mystery, based on Gerald Walker's homophobic novel, is set in New York's sex and S&M underground. Nasty, exploitative film which suggests that homosexuality can be acquired through contact.

PARTNERS (1982), directed by James Burrows. Ryan O'Neal and John Hurt, a straight and a gay police officer, pretend to live "as homosexuals" in order to trap a killer. Every neanderthal stereotype in the book.

THE SERGEANT (1968), directed by

John Flynn. Rod Steiger as the officer in love with handsome young John Philip Law. A textbook case of the tortured, self-hating homosexual who commits suicide after giving in to his unnatural desires. The film implicitly approves of suicide as a solution to homosexuality.

STAIRCASE (1969), directed by Stanley Donen. Relentlessly grim portrait of two bitter, aging homosexual barbers facing a crisis when one is arrested for soliciting. The film and the play upon which it is based blame their misery not on their problems but on their sexuality.

TERRY HELBING'S TEN BEST AND FIVE WORST GAY AND LESBIAN PLAYS

Terry Helbing has been active in gay theater in various capacities since he acted in the Boston and New England touring company of Jonathan Ned Katz's *Coming Out!* in 1973. He has worked as a producer, actor, and dramaturge for The Glines, was a co-founder and co-artistic director of Meridian Theatre, and was a co-founder of Gay Presses of New York. For the past seven years, he has been theater editor for the *New York Native*.

Read any critic's year-end ten best list, and you know how hard it is to restrict such a compilation to just ten selections. The staggering proliferation of gay theater in the twenty years since Stonewall (the focus here) makes that especially true of a ten best gay plays list. It seems logical to select works that are, first of all, excellent plays, but that also portray gays and lesbians with a positive, open attitude. Gay plays written before Stonewall were most often homophobic, largely because of the prevailing social climate which required that plays conform to popular morality. Some of the most homophobic plays are listed after my list of "best" plays.

Whole articles could be written on how to define a "gay" play, but for the purposes of this listing, I've chosen the straightforward definition of "having a major gay character or theme." This definition puts the emphasis on the play as literature, rather than as a production, and eliminates works that might be classified under the broader heading of "gay theatre," including the work of Charles Busch, the late Charles Ludlam, Ethyl Eichelberger, and the English troupe Bloolips. This list represents a very small sampling of the many worthwhile gay and lesbian plays of the past twenty years. It is therefore meant only to give a general idea of how gay men and lesbians have been depicted on the stage. Beyond that, I hope that it will arouse your interest enough to read other plays. My selections are listed in alphabetical order:

BEST

BENT by Martin Sherman. Not only does Sherman's play dramatize the little-known Nazi persecution of gays, but it also allows the two gay protagonists (who develop a relationship in a concentration camp and have orgasms while standing at attention and not touching each other) to demonstrate that "the joyous affirmation of the human spirit" is not strictly a heterosexual phenomenon.

COMING OUT! by Jonathan Ned Katz. Like his two gay history books that were published subsequently, Katz's play takes a documentary look at the history of gays and lesbians, with scenes about Walt Whitman, Willa Cather, Horatio Alger, female-to-male transvestism, and the early days of gay liberation. This truly cosexual play, performed with a cast of five women and five men, played in New York City in 1972, and a separate cast played and toured New England in 1973.

JERKER by Robert Chesley. Part of what might be called the "second generation" of gay playwrights, Chesley tackles the subject of AIDS from as distinctive and liberating a viewpoint as the city he calls home, San Francisco. Two men meet and develop a "buddy" relationship entirely through a series of telephone calls — "many of them dirty," as his subtitle indicates — without ever meeting face to face.

LAST SUMMER AT BLUEFISH COVE and **A LATE SNOW** by Jane Chambers. Frequently described as "the breakthrough lesbian play," *Bluefish Cove* is about a tightly knit group of women who spend their summers together in a resort community. For one, dying of a brain tumor, it is her last summer there. (The play had been written and produced before playwright Chambers died of a brain tumor in 1983.) *A Late Snow* concerns, in the playwright's own words, "five women snowbound in an isolated cabin: Ellie and her first, last, current and next lover." Both plays — along with the handful of other plays and novels she wrote — reflect Chambers's warmth, genuineness, and terrific sense of humor.

NIAGARA FALLS by Victor Bumbalo. In two one-act plays under this collective title, Bumbalo details how an upstate New York Italian-American family comes to terms with their son's gayness. In "American Coffee," the parents discuss their gay son without his ever appearing, while in "The Shangri-La Motor Inn," the parents' daughter's new married life is set to rights by an understanding gay man.

THE NORMAL HEART by Larry Kramer. As the tragic AIDS epidemic continues to worsen, there might soon be reason to compile a separate list of "Best AIDS Plays" that would include such moving efforts as William M. Hoffman's *As Is*. But screenwriter-novelist Kramer's play, detailing the onset of AIDS and the New York City gay community's activist response to it, is included here because it is among the rare works of political theater that are as effective theatrically as they are politically.

STREET THEATER by Doric Wilson. Wilson's play, set on Christopher Street the two hours before the Stonewall riots, concerns the drag queens, bull dykes, leathermen, and closet cases who came together that fateful "full-moon Friday night" in 1969. Like his other plays — *A Perfect Relationship* and *Forever After* — *Street Theater* is full of witty one-liners, clever farce, and characters so right that they are archetypes rather than stereotypes.

T-SHIRTS and **BLUE IS FOR BOYS** by Robert Patrick. Playwright Patrick has written hundreds of plays, many of them with gay characters or themes, and these are two of his best. The semi-autobiographical *T-Shirts* evokes as well as any play the state of urban gay male life in the late 1970s, while *Blue is for Boys,* set in a college dormitory, is as giddy and funny a contemporary sex farce as you could ever hope to find, gay or straight. Both plays reflect Patrick's fascination with language; his wordplay is as clever and complex as that of the best pundits and satirists.

THANKSGIVING by Loretta Lotman and **PATIENCE AND SARAH** by Isabel Miller. Both of these lesbian plays are classified in the "coming out" genre, of which there are many examples, but their superior writing distinguishes them from the rest. *Thanks-*

giving, the winner of the first Jane Chambers Memorial International Gay Playwriting Contest, feaures a pretty standard coming out situation — lesbian reveals she's gay to her family at a major holiday (in this case, Thanksgiving) — while Miller's adaptation of her popular novel concerns two nineteenth-century New England farm women who discover their love for one another, reveal it to their respective families, and go off to make a life together.

TORCH SONG TRILOGY by Harvey Fierstein. Fierstein's three full-length plays, *The International Stud, Fugue in a Nursery,* and *Widows and Children First!* — originally performed separately at La Mama ETC — won two Tony Awards for the author/star when performed on Broadway in a slightly abridged form under this collective title. The plays chronicle the life of ex-drag queen Arnold Beckoff, and in their own way espouse "traditional family values," but in a most nontraditional and tolerant kind of extended family.

WORST

Not surprisingly, most of these plays were written before Stonewall, when it seemed quite natural that the only logical conclusion for a play about a tortured faggot or dyke was for him or her to commit suicide. We've come a long way since then, but that doesn't mean that homophobic plays aren't still being written. Once again, the plays are listed in alphabetical order.

THE BOYS IN THE BAND by Mart Crowley. Some people might find it surprising that the very play that brought homosexuals to the attention of a wider theatrical audience is included on a list of homophobic plays. But with its self-loathing characters and its bitchy dialogue (one of the reasons why some people still like the

play so much), the play was already a dated period piece when it was first performed in 1968, and it's surprising that anyone is still bothering to produce it today.

THE CHILDREN'S HOUR by Lillian Hellman. A malicious child's false accusation of a lesbian relationship between two teachers is enough to make one of the women wonder if, indeed, it might be true and feel so guilty that she must, of course, commit suicide.

THE KILLING OF SISTER GEORGE by Frank Marcus. Marcus wallows in some of the worst stereotypes about lesbians as he presents Sister George, a character in a BBC soap, whom he portrays as a cigar-smoking, gin-drinking, hard-cursing bull dyke who makes her lover wait on her hand and foot. A truly disgusting portrayal of gay women.

THE KNIFE by David Hare. Joseph Papp's Public Theatre was virtually silent on the subject of gay men and lesbians for many years, but has more than made up for it lately with productions of Larry Kramer's *The Normal Heart,* Albert Innaurato's *Coming of Age in Soho,* Harry Kondoleon's *Zero Positive,* and other plays. But Papp also produced this 1987 work, which is more implicitly than explicitly homophobic. In this musical about a male-to-female transsexual sex change, Hare refuses to allow his "new woman" to have a lesbian relationship with "his" former girlfriend. Seemingly such a relationship is impossible because "s/he" no longer has the requisite equipment. In addition, the musical contains a number by a group of gay waiters in which, to quote one critic, they are portrayed as "simpering, disagreeable fags."

TEA AND SYMPATHY by Robert Anderson. At a boys' school, the head-

Terry Miller

In 1983 the Meridian Gay Theatre produced Jane Chambers's *A Late Snow*, which Terry Helbing describes as reflecting the playwright's "warmth, genuineness, and terrific sense of humor."

master's wife "sacrifices" her marital fidelity and sleeps with a boy who is constantly being called a sissy, thus assuring him of his manhood. In the world of this play, gayness and manhood could not possibly be synonymous! This is the play that contains the dreaded line, "When you remember this years from now, and you will, be kind."

ADAM BLOCK'S FIVE HOMO-NEGATIVE AND TEN PRO-HOMO POP SONGS

Adam Block is a widely published San Francisco-based journalist, a columnist for the San Francisco *Sentinel*, and the pop music editor for *The Advocate*.

Growing up, listening to the radio, I heard all kinds of wonder and weirdness, freedom and delight pumping out of the local rock station. But in thousands of doomed romances, one subject never came up; homos and lesbians simply didn't exist. Nearly thirty years later the subject still makes the pop scene squeamish. Gay singers long believed that honesty would spell commercial suicide. Most still do. That fear has generally left it up to heteros to address the subject . . . or to let it lie.

HOMO-NEGATIVE POP

Fact is that homophobic lyrics are a lot rarer than pop homophobia. Gays inspired by the songs of Donna Summer or Bob Marley would discover the artist's intolerant fundamentalism only from interviews. Fans of Neil Young and the Beastie Boys read their bigoted bile in magazines, not on lyric sheets. Metal morons like Sammy Hagar confined their queer-bashing to crowd-pleasing cracks in concert. The vinyl evidence is only the iceberg's tip.

MONEY FOR NOTHING and **LES BOYS** by Dire Straits. Songwriter Mark Knopfler insisted that the line "That little faggot has his own jet airplane" represented the voice of a blue-collar bigot with whom he had no sympathy. Anyone who had heard his earlier smug affront, "Les Boys," knew better.

THE MESSAGE by Grandmaster Flash & The Furious Five. This rap classic bit the bigot's hand, but took time out to level disdain on gays, sneering about a "fag hag" and evoking a prison rape that turns a man into that most horrible of all creatures: a limp-wristed queen.

MACHO MAN by The Village People. Originally a gay-concept-novelty (doing male drag to disco instead of female drag to showtunes, thereby portraying queers who would no longer live according to cherished stereotypes), crossover success sent the combo diving for their closets. With this song they celebrated the most moronic, narcissistic vision imaginable. Suddenly, the group became a eunuched family cartoon, neutering the spectre that had inspired them.

I LOVE WOMEN by Lou Reed. Of all the glitter gang, Reed was the only one to live openly with a male lover (even if it was a creature named Rachel), but this song marked his apostasy. It wasn't so much his marriage that galled — or the declaration, "I love women. I've always loved women" — but his insistence that "We all love women. We have always loved women." I figure Reed had the right to disown his own gay past, but I draw the line at his claim that the rest of us are simply deluding ourselves ... until the right woman comes along.

ON ANY OTHER DAY by The Police. Sting offered a litany of disasters: "My wife just burned the scrambled eggs, my daughter ran away, my son just said he's gay; it's been a terrible day." Later he would sing backup on the infamous "Money for Nothing," and release a film where his band slagged

homos. Some suggest that his tribute to the distinctly old-school homo Quentin Crisp, "An Englishman in New York," was calculated to clear his name.

PRO-HOMO POP

This list doesn't pretend to be definitive. Many will miss the noble, if little-heard, independents like Steve Grossman, Blackberri, Charlie Murphy, Tom Wilson, Romanovsky & Phillips, Michael Callen, or any of the women on Redwood or Olivia. And where are such gay pop wonders as Sylvester, Boy George, and Marc Almond? As for "Lola" by the Kinks, endlessly cited by critics as "everybody's favorite," I never thought that old-school-homo sing-along about a seduction by a drag queen had *anything* to do with gay lib.

REBEL REBEL and **QUEEN BITCH** by David Bowie. A bitch with a boner, a boy on a tear: scary, sexy declarations of possibility as shameless as squealing tires and as hungry as true love.

THIS CHARMING MAN and **DIAL A CLICHE** by The Smiths. The great fey loner Morrissey's grandiose misery is illuminated by savage wit and erotic visions find the elegant outsider repeatedly betrayed by rough trade and still coming back for more. Boys flock to the vegan-celibate Morrissey with the same fervor their big brothers brought to Bowie.

SWIM TEAM by Phranc. The brush-cut lesbian emerged from L.A.'s punk scene as a tough but disarming folksinger who "enjoys using the 'L' word." She won over young audiences when she opened for Husker Du and for The Smiths.

GLAD TO BE GAY and **THE WEDDING** by Tom Robinson. The first song, which he did with his band in 1978, was a black blast at gay apathy masquerading as an anthem. The second, a solo piece done nine years later, is a venomous, brilliant account of attending his boyfriend's wedding.

JOHNNY ARE YOU QUEER? by Josie Cotten. The Go Go's passed on this blast of pure pop which sweetly acknowledges that there *are* girls in high school who are confused by their gay boyfriends. Radical whimsy with a heart.

THE ALTAR BOY AND THE THIEF by Joan Baez. An astonishingly astute portrait of a 1970s gay bar, which climaxes with two youths dancing as Joan declares, "to me they will always remain: unclaimed, unchained, and unblamed — the altar boy and the thief — grabbing a little relief." Bravo.

SMALLTOWN BOY and **WHY?** by The Communards. This unglamorous trio laid down a propulsive disco rhythm as Jimi Sommerville's falsetto soared on. A tale of a gay boy kicked out of his home in the industrial north of England and a toe-tapper assaulting gay bashing and bigotry. The first gay socialist guerrillas to top the dance charts.

I AM WHAT I AM by Gloria Gaynor. The lady who cut "Never Can Say Goodbye" and "I Will Survive" takes the climactic number from *La Cage Aux Folles* to the dance floor, and makes the coming-out anthem an endless celebration.

GIMME, GIMME, GIMME (A Man After Midnight) by Erasure. Andy Bell, the U.K. duo's brazen gay vocalist, turns Abba's confection into a glistening carousel with rugged studs in the place of ponies.

CIRCLE JERK and **I WANNA FUCK YOUR DAD** by The Impotent Sea Snakes. The Tampa, Florida combo were on a tear when "13" wrote the lyrics to this unlikely LP. The music is generic speed/thrash, but the words are inspirational — like that of the boy so smitten with his girlfriend's pa that he rants, "I don't want your tits and cunt. Your fuckin' dad is all I want. I know your dad, he ain't no fool. He can't live without my love tool," and the paean to communal boy sex, which details a complex orgy, and then choruses, "Circle Jerk! Let's all: Circle Jerk! C'mon, c'mon and jack off with me. Whores cost money but friends are free!" are unparalleled in pop music's rocky relationship with queerdom.

NATIONAL ORGANIZATIONS

The organizations listed here operate on a national level. Some provide services directly to individuals; others to local groups. Organizations that did not return a brief questionnaire from us, and which could not be contacted by telephone, are not included.

When requesting more information from any of these organizations, we suggest you enclose a stamped, self-addressed, business-size envelope.

— AIDS-RELATED —

AIDS Action Council, 729 Eighth St. SE, Suite 200, Washington, DC 20003; (202) 293-2886.
Founded: 1983
Purpose: To work with the federal government to create a sound national AIDS policy, and lobby for funding of AIDS research and treatment.

AIDS Coalition to Unleash Power (ACT-UP), 496-A Hudson St., Suite G-4, New York, NY 10014; (212) 533-8888.
Founded: 1987
Purpose: A diverse, non-partisan group united in anger and committed to direct action to end the AIDS crisis.

American Foundation for AIDS Research (AmFAR), 40 W. 57th St., #406, New York, NY 10019; (212) 719-0033; or 5900 Wilshire Blvd., 2nd Floor, Los Angeles, CA 90036; (213) 857-5900.
Founded: 1985
Purpose: To provide funding for research into the cure, prevention, and treatment of AIDS, and to produce educational materials for the general public, medical and scientific professionals, and people with AIDS.

American Run for the End of AIDS, 2350 Broadway, New York, NY 10024; (212) 580-7668.
Founded: 1985
Purpose: To provide public education about AIDS and fundraising for AIDS service groups.

Community Research Initiative, 31 W. 26th St., New York, NY 10010; (212) 481-1050.
Founded: 1986
Purpose: To sponsor and run trials on new, and often alternative, AIDS drugs.

National Association of People With AIDS, 2025 Eye Street NW, #415, Washington, DC 20006; (202) 429-2856.
Founded: 1986
Purpose: To provide information and referrals to member organizations and to advocate for rights for people with AIDS.

National AIDS Network, 2033 M St. NW, #800, Washington, DC 20036; (202) 293-2437.
Founded: 1986
Purpose: To provide technical assistance, referral services, and grants to its member organizations, which include community-based AIDS organizations, hospitals, and educational facilities.

National Leadership Coalition on AIDS, 1150 17th Street NW, #202, Washington, DC 20036; (202) 429-0930.
Founded: 1987

Purpose: To increase public and private sector cooperation on AIDS issues. Works especially to improve the response of employers and employees to AIDS and to encourage balanced and informed consideration of public policies affected by the disease.

— BUSINESS/PROFESSIONAL —

Alliance for Gay and Lesbian Artists in the Entertainment Industry, PO Box 69A18, West Hollywood, CA 90069; (213) 273-7199.
Founded: 1979
Purpose: To ensure that the gay and lesbian community is accurately portrayed in film, television, and theater.

American Association of Physicians for Human Rights, 2940 16th Street, #105, San Francisco, CA 94103; (415) 255-4547.
Founded: 1980
Purpose: To provide an organization in which lesbian and gay physicians and medical students can find a source of professional and personal support and affiliation.

Association for Gay, Lesbian, and Bisexual Issues in Counseling, Box 216, Jenkintown, PA 19046.
Founded: 1975
Purpose: To educate those in the counseling profession about issues of lesbian, gay, and bisexual concern.

Association of Gay and Lesbian Psychiatrists, 1721 Addison Street, Philadelphia, PA 19146.
Founded: 1978
Purpose: A professional, educational, and social organization for psychiatrists who are gay or lesbian and/or who are involved in treating gay and lesbian patients.

Gay Task Force, American Library Association, 50 East Huron, Chicago, IL 60611.
Founded: 1970
Purpose: To put more and better gay material into libraries and to oppose discrimination against gay librarians and library patrons.

High Tech Gays, P.O. Box 6777, San Jose, CA 95150; (408) 993-3830.
Founded: 1982
Purpose: To increase awareness of the presence of gays in the high tech industry, and to provide support to members.

Lesbian, Gay, and Bisexual People in Medicine, 1890 Preston White Drive, Reston, VA 22091; (703) 620-6600.
Founded: 1976
Purpose: To give support to lesbian and gay medical students.

National Association of Lesbian and Gay Alcoholism Professionals, 204 West 20th Street, New York, NY 10011; (212) 713-5074.
Founded: 1979
Purpose: To create and sustain a support network for alcoholism professionals, and to advocate a non-homophobic treatment of chemically dependent lesbians and gay men.

— EDUCATIONAL —

Fund for Human Dignity, 666 Broadway, Suite 410, New York, NY 10012; (212) 529-1600.
Founded: 1974
Purpose: To administer and operate the National Gay & Lesbian Resource Center, the National Gay/Lesbian Crisisline/AIDS 800, and the Lesbians and Gays in the Arts Project.

National Federation of Parents and Friends of Gays, 8020 Eastern Ave. NW, Washington, DC 20012; (202) 726-3223.
Founded: 1979
Purpose: To provide educational materials to anyone searching for an improved understanding of issues surrounding human sexuality.

National Lesbian/Gay Health Foundation, 1638 R St. NW, #2, Washington, DC 20009; (202) 797-3708.
Founded: 1978
Purpose: To provide comprehensive information and service delivery models to the lesbian and gay community and to the American health care system.

—LEGAL AND POLITICAL—

ACLU Lesbian and Gay Rights Project, 132 W. 43rd St., New York, NY, 10036; (212) 944-9800.
Founded: 1986
Purpose: To defend the civil rights of lesbians and gay men.

Fairness Fund. The Fairness Fund was absorbed by the Human Rights Campaign Fund in March 1988.

Gay and Lesbian Advocates and Defenders, P.O. Box 218, Boston, MA 02112; (617) 426-1350.
Founded: 1978
Purpose: To provide litigation and education in support of gay and lesbian civil rights.

Gay and Lesbian Democrats of America, 114 15th St. NE, Washington, DC 20002; (202) 543-0298.
Founded: 1982
Purpose: A nationwide federation of local groups and activists working to involve lesbians and gay men in electoral politics. (Formerly called the National Association of Gay and Lesbian Democratic Clubs.)

Human Rights Campaign Fund, P.O. Box 1396, Washington, DC 20013; (202) 628-4160.
Founded: 1980
Purpose: To educate and elect congressional candidates who support lesbian and gay civil rights and full funding for AIDS research and treatment.

Lambda Legal Defense and Education Fund, 666 Broadway, New York, NY 10012; (212) 995-8585.
Founded: 1973
Purpose: To pursue litigation to counter discrimination against gay men and lesbians, as well as to organize educational programs to raise public awareness of gay legal rights.

Lesbian Mothers National Defense Fund, P.O. Box 21567, Seattle, WA 98111.
Founded: 1974
Purpose: To secure fair and equitable judgments in child custody and visitation disputes based on the best interests of the children and to completely eliminate the consideration of sexual preference in court decisions regarding custody and visitation.

Lesbian Rights Project, 1370 Mission St., 4th floor, San Francisco, CA 94103; (415) 621-0674.
Founded: 1977
Purpose: A public interest law firm dedicated to eradicating discrimination against lesbians and gay men.

National Association of Gay and Lesbian Democratic Clubs. This group is now known as Gay and Lesbian Democrats of America; see listing under that name.

National Gay and Lesbian Task Force, 1517 U St. NW, Washington, DC 20009; (202) 332-6483.
Founded: 1973
Purpose: A national gay rights organization working to create a society in which lesbians and gay men can live openly and free from violence, bigotry, and discrimination.

National Gay Rights Advocates, 540 Castro St., San Francisco, CA 94114; (415) 863-3624.
Founded: 1978
Purpose: A public interest law firm created to expand and defend gay civil rights.

—RELIGIOUS—

Affirmation: United Methodists for Lesbian and Gay Concerns, P.O. Box 1021, Evanston, IL 60204; (312) 475-0499.
Founded: 1976
Purpose: To eliminate homophobia, racism, classism, and sexism from the United Methodist Church and from society in general, and to be a support group for lesbians, gay men, and their friends.

Affirmation: Gay and Lesbian Mormons, P.O. Box 46022, Los Angeles, CA 90046; (213) 255-7251.
Founded: 1977
Purpose: To provide a social and support group for gay and lesbian Latter-Day Saints.

American Baptists Concerned, 870 Erie Street, Oakland, CA 94610; (415) 465-8652.
Founded: 1972
Purpose: To provide education and support for gay and lesbian members of the American Baptist Church, as well as to their friends and families.

Brethren/Mennonite Council for Lesbian and Gay Concerns (BMC), P.O. Box 65724, Washington, DC 20035; (202) 462-2595.
Founded: 1976
Purpose: To provide support for Brethren and Mennonite gays and lesbians, their families, and friends, and to provide accurate information about homosexuality to the churches.

Catholic Coalition for Gay Civil Rights, P.O. Box 1985, New York, NY 10159; (718) 629-2927.
Founded: 1978
Purpose: A national movement of Roman Catholic individuals and organizations who have publicly endorsed civil rights for homosexual people.

Center for Homophobia Education, P.O. Box 1985, New York, NY 10159.
Founded: 1988
Purpose: A resource group for seminars on the societal and ecclesiastical roots of homophobia and a strategy group for combatting homophobia in personal and institutional manifestations.

Conference for Catholic Lesbians, P.O. Box 436, Planetarium Station, New York, NY 10024; (718) 353-7323.
Founded: 1983
Purpose: An international organization for women who recognize the importance of the Catholic tradition in their lives, and who seek to develop a spiritual life which enhances and affirms their lesbian identity.

Dignity/USA, 1500 Massachusetts Ave. NW, #11, Washington, DC 20005; (202) 861-0017.
Founded: 1969
Purpose: To unite all gay and lesbian Catholics to develop leadership, and to be an instrument through which they might be heard by the Church as well as by society at large.

Friends for Lesbian and Gay Concerns, P.O. Box 222, Sumneytown, PA 18084.
Founded: 1972
Purpose: An organization for gay and lesbian Quakers and their friends, including those who would like to know more about Quakers.

New Ways Ministry, 4012 29th Street, Mt. Rainier, MD 20712; (301) 277-5674.
Founded: 1977
Purpose: To provide a ministry of advocacy and justice for lesbian/gay Catholics and the larger Christian community.

Presbyterians for Lesbian and Gay Concerns, c/o James Anderson, P.O. Box 38, New Brunswick, NJ 08903.
Founded: 1974
Purpose: To work toward the full

participation of lesbian and gay people in the Presbyterian Church.

Unitarian/Universalists for Lesbian and Gay Concerns, 25 Beacon Street, Boston, MA 02108; (617) 742-2100, ext. 522.
Founded: 1978
Purpose: To integrate and educate, and to make gay and lesbian influence felt in the Unitarian Universalist Church and in society at large.

United Church Coalition for Lesbian and Gay Concerns, 18 N. College Street, Athens, OH 45701; (614) 593-7301.
Founded: 1972
Purpose: To provide a special ministry to and to promote justice for lesbian, gay, and bisexual members of the United Church.

Universal Fellowship of Metropolitan Community Churches, 5300 Santa Monica Blvd., #304, Los Angeles, CA 90029; (213) 464-5100.
Founded: 1968
Purpose: An ecumenical religious denomination which welcomes all worshippers, with a special outreach to the gay and lesbian community.

— SPECIAL-INTEREST —

Federation of Parents and Friends of Lesbians and Gays, P.O. Box 27605, Washington, DC 20038; (202) 638-4200.
Founded: 1981
Purpose: To help parents and friends of gay men and women understand homosexuality.

Gay and Lesbian Parents Coalition International, PO Box 50360, Washington, DC 20004; (703) 548-3238.
Founded: 1976
Purpose: To provide support and social activities for members and their children.

Gay Married Men's Association, P.O. Box 28317, Washington, DC 20038; (703) 548-3238.
Founded: 1978
Purpose: A support group for men who have just come out to their wives, either intentionally or accidentally.

Gay Veterans Association, 346 Broadway, #814, New York, NY 10013; (212) 787-0329.
Founded: 1984
Purpose: To advocate for the civil rights of those presently in military service and for former members of military service.

International Advisory Council for Homosexual Men and Women in Alcoholics Anonymous, P.O. Box 90, Washington, DC 20044; (202) 544-1611.
Founded: 1981
Purpose: To provide experience, strength, and hope to any arm of AA when called upon to do so.

National Association of Black Lesbians and Gays, 19641 West Seven Mile, Detroit, MI 48219; (313) 537-0484.
Founded: 1978
Purpose: To help black gay men and lesbians in local organizing efforts, networking, and empowering one another.

National Gay Youth Network, P.O. Box 846, San Francisco, CA 94101.
Founded: 1979
Purpose: To provide a network of lesbian and gay youth and student groups throughout the United States and Canada.

Network of Gay and Lesbian Alumni/ae Associations, P.O. Box 15141, Washington, DC 20003.
Founded: 1985
Purpose: To serve as a clearinghouse for college lesbian and gay alumni organizations and to eliminate homophobia within universities.

NATIONAL AWARDS

AGLA MEDIA AWARDS

The Alliance for Gay and Lesbian Artists in the Entertainment Industry (AGLA) presents awards each year for the responsible portrayal of gay and lesbian characters and issues in the entertainment industry. In 1988, awards were presented for the following motion pictures, television programs, and Los Angeles area theatrical productions exhibited or broadcast during 1987:

The play *Bent*

The play *Burn This*

Celebration Theatre — 1987 Season

The short film *A Death in the Family*, as presented on PBS

The "Killing All the Right People" episode of *Designing Women*

The television show *Hooperman*, as presented on ABC

The film *Maurice*

The "One of the Girls" episode of *Nine to Five*

Not All Parents Are Straight, as presented on PBS

Bill Press
for his Eyewitness News commentary on the 1987 March on Washington

The film *Prick Up Your Ears*

Purple Stages, a celebration of gay and lesbian culture presented as part of the 1987 Fringe Festival in Los Angeles

The "Gay Married Couples" and the "I Was Beaten Up for Being Gay" episodes of the *Sally Jesse Raphael* show

St. Elsewhere, as presented on NBC

The Truth About Alex, as presented on HBO Family Playhouse

Too Little, Too Late, as presented on PBS

What If I'm Gay, as presented on CBS

The AGLA Special Award
was presented to Steven Bochco for his ongoing creation and achievement in promoting the responsible portrayal of gay and lesbian characters and issues on national prime-time network television.

The AGLA Humanitarian Award
was presented to Dr. Mathilde Krim for her achievement, dedication, and compassion in raising consciousness, protecting human rights, and preserving human life throughout the world.

NATIONAL BLACK GAY AND LESBIAN CONFERENCE AWARDS

At the National Black Gay and Lesbian Conference in Los Angeles, co-sponsored by local chapter of Black and White Men Together and by National Coalition of Black Lesbians and Gays, the following awards were presented:

James Baldwin Memorial Arts and Letters Award
to Audre Lorde

National Black Gay and Lesbian Conference Award
to The Kupona Network

Bayard Rustin Memorial Award
to Gil Gerald
for his work in the gay movement.

Frederick Garnett Memorial Award
to Dionne Warwick
for her fundraising work.

The Lambda Legal Defense and Education Fund staff with the 1988 Liberty Award recipients. From left: Honorees Judith Peabody and Karen Thompson, Nan D. Hunter, Honoree Perry Watkins, Tom Stoddard, Liz Smith, and Frederick A. O. Schwarz, Jr.

THE LIBERTY AWARD

The Lambda Legal Defense and Education Fund, Inc. presents its annual Liberty Award to individuals who have worked to uphold individual rights. In 1988, Lambda presented the award to the following three people, with these comments:

Karen Thompson, of Minneapolis, who has spent nearly five years urging the importance of legal agreements between lesbian or gay partners. Her own relationship was disrupted in 1983 after her partner, Sharon Kowalski, was severely brain-damaged in an automobile accident and Sharon's parents refused to acknowledge Karen's rights.

Perry Watkins, of Tacoma, Washington, who had served with distinction in the U.S. Army since 1969. In 1981, he was denied the opportunity to re-enlist solely because he is gay. A U.S. Circuit Court of Appeals in San Francisco recently ruled that the denial was unconstitutional.

Judy Peabody, whose work helping people

with AIDS has raised the visibility of volunteers across the nation, including New York City, where she lives, through her work with the Gay Men's Health Crisis, the PWA Coalition, and Lambda Legal Defense and Education Fund, among others.

NATIONAL GAY RIGHTS ADVOCATES

The National Gay Rights Advocates, the nation's leading public interest law firm promoting equality for gay men and women, honored four individuals at their tenth anniversary celebration in April 1988. Included here are summaries of NGRA's comments about each.

Lifetime Achievement Award
to Midge Costanza

Costanza made history when President Jimmy Carter appointed her Assistant to the President for Public Liaison; she was the first woman to hold that prestigious position. Costanza used that forum to work on behalf of a wide range of groups that had experienced limited access to the executive office in the past, including women, youth groups, senior citizens, veterans, gay men, lesbians, minorities, and the handicapped. Twenty months into her often stormy tenure, feeling that her ideas on human rights were no longer welcome in the White House, she submitted her highly publicized resignation to President Carter.

Lifetime Achievement Award
to Laurence Tribe

Tribe has taught at Harvard Law School since the age of 27. In 1977, *Time* magazine named him one of the country's ten best law professors. Tribe, who has repeatedly supported lesbian and gay civil rights, has been described by *The New Republic* as "the premier Supreme Court litigator of the decade."

Humanitarian Award
to Cleve Jones

One of the thousands of gay young people drawn to San Francisco in the early 1970s, Cleve Jones was befriended by pioneer gay rights activist Harvey Milk, who was elected to the San Francisco Board of Supervisors in 1977 as one of the first openly gay elected officials. In 1982, Jones helped establish the San Francisco AIDS Foundation, and in November of 1985, he conceived the idea of the AIDS Quilt, which was displayed on the Capitol Mall in Washington, D.C. on October 11, 1987. For his work with the quilt, ABC News named him "Person of the Week."

Posthumous Award
to Michael Bennett

Tony Award-winning Michael Bennett was the most influential director and choreographer of his generation in musical theater, rising to near mythic stature with *A Chorus Line.* The musical won a Pulitzer Prize and the New York Drama Critics Circle Award, as well as nine Tonys. It broke all Broadway records for number of performances.

ASSOCIATION OF GAY AND LESBIAN PSYCHIATRISTS

The Association of Gay and Lesbian Psychiatrists presents an annual award to an individual who has had a major impact on the treatment, care, or status of gays and lesbians. In past years it has been given to Representative Barney Frank; to Judd Marmor, one of the psychiatrists who pushed for the removal of homosexuality from the diagnostic manual listing pathological mental illnesses; and to Dr. Marmor's colleague John Spiegel.

In 1989, the award will go posthumously to Dr. Emory Hetrick. Dr. Hetrick was a member of the AGLP at its beginning and was active in the early gay movement. He was a practicing psychiatrist in New York for many years and co-founded the Institute for the Protection of Lesbian and Gay Youth, now known as the Hetrick-Martin Institute.

THE GAY AND LESBIAN PRESS ASSOCIATION

The Gay and Lesbian Press Association each year presents a number of awards to individuals, publications, and broadcasts. Publications honored in 1988 included *Frontiers* of Los Angeles, the San Francisco *Sentinel,* *The News* of Los Angeles, and *Guide to the Gay Northeast.* Individuals honored included Don Volk, for work in *Frontiers;* Tommi Avicolli, for work in *Philadelphia Gay News;* Jon Robbins, for work in *Frontiers;* Daniel Mangin, for work in the San Francisco *Sentinel;* Jane Rosett, for work in several publications; Garland Richard Kyle, for work in *Frontiers;* Victoria Brownworth, for work in the *Philadelphia Gay News;* and David France, for work in *The Advocate.*

THE NAMES PROJECT

Cleve Jones was devastated when his best friend died of AIDS in the fall of 1986. For months afterwards, he found himself on the edge of despair. The memory of his friend was so painful that he found it difficult to carry on in his everyday life. Then, one day Cleve and a friend spread fabric across his back patio and began painting names and designs with paint they had found in the garage. While doing so, they talked, laughed, and reminisced about the friends they had lost to AIDS. Cleve found the experience so therapeutic that he asked friends to join him in creating a giant quilt to commemorate those who had died of AIDS. Thus began The NAMES Project.

The NAMES Project has become a national AIDS memorial, taking the form of a huge quilt, made up of individual three-foot by six-foot panels, each bearing the name of a person lost to AIDS.

The Quilt was first displayed on the Capitol Mall in Washington, D.C., in October 1987. The memorial is an ongoing project, and panels continue to be added. As the toll on lives of men, women, and children rises, the Quilt is offered as a compassionate response to the epidemic.

The goals of the Quilt are:

•To illustrate the impact of the AIDS epidemic by showing the humanity behind the statistics;

•To provide a positive and creative means of expression for those whose lives have been touched by the epidemic; and

•To raise vital funds and encourage support for people with AIDS and their loved ones.

The NAMES Project is now taking these messages to every corner of America. Between April 8 and October 10, 1988, the Quilt was displayed in twenty cities, beginning in Los Angeles and ending in Washington. Hundreds of thousands of people have visited the Quilt, and hundreds of thousands of dollars have been raised for direct care services for people with AIDS. These funds remain in the local communities where the Quilt is displayed and are distributed through local AIDS organizations.

HOW TO CREATE A MEMORIAL PANEL:

1. Select a durable, lightweight fabric for the background. Cut and hem the fabric to 3' by 6'. (The NAMES Project staff will hem it for you if you leave three inches extra fabric on each side.)

2. Design the letters. Some suggestions:
• Appliqué: sew letter to background fabric
• Painting: brush letters on with paint, dye, or ink
• Stencil: spray paint cut-out letters
• Collage: glue on material with fabric glue
• Embroider: sew on beads, sequins, or rhinestones

3. When the panel is complete, write a one- or two-page description of the person you have memorialized. Enclose a photograph of the person if you're willing to part with it.

4. Wrap the panel securely before mailing it to: The NAMES Project, P.O. Box 14573, San Francisco, CA 94114.

5. Please include as generous a contribution as possible.

Have any questions? Call The NAMES Project at 415-863-5511.

NATIONAL HOTLINES

AIDS ACTION HOTLINE: (800) 257-4900; ask for operator 9184. Sponsored by the Human Rights Campaign Fund. This hotline was set up in 1987 to encourage constituent pressure on Congress. By phoning the hotline, you can have a fifty-word message about AIDS issues sent to the member of Congress you wish to reach; the charge of about $4.50 will be billed to your home telephone number.

FAIRNESS HOTLINE: (800) 257-4900; ask for operator 9188. Sponsored by the Human Rights Campaign Fund. By phoning this hotline, you can have a fifty-word message about gay and lesbian rights issues sent to the member of Congress you wish to reach; the charge of about $4.50 will be billed to your home telephone number.

NATIONAL AIDS HOTLINE: (800) 342-AIDS. Sponsored by the American Social Health Association. Operates twenty-four hours a day. Provides information about AIDS, and referrals to other groups, especially local AIDS organizations and hotlines.

NATIONAL GAY AND LESBIAN CRISISLINE: (800) 221-7044; in New York, Alaska, and Hawaii: (212) 529-1604. Weekdays 5 p.m. to 10 p.m.; Saturdays 1:00 p.m. to 5:00 p.m. (east coast time). Sponsored by the Fund for Human Dignity. Answers questions about all concerns related to the gay and lesbian community, including questions about AIDS.

STD NATIONAL HOTLINE: (800) 227-8922; in California: (800) 982-5883. Weekdays from 8 a.m. to 8 p.m., (west coast time). Sponsored by the American Social Health Association. Offers information about sexually-transmitted diseases, and referrals to doctors and public health services.

CELEBRATION '90: THE GAY GAMES

In the summer of 1990, one of the world's largest amateur sports events will take place in Vancouver, Canada, as thousands of lesbians and gay men come together for Celebration '90: Gay Games and Cultural Festival.

BACKGROUND: Dr. Tom Waddell first conceived of the idea of a "Gay Olympics" in 1980. When the event took place two years later, in San Francisco, it had caught the imagination of far more people than Waddell or anyone else had dreamed. Over 1300 athletes from 179 cities participated in 14 sports. The emphasis was on participating in sports with other gay people and doing one's personal best, rather than winning medals, and that emphasis has continued.

Roy Coe, A Sense of Pride

The Cambridge, Massachusetts Volleyball Team competing at Gay Games II in San Francisco, August 1986.

THE FOUNDER: In 1968, Dr. Tom Waddell represented the U.S. at the Olympic Games in Mexico City, placing sixth in the decathlon. During those games he also supported the American sprinters John Carlos and Tommie Smith when they gave a clenched-fist black power salute during the medal ceremonies. In doing so, Waddell incurred the enduring animosity of the U.S. Olympic Committee.

In 1980, Waddell began work on what was then called the Gay Olympics. "To do one's personal best is the ultimate of all human achievement," said Waddell, who participated in the 1982 and 1986 events. But only a month before the 1986 games opened in San Francisco, Waddell was diagnosed with AIDS; he died the following year. In honor of Waddell's achievements, the city of San Francisco held memorial services for him in the rotunda of City Hall.

THE NAME: Waddell originally called these events the "Gay Olympics." But the U.S. Olympic Committee, just two weeks before the 1982 Games were to open, obtained an injunction prohibiting the organizers from using the word "Olympics" in describing the events. The U.S.O.C. had allowed dozens of other groups, ranging from the Special Olympics and the Police Olympics to the Rat Olympics and the Eskimo Olympics, to use the word without facing such action, but the juxtaposition of "Gay" and "Olympics" was unacceptable to them.

The Olympic Committee also obtained a $96,000 lien against Waddell's house, to cover legal costs they might incur. (The lien was eventually withdrawn.) In 1987, after five years of legal battle, the U.S. Supreme Court passed down a five-to-four decision against Waddell and the Gay Games. A few weeks later, Waddell died.

THE 1986 GAMES: The 1986 Games had already grown considerably from 1982. San Francisco again sponsored them, as 3482 athletes from 259 cities participated in 17 sports. They were the largest international amateur sporting event held that year in North America.

THE 1990 GAMES: The 1990 Games are expected to grow even more dramatically. Some 10,000 people are expected to come to Vancouver for eight days of athletic competition and cultural activities, beginning Saturday, August 4. The organizers are emphasizing inclusiveness; gay and straight participants are all welcome. The official sports will include:

Badminton	Race walking
Basketball	Racquetball
Billiards	Soccer
Bowling	Softball
Croquet	Squash
Cycling	Swimming
Darts*	Tennis
Diving	Touch football
Equestrianism	Track and field
Golf	Triathlon
Hockey*	Water polo
Marathon	Wrestling
Martial arts	Volleyball
Physique	
Power lifting	* Exhibition events

TO PARTICIPATE: Sport registration will begin July 1, 1989. Housing and other information about participation is available from the planners in Vancouver. You can support Celebration '90 and stay informed of its progress with a $10 membership. Send $10 with your name and address to Celebration '90, 1170 Bute St., Vancouver, BC, Canada V6E 1Z6. The phone number for information is (604) 684-3303.

NATIONAL PUBLICATIONS

Compiled by Leigh Rutledge

THE ADVOCATE. Liberation Publications Inc. Executive Editor: Stuart Kellogg. Published twenty-six times a year. Editorial Offices: 6922 Hollywood Blvd., Tenth Floor, Los Angeles, CA 90028; (213) 871-1225. Subscriptions: P.O. Box 4371, Los Angeles, CA 90078. Newsstand price: $2.95. Subscription rate: $44.97 per year. Biweekly newsmagazine for gay men and lesbians, featuring national and regional news, book, film, theater, and music reviews, interviews, and large classified ads section.

ADVOCATE MEN. Liberation Publications Inc. Editor: Gerry Kroll. Published twelve times a year. Editorial Offices: 6922 Hollywood Blvd., Tenth Floor, Los Angeles, CA 90028; (213) 871-1225. Subscriptions: P.O. Box 4371, Los Angeles, CA 90078. Newsstand price: $5.95. Subscription rate: $54.00 per year. Monthly glossy magazine for gay men, featuring male nudes and erotic fiction.

BGM. Editor: Sidney Brinkley. Published four times a year. Editorial Correspondence and Subscriptions: P.O. Box 9391, Washington, DC 20005; (202) 232-5796. Single copy price: $5.95. Subscription rate: $23.80 per year. Quarterly periodical dealing with problems and issues of black gay men.

BOLT. Lifestyle International Communications Inc. Editor: Chad Martin. Published twelve times a year. Editorial Offices and Subscriptions: 2210 Wilshire Blvd., #610, Santa Monica, CA 90403; (800) 562-5497. Newsstand price: $4.95. Subscription rate: $45.00 per year. Monthly glossy magazine for gay men, featuring male nudes and erotic fiction.

CHRISTOPHER STREET. That New Magazine Inc. Editor: John Hammond. Published twelve times a year. Editorial Correspondence and Subscriptions: P.O. Box 1475, Church Street Station, New York, NY 10008; (212) 627-2120. Newsstand price: $3.00. Subscription rate: $27.00 per year. Monthly general interest magazine for gay men, featuring quality fiction, reviews, interviews, and nonfiction feature articles.

DRUMMER. Desmodus Inc. Editor: Anthony F. DeBlase. Published twelve times a year. Editorial Correspondence and Subscriptions: P.O. Box 11314, San Francisco, CA 94101; (415) 978-5377. Newsstand price: $4.95. Subscription rate: $50.00 per year third class bulk mail, $70.00 per year first class mail. Monthly magazine covering erotic aspects of leather, S/M, and other masculine fetishes for gay men; features erotic fiction, news of the leather community, some nudes, informational and how-to articles, and large classified ads section.

DUNGEONMASTER. Desmodus Inc. Editor: Anthony F. DeBlase. Published four times a year. Editorial Correspondence and Subscriptions: P.O. Box 11314, San Francisco, CA 94101; (415) 978-5377. Newsstand price: $4.95. Subscription rate: $18.00 per year third class bulk mail, $24.00 per year first class mail. Quarterly magazine covering gay male S/M, with emphasis on how-to articles exploring equipment for S/M scenes, safe bondage, and S/M techniques.

FIRST HAND. Firsthand Ltd. Editor: Lou Thomas. Published twelve times a year. Editorial Offices: 310 Cedar Lane, Teaneck, NJ 07666; (201) 836-9177. Subscriptions: P.O. Box 1314, Dept. B, Teaneck, New Jersey 07666. Newsstand price: $3.50. Subscription rate: $39.00 per year. Monthly magazine dealing with gay male sexuality and related issues, with emphasis on readers' letters describing personal sexual fantasies and experiences; some erotic fiction and short general interest articles and reviews.

FQ: FORESKIN QUARTERLY. Desmodus Inc. Editor: Anthony F. DeBlase. Published four times a year. Editorial Correspondence and Subscriptions: P.O. Box 11314, San Francisco, CA 94101; (415) 978-5377. Newsstand price: $3.50. Subscription rate: $15.00 per year third class bulk mail, $21.00 per year first class mail. Quarterly magazine devoted to all aspects of foreskin/circumcision; includes fiction, non-fiction, photographs.

FRICTION. Liberation Publications Inc. Editor: Gerry Kroll. Published twelve times a year. Editorial Offices: 6922 Hollywood Blvd., Tenth Floor, Los Angeles, CA 90028; (213) 871-1225. Subscriptions: P.O. Box 4371, Los Angeles, CA 90078. Newsstand price: $3.95. Subscription rate: $27.00 per year. Monthly magazine of gay erotic fiction, readers' letters describing personal sexual fantasies and experiences, some male nudes.

GAY COMMUNITY NEWS. Coordinating Editor: Marc Stein. Published forty-nine times a year. Editorial Offices and Subscriptions: 62 Berkeley Street, Boston, MA 02116; (617) 426-4469. Newsstand price: $1.00. Subscription rate: $33.00 per year. Weekly national newspaper with strong political focus for lesbians and gay men.

HONCHO. Mavety Media Group. Editor-in-Chief: Stan Leventhal. Published twelve times a year. Editorial Offices and Subscriptions: 462 Broadway, Fourth Floor, New York, NY 10013; (212) 966-8400. Newsstand price: $4.95. Subscription rate: $49.95 per year. Monthly glossy magazine devoted to male nudes and erotic fiction, with some emphasis on leather sex.

HONCHO OVERLOAD. Mavety Media Group. Editor: Jake Savage. Published nine times a year. Editorial Offices and Subscriptions: 462 Broadway, Fourth Floor, New York, NY 10013; (212) 966-8400. Newsstand price: $2.95. Subscription rate: $24.00 per year. Magazine for gay men, featuring erotic fiction, readers' letters and fantasies, black-and-white male nudes.

HOT/SHOTS. Sunshine Publishing Co. Editor-in-Chief: John Blanda. Published twelve times a year. Editorial Offices and Subscriptions: 6695 Convoy Court, San Diego, CA 92111; (619) 278-9086. Newsstand price: $3.50. Subscription rate: $29.95 per year. Monthly gay magazine featuring erotic fiction, extensive video reviews, some black-and-white male nudes.

IN TOUCH FOR MEN. In Touch Publications International Inc. Editor-in-Chief: Bob Stanford. Published twelve times a year. Editorial Offices and Subscriptions: 7216 Varna, North Hollywood, CA 91605; (818) 764-2288. Newsstand price: $4.95. Subscription rate: $43.50 per year. Monthly glossy magazine covering the gay male lifestyle, gay male humor, and erotica; features younger (18-21) male nudes, fiction, and non-fiction articles and reviews.

INCHES. Inches Inc. Editor: John W. Rowberry. Published twelve times a

year. Editorial Offices and Subscriptions: 1156 Howard Street, San Francisco, CA 94103; (415) 621-6069. Newsstand price: $4.95. Subscription rate: $39.95 per year. Monthly glossy magazine devoted to male nudes and erotic fiction, with emphasis on men with "large endowment."

JAMES WHITE REVIEW. Editors: David Lindahl and Greg Boeshans. Published four times a year. Editorial Correspondence and Subscriptions: P.O. Box 3356, Traffic Station, Minneapolis, MN 55403; (612) 291-2913. Single copy price: $2.50. Subscription rate: $10.00 per year. Gay men's literary quarterly featuring fiction, book criticism, and interviews.

JOCK. Klinger International Inc. Editor: Robert Leighton. Published twelve times a year. Editorial Offices and Subscriptions: 7715 Sunset Blvd., Second Floor, Los Angeles, CA 90046; (213) 850-5353. Newsstand price: $4.95. Subscription rate: $59.00 per year. Monthly glossy magazine devoted to male nudes, erotic fantasies, readers' letters describing true sexual adventures.

JOURNAL OF GAY/LESBIAN PSYCHOTHERAPY. Editor: Dr. David Scasta. Published four times a year. Editorial Correspondence: 1721 Addison Street, Philadelphia, PA 19146. Subscriptions: Journal of Gay/Lesbian Psychotherapy, c/o Haworth Press, 12 West 32nd Street, New York, NY 10001. Subscription rate: $36.00 per year for institutions, $24.00 per year for individuals. Professional journal covering gay and lesbian issues in psychotherapy.

JOURNAL OF HOMOSEXUALITY. Editor: Dr. John DeCecco. Published four to eight times a year. Editorial Correspondence: CERES, San Francisco State University, San Francisco, CA 94132; (415) 338-1137. Subscriptions: Journal of Homosexuality, c/o Haworth Press, 12 West 32nd Street, New York, NY 10001. Subscription rates: $32.00 per year for individuals, $90.00 per year for institutions, $132.00 per year for libraries. Research journal dealing with homosexuality in the social sciences, humanities, law, and religion.

LAMBDA RISING BOOK REPORT. Editor: Jane Troxell. Published six times a year. Editorial Correspondence and Subscriptions: 1625 Connecticut Ave., NW, Washington, DC 20009; (202) 462-6969. Newsstand price: $2.00. Subscription rate: $18.00 for twelve issues. Bimonthly newspaper featuring reviews of lesbian- and gay-themed books.

MANDATE. Mavety Media Group. Editor-in-Chief: Stan Leventhal. Published twelve times a year. Editorial Offices and Subscriptions: 462 Broadway, Fourth Floor, New York, NY 10013; (212) 966-8400. Newsstand price: $4.95. Subscription rate: $49.95 per year. Monthly glossy magazine devoted to male nudes and erotic fiction.

MANSCAPE 2. Firsthand Ltd. Editor: Lou Thomas. Published six times a year. Editorial Offices: 310 Cedar Lane, Teaneck, NJ 07666; (201) 836-9177. Subscriptions: P.O. Box 1314, Dept. B, Teaneck, NJ 07666. Newsstand price: $4.95. Subscription rate: $22.00 per year. Bimonthly magazine of male nudes, erotic fiction, and general interest features, with emphasis on gay male sexual fetishes and leather sex.

OBSESSIONS. Klinger International Inc. Editor: Kevin C. Watson. Published twelve times a year. Editorial Offices and Subscriptions: 7715 Sunset Blvd., Second Floor, Los Angeles, CA 90046; (213) 850-5353. Newsstand price: $4.95. Subscription rate: $59.00 per year. Monthly glossy magazine devoted to male nudes.

ON OUR BACKS. Editor: Susie Bright. Published four times a year. Editorial Offices and Subscriptions: 526 Castro Street, San Francisco, CA 94114; (415) 861-4723. Newsstand price: $5.00. Subscription rate: $19.00 per year. Quarterly magazine featuring "sexual entertainment for the adventurous lesbian."

OUT/LOOK. Managing Editor: Debra Chasnoff. Published four times a year. Editorial Correspondence and Subscriptions: P.O. Box 460430, San Francisco, CA 94146; (415) 626-7929. Newsstand price: $5.00. Subscription rate: $19.00 per year. National quarterly publication of lesbian and gay opinion, politics, and culture; features non-fiction, fiction, and poetry.

PLAYGUY. Mavety Media Group. Editor-in-Chief: Stan Leventhal. Published twelve times a year. Editorial Offices and Subscriptions: 462 Broadway, Fourth Floor, New York, NY 10013; (212) 966-8400. Newsstand price: $4.95. Subscription rate: $49.95 per year. Monthly glossy magazine for gay men, featuring younger (18-21) male nudes and erotic fiction.

STALLION. Mavety Media Group. Editor-in-Chief: Stan Leventhal. Published twelve times a year. Editorial Offices and Subscriptions: 462 Broadway, Fourth Floor, New York, NY 10013; (212) 966-8400. Newsstand price: $4.95. Subscription rate: $49.95 per year. Monthly glossy magazine devoted to male nudes and erotic fiction.

STUDFLIX: The Gay Video Magazine. Fan Magazines Inc. Editor: John W. Rowberry. Published six times a year. Editorial Offices and Subscriptions: 1156 Howard Street, San Francisco, CA 94103; (415) 621-6069. Newsstand price: $5.95. Subscription rate: $29.95 per year. Bimonthly glossy magazine featuring gay male erotic video reviews and previews, and male nudes.

SWAN. Patrick H. Colley Inc. Editor: Patrick H. Colley. Published six times a year. Editorial Offices and Subscriptions: 4864 Luna, #191, Phelan, CA 92371. Subscription rate: $26.00 per year. Bimonthly magazine "in praise of the older gay man," featuring non-fiction articles, erotic fiction, artwork, some photography, and personal ads section.

TORSO. Mavety Media Group. Editor-in-Chief: Stan Leventhal. Published twelve times a year. Editorial Offices and Subscriptions: 462 Broadway, Fourth Floor, New York, NY 10013; (212) 966-8400. Newsstand price: $4.95. Subscription rate: $49.95 per year. Monthly glossy magazine devoted to male nudes and erotic fiction.

UNCUT. Crete International Inc. Editor: John W. Rowberry. Published six times a year. Editorial Offices and Subscriptions: 1156 Howard Street, San Francisco, CA 94103; (415) 621-6069. Newsstand price: $4.95. Subscription rate: $24.95 per year. Bimonthly glossy magazine devoted to male nudes and erotic fiction, with emphasis on men who are uncircumcised.

VISIBILITIES. Editor: Susan T. Chasin. Published six times a year. Editorial correspondence and Subscriptions: P.O. Box 1258, Peter Stuyvesant Station, New York, NY 10009; Single-issue price: $2.00. Subscription rate: $15.00 for eight issues (Domestic U.S. postage). Bimonthly magazine for lesbians, seeking to promote a positive image of lesbianism; includes non-fiction features, profiles, columns, reviews, poetry.

YONI. Editor: Bee Fidds. Published four times a year. Editorial Correspondence and Subscriptions: P.O. Box 19316, Oakland, CA 94619; (415) 635-6137. Newsstand price: $3.50. Subscription rate: $13.00 per year. Quarterly magazine of lesbian erotica.

NOTE: Not included in the above listing are national newsletters for clubs and organizations; feminist publications that include, but do not focus on, lesbian concerns; publications whose focus is primarily regional; publications whose publishing information could not be confirmed either by telephone or by mail, due to disconnected numbers, lack of address, or lack of response to inquiries.

ADVICE
FOR EVERYDAY LIFE

The skills and knowledge that we gain while growing up — from family and friends, school and church — don't always meet our later needs as lesbians and gay men. These six short essays fill in some of the gaps. The article on coming out was written from a specifically gay male perspective, and Carol Becker's essay about ending a relationship was based on a study of lesbian couples. We hope you'll read both, however, and that you'll agree with us that the similarities between lesbians and gay men in these situations are greater than the differences.

FINANCIAL PLANNING FOR LESBIANS AND GAY MEN
by Harold Gunn

Few people realize how much the financial planning and insurance concerns of gay people differ from those of straight people. While homosexuals *and* heterosexuals are concerned with saving taxes, making the right investments, and planning for a secure future, gay people often need to use different techniques to achieve these goals.

For example, when a man and woman marry, the laws of the state in which they live do some benevolent financial planning for them. Though the couple may choose to arrange things otherwise, the state dictates how property acquired during their marriage is owned and how it will be distributed after one of them dies. This intervention by the state is designed to protect each party and encourage the institution of marriage. A gay couple, however, must actively construct this framework for themselves, yet few know how to go about it.

Similarly, insurance coverage is structured to favor married couples. As the number of AIDS cases increases, life, health, and disability insurance are becoming harder to get, just at the very time they are more crucial to our financial security. There *are* ways around these obstacles.

Another often overlooked part of planning for a secure future involves executing a will. Without such a safeguard, your lover or friends would almost certainly get nothing from your estate. Even with a will, disgruntled relatives can thwart the wishes of the deceased by contesting the document's validity. Taking precautions now can eliminate these problems.

Planning for a life together

The delights of living together can mask some of the financial complications caused by the legal system's bias towards heterosexual couples. The financial advantages that our laws grant to married couples include the right to financial support from a spouse, the right to inherit from a spouse without a will, and the right to recover damages for a spouse's wrongful death. Without these protections gay couples are at a disadvantage, but there are alternative ways to secure the financial benefits associated with marriage.

First, the couple should work out the money details of their relationship before they move in together. Gay lovers tend to live together with only an ambiguous understanding about how they will share expenses. The wise couple will sit down together, discuss their financial concerns and expectations, and come to an agreement in the form of a living-together contract.

Recent litigation might make such a contract legally enforceable, although that cannot be taken for granted. In any case, consider such an agreement a useful tool to avoid or help resolve disputes.

In addition to living-together contracts, gay couples should seriously consider the advantages and disadvantages of joint savings, checking, and credit card accounts. The primary advantage of joint accounts are their convenience. However, a joint account means that each person is responsible for the debts incurred on that account by the other. A disgruntled lover could charge thousands of dollars on a joint credit card or withdraw everything from a joint checking account and skip town. One solution: hold credit cards and bank accounts separately, but open a joint checking account in which only a moderate amount is maintained to cover joint expenses.

Gay couples should know that leases obligating both of them to pay the rent, or loan agreements obligating both of them to pay the amounts due, offer both risk and legal protection. These are called "joint and several" obligations, which means that the creditor can choose to sue both partners — or either of them alone — for the full amount owed. If the creditor collects from only one partner, however, the lover who paid the joint obligation would generally have the right to look to her partner for a share of the debt.

Purchasing a home with a lover also requires careful planning. Ownership by two persons may take several forms, each with its own financial consequences:

• *Joint tenants* each own an equal, undivided interest in the whole property during their lives. Upon the death of a joint tenant, his interest will automatically pass to the survivor, even overriding a provision in his will to the contrary. If a joint tenant sells his interest to someone else, the new owners automatically become "tenants in common."

• *Tenants in common* each own a separate, undivided interest in the property. "Tenants in common" can own property in unequal shares and can bequeath their interests to whomever they specify in their wills.

• *Tenants by the entirety* are married joint owners. (Essentially, this is the same as a joint tenancy, except it is more difficult to sever the ties of joint ownership.)

Unless you specify which type of ownership you are taking when purchasing, the form will be determined by the law of the state in which the property is located. In many states the law presumes that unmarried joint property owners are "tenants in common" — unless you explicitly indicate otherwise.

Planning for the Unexpected: Health, Life, and Disability Insurance

A person wihtout health insurance courts financial ruin. Though Medicaid can help pay medical expenses, the patient must first exhaust practically all other personal resources. Group health insurance plans provide coverage for employees of most larger businesses, but all other individuals should purchase their own policy.

Purchasing a new policy, or making a claim on an existing one may present difficulties. "Pre-existing conditions" are the most common problem. An insurance company may refuse to pay a claim if, at the time she purchased the policy, the claimant knew or should have known that she had the condition which gave rise to the claim. Most health insurance contracts provide a period of time after which claims on pre-existing conditions must be honored — usually eleven months, although some are as long as two years.

An insurance company may also deny a claim if the claimant made a "material misrepresentation" on his application. For this move to succeed, the misrepresentation must be serious and sufficiently related to the illness that, if the company had known, it would not have issued the policy. In most states, however, an insurance company has two years from the time the policy is issued to raise an objection to the misrepresentation. After that time, a claim must be paid.

These issues take on a new significance in light of the AIDS epidemic. Some insurers have expanded their definition of a pre-existing condition so as to withhold benefits from policyholders with AIDS who exhibited certain ailments prior to their diagnosis. The best advice would be to answer the questions on the insurance application honestly and completely, but without volunteering any unrequested information. For example, you would not want to disclose that you have tested positive for the HIV antibody. (A number of states currently forbid insurers from asking this question, although the industry would like that changed.)

As you change jobs, be sure your health coverage follows you. In many states you can convert group health insurance to an individual policy with the same company without having to provide new proof of insurability. Though an individual policy is more expensive and provides less coverage, at least the coverage continues.

Congress has also passed COBRA (Consolidated Omnibus Reconciliation Act) which allows any employee leaving a job to stay on the company's group insurance plan by paying the group premium. Though this option is less expensive than converting to an individual policy, an ex-employee may only continue with the group coverage under COBRA for a period of eighteen months.

Health insurance, though essential, is not helpful if, through disease or workplace accident, you should lose the ability to work. This kind of protection is provided by disability insurance. For the single gay person, disability insurance is far more important than life insurance. According to insurance industry statistics, if your age is between thirty-five and sixty-five, you have a fifty percent chance of becoming disabled for at least ninety days prior to your sixty-fifth birthday. Make certain that your disability coverage is adequate.

If others depend on your income, purchase enough life insurance to be sure that they will not face a serious financial setback in the event of your death. This is becoming trickier than it sounds. In response to the AIDS crisis, insurance companies are making special efforts to identify those applicants believed to be at high risk for contracting the disease, then requiring them to take the HIV antibody test. Those who test positive are denied life insurance. This is completely legal in most states.

Insurance companies examine a number of factors to determine a high-risk applicant, including marital status, occupation, history of sexually transmitted diseases, and naming an unrelated person of the same sex as a beneficiary. Again, while you should answer all of the questions on the application honestly, do not volunteer information. Avoid naming your lover as a beneficiary: name your estate instead, and make a will that leaves your estate to him or her.

Finally, any information that you supply to an insurance company may be made available to other insurance companies through the Medical Information Bureau, Inc. (MIB). MIB attempts to reduce underwriting costs by uncovering dishonest applicants. MIB maintains files of personal medical information, and other "nonmedical information of a very restricted nature regarding insurability."

The Fair Credit Reporting Act of 1970 assures your access to the file MIB may be keeping on you. You may request this information by filling out a special form, which can be obtained by writing MIB, PO Box 105, Essex Station, Boston, MA 02112. The records, once released, may only be sent to a "licensed medical professional" which you designate. After reviewing the file with your doctor, you may submit corrections to MIB.

Planning for Your Estate

By failing to draft a will, you agree to let the state dispose of your earthly possessions. Since state laws are based on the assumption that your family is the natural object of your affection, your estate would go to your closest blood relative. Lovers and close friends would receive nothing.

It is possible to direct the disposition of property by means other than a will: recall that property held as joint tenants passes to the survivor automatically. However, for assets that are not held jointly, there is no reliable substitute for a carefully drafted will.

Contrary to popular belief, there is no law *requiring* that a certain portion of your estate go to your relatives. If you do leave them little or nothing, they can initiate legal proceedings in an attempt to have the will declared invalid. This can be successfully argued by proving that 1) the will was improperly executed, 2) someone used undue influence to coerce you into executing the will, 3) you were mentally incompetent to execute a will, or 4) someone deceived you as to how the will would dispose of your property. A careful will and estate plan can thwart such arguments ahead of time. Another device that can avoid will contests is the *in terrorem* clause. When put in a will, this clause disinherits anyone who contests the legality of the document.

As you plan your estate, seriously consider making a bequest to charitable or political organizations that promote the health, civil rights, and vital interests of the gay community. There are dozens of worthwhile groups that depend on our contributions for their survival. A generous bequest would help ensure that they have the resources to continue with their important work.

Gay men and women can generally achieve their financial planning goals, but it takes advance information and thought, a bit more work, and a little ingenuity. The key is to plan ahead, before calamity strikes.

———

Harold Gunn is an attorney in New York City specializing in wills and trusts.

FINDING A GAY-AFFIRMATIVE THERAPIST
by Marny Hall

Perhaps the most important quality that lesbians and gay men shop for in a therapist — an affirmative attitude towards our sexuality — is also the most difficult to find. After all, "gay" or "lesbian" is not a single kind of behavior. Each represents a whole cluster of styles, sexual practices, tastes, social environments, and political networks. Obviously, there can be no single, monolithic attitude towards such a behavioral mix on the part of any therapist.

Likewise, there is no single profile of a gay-affirmative therapist. Such therapists, like any other counselors, run the gamut of experience and training. "Gay-affirming" simply represents an additional layer on top of their particular therapy orientation. Such therapists share a determination not to reinforce in gay and lesbian clients the devaluing messages issuing from the culture. Instead, they offer clients the view that being lesbian or gay is a positive choice.

Not all these therapists are themselves lesbian or gay. In some parts of the country, lesbian or gay therapists may be difficult, even impossible, to find. There's no rule that says a heterosexual therapist can't be helpful to us — and none that promises competence and nurturing from a therapist who is gay.

How to Check a Counselor's Attitude

Obviously, a referral is the fastest — and least risky — way to meet a gay-affirmative therapist. When there's no such referral, and no other evidence is forthcoming — no gay periodicals in the waiting room and no clearly affirmative statements from the counselor — you need to look for subtler clues.

How does the therapist say your lover's name? What expressions and body language do you notice when you describe something sexually explicit? How does the counselor react to words like "dyke" and "faggot?" How does the counselor respond when you discuss AIDS or becoming a gay or lesbian parent?

If your therapist is not affirmative about lesbian and gay experiences, it will be difficult to help the client become and remain so. The focus of work with gay clients is to flush out the old, demeaning standards and hold them up for examination. It means helping the client realize the inapplicability and irrelevance of many non-gay values. A therapist who has any doubt, hesitation, or ambivalence about this is probably the wrong one for you; such a therapist may only reinforce the homophobia that is inside and around you. In the absence of any clear-cut statements by your therapist, your intuition is probably your best guide. Use it.

Shopping for a Bi-focal Approach

Gay affirmation is an indispensable part of effective therapy with lesbians and gay men. Good therapy, however, is not limited to lesbian and gay issues. Plenty of problems, although they may be indirectly related to sexual orientation, have a reality independent of lesbianism or gayness. Such problems, which must be dealt with separately, include: drug or alcohol abuse; parenting or career issues; aging; and illness.

A gay or lesbian counselor, to be most effective, must have a bi-focal approach, an ability to move easily from a gay perspective to one where homosexuality is incidental. A therapist without this ability can do limited good. Such a therapist may overidentify with a client, flatten the differences among clients, rob each client of her or his uniqueness, and provide too limiting or too comforting an environment.

How to Find a Gay-Affirmative Therapist

Bookstores, Coffeehouses, Newspapers. These will often provide leads through bulletin boards, conversations, or advertisements.

Ads are a legitimate way to find a therapist. Some offer initial consultations free — a good way to start the shopping process. Many therapists who don't advertise free first sessions will offer one if you ask.

Switchboards. Operating in many urban areas, switchboards provide a source of lesbian and gay counselors. They are usually listed in the phone book under "Feminist," "Gay," "Lesbian," or "Women." In areas without visible gay or feminist communities, switchboards for crisis intervention, substance abuse support, or even peace groups may offer the information you need.

Lesbian and Gay Directories. The professional organizations to which psychotherapists belong frequently have lesbian and gay caucuses, which offer, upon request, listings of lesbian and gay therapists across the country. Several other directories for lesbians and gay men also list lesbian and gay mental health resources. See the Resource Section of this book for details.

Sleuthing. The difficulty of finding a gay-affirmative therapist is compounded by closetry — the conviction on the part of some therapists (particularly those who work in agencies or clinics) that they dare not come out at work.

If you get the name of someone in a clinic, call the person directly. If the person is lesbian or gay and closeted, a comment like "you've been recommended to me as a therapist and I want to know if I can arrange for you to see me," is a nonthreatening introduction. Approached in this way, therapists will often either arrange to see you, or alert the intake worker to assign you to him or her.

Country Ways

The task for rural gay people seeking therapy is different from their urban counterparts. Some rural lesbians and gay men have located therapists in nearby cities whom they drive to see.

If driving long distances for therapy is not feasible, country dwellers may elect, instead, to have telephone therapy. Some therapists who live in urban areas are open to negotiating regular telephone sessions with clients who don't have access to their offices.

Social contact with other lesbians and gay men who are not necessarily counselors may be especially important for rural lesbians and gay men.

How do you find someone who — even if not lesbian or gay — is sympathetic, warm, and supportive? Such a search means getting involved in aspects of local community work which reflect shared values, and cultivating friendships with people who have the qualities you would seek in any therapist. Such people are "natural helpers": those whose listening ability, tolerance, and empathy make them sought-out "counselors" within their communities.

The search for a lesbian/gay-affirmative therapist may be quick and direct, or arduous and time-consuming. The search will be facilitated by drawing on available resources such as referrals and national publications, by assertive interview techniques, and most importantly, by your own creativity and intuition.

Anyone may receive referral information from the Association of Gay and Lesbian Psychiatrists by contacting: AGLP Referral Service, c/o Phillip Cushman, 2830 N.W. 41st Street, Suite B, Gainesville, FL 32606, (904) 372-0387.

———

Marny Hall is a practicing psychotherapist in the San Francisco Bay Area. This essay is excerpted from her book *The Lavender Couch: A consumer's guide to psychotherapy for lesbians and gay men.*

FINDING A GAY-AFFIRMATIVE DOCTOR OR LAWYER
by Wayne Curtis

There is no assurance that a gay doctor or lawyer is, by definition, better than a straight one, but there are compelling reasons for searching out gay-identified, or at least gay-affirmative, legal and health care professionals. In some urban areas this is as simple as turning to your local gay community publication's service guide. But for many of America's gay men and lesbians, no such community listing is readily available.

Why should I bother to look for a gay doctor or lawyer?

While many medical and legal situations have nothing to do with sexual preference, you won't get the best possible service from a doctor or lawyer if you don't feel free to talk about every aspect of your life. Also, as a consumer, you have the right to expect treatment unclouded by the professional's personal prejudices.

From a health care standpoint, this means a thorough understanding of your special needs as a gay man or lesbian, whether single or coupled. A doctor or health care worker should not only understand whatever physical health problems you may have, but also needs to be sensitive to the types of "legal" discrimination that can be based on a gay individual's medical history. If you have a lover, your doctor should respect your visitation rights if one of you becomes seriously ill.

Similarly, your legal needs are influenced by the generally heterosexist bias of our legal system. Non-traditional family units do not get the legal status or prerogatives of a married couple, and gay people must construct a more elaborate protective framework to make up for that disadvantage. A sympathetic lawyer can also provide the best defense of your rights should you be victimized by anti-gay discrimination or violence.

Where can I look to find a gay-affirmative lawyer or doctor?

The recommendation of a trusted friend is often the easiest, and best, place to start. Another option is to use a locally-produced gay or lesbian paper or community service guide. Keep in mind, however, that just because someone advertises in a local gay publication, that doesn't make them qualified.

Several national organizations can also provide you with recommendations. Gay and Lesbian Advocates and Defenders (GLAD), a non-profit law firm, publishes the *National Attorney Directory for Lesbian and Gay Rights,* now in its fourth edition. It's available for $12 (postpaid) from GLAD, P.O. Box 218, Boston, MA 02112. Two sources exist for finding a gay-affirmative doctor or clinic. The American Association of Physicians for Human Rights (AAPHR) can refer you to one of their members. Write the AAPHR at 2940 16th Street, #105, San Francisco, CA 94103. Also, the National Lesbian and Gay Health Foundation publishes *The*

Sourcebook on Lesbian/Gay Health Care, now in its second edition. Along with articles about gay and lesbian physical and mental health, the *Sourcebook* also has an extensive listing of doctors, psychiatric services, and health clinics which serve the gay community, as well as their locations, specialties, and hours. This helpful publication is available for $20 (postpaid) from the National Lesbian and Gay Health Foundation, PO Box 65472, Washington, DC 20035.

———

Wayne Curtis is on the staff of Alyson Publications. He is the editor of *Revelations: A collection of gay male coming out stories.*

Bob Young

THE FIVE STAGES OF A RELATIONSHIP
by Larry Uhrig

The joy of a relationship is discovered only with time. As we live together and pursue our vocations, something wonderful happens to us. We begin to develop our corporate identities. This happens as lives merge into shared goals, property, feelings, hopes, and friends. An extended family may develop to include the relatives and parents of the couple as well as close intimate friends. This bonding process unfolds in stages. These stages can be viewed as (1) discovery, (2) disappointment, (3) decision, (4) development, and (5) destiny.

Discovery.

The discovery stage includes the initial meeting and introduction of the two people. This stage incorporates all of the courting and dating dynamics and customs of our culture. It is the one stage most filled with passion and wonder; this is the stage most often exploited by the Hollywood myth. Here is the phase where so many of us get stuck. It is in the discovery period that infatuation is strong and love not yet defined. While this stage is filled with energy, joy, and excitement, it is also filled with ambiguity and confusion.

Disappointment.

Stage two is the point at which many couples decide not to continue the relationship. In this stage, the two people encounter reality. The limits and shortcomings of the other become more focused and for a time these shortcomings dominate the horizon. This is a two-way street as both encounter the other's weaknesses. Here, the conflict usually occurs between the myth of a "shopping list lover" and the real qualities of the person at hand. The temptation is to get rid of the one at hand and go out to find the personification of the myth. It is essential to know that this process will repeat itself again and again. Discovery is always followed by disappointment and it sometimes appears easier to leave the relationship than to stay.

Decision.

Disappointment always brings both people to the point of decision. At this intersection, each must evaluate their goals and assumptions. Here, clear communication is required to perceive accurately where the other person is. This is a time to take "inventory" as to what you each have invested in the other. Are your assumptions about the relationship open and shared, or is one or both operating on the basis of assumptions not disclosed to the other? Decision is an essential stage in establishing a long-term commitment. The way you encounter this decision will set the pattern for how you resolve future conflicts.

Disappointment and decision are recurring cycles in any relationship. We must realize that this is not a sad reality to escape but an inevitable human process which can enrich each person's life as each accepts the other partner with all his or her weaknesses and grants the other the freedom to grow and change.

Development.

Development is the term I choose to refer to the often extensive period following the decision to continue the relationship. This is a period of nitty-gritty living, change, and growth. It is often characterized by higher levels of security and the growth of trust between two people. The choice to stay carries with it a mutual acknowledgment of each other as persons of worth, persons who are loved.

The development stage of the relationship is often the time when the couple begins to publicly acknowledge their pair-bonding to friends, co-workers and families. The time between the discovery and the development stage of a relationship is about six months to one year. Understanding that this is a natural process which takes time to develop will ease pressure.

Destiny.

The final stage — which may follow a series of decision stages — I am calling "destiny." This is the stage of mutual trust and honesty. At this point in a relationship there will be regular and clear communication, a developing ability to face conflict and resolve it, an absence of jealousy and possessiveness, and a mutual independence and freedom. This is a stage of "good health"

which allows the future to be a blessing and challenge to be faced together.

This stage of a relationship does not occur until after an extensive period, usually not until the third year or later.

A major problem in gay relationships is our impatient desire to hurry the process along. We cannot leapfrog any stage nor even greatly shorten it. Each must be allowed to unfold naturally. Sometimes, however, the process can be enhanced; this occurs when two people begin the process at the discovery stage with maturity, respect and high levels of trust. This often results from the successful resolution and completion of former relationships. The resolution of previous pair-bonding is imperative for the success of our present relationship. A hopeful word here is that one's present relationship, when based on honesty, greatly helps heal the pain and hurt carried over from a previous relationship.

Destiny is the intention to spend a life together in a relationship bonded through time, testing, trust, and honesty.

———

Larry Uhrig is the pastor of the Metropolitan Community Church in Washington, D.C. This essay is from his book *The Two of Us: Affirming, celebrating and symbolizing gay and lesbian relationships.*

A GAY MAN'S GUIDE TO COMING OUT
by Wes Muchmore and William Hanson

First you come out to yourself. You admit that erotically your primary interest is in other men.

Men new to their gayness sometimes believe that if they have sex with a male, or even think about it, some terrible Jekyll-Hyde change will come over them. The truth is that nothing special will happen. You will not turn into anything, develop a sudden, unconquerable yen to wear dresses, jewelry, or makeup, or become a woman. You will not now lust for little boys, turn girlish, or begin to talk in a lisping manner. You will not start to hate females, lose your sense of morality, or go wild over the colors purple, lavender, pink, or green. That's all nonsense. If nobody could tell about you before, nobody can tell about you after.

Coming out is not always pleasant even under the best of circumstances, and it can be an extremely difficult process. Very often a man has to completely reassess and restructure his whole existence.

Along with the strains of adjustment several problems may arise from within. Difficulties frequently have two sources. First, in American society where virtually everyone is raised to be heterosexual, we all learn as children that homosexuality is a sickness or a sin. At the least we are led to view it as a faintly amusing misfortune. When a man realizes that *he* is one of *them*, a certain degree of self-hatred is almost inevitable.

Second, many gays feel that they have had very much less than idyllic upbringings. Anyone who has grown up in an atmosphere of unusual conflict and hostility is more apt to have unresolved tensions which can affect his adult relationships.

With all the negative emotions it can raise, the discovery of oneself as gay usually brings to an end months or even years of doubts, confusion, and anguish. A dizzying sense of elation may take their place. Remember that other people in your life may find it difficult or impossible to share whatever feelings of release you may have.

Coming out to friends

Be prepared for some surprises. The friend you've regarded as the most liberal may turn out to be the one who can't handle the idea that you're gay. Others may accept it intellectually but will become uneasy when confronted by tangible evidence of your sex life, such as your lover.

Roughly speaking, your straight male friends who do not feel secure about their own sexual identification are likely to reject you. Even those straight men who are not hung up about gayness may fear guilt by association if they are known to be friends with someone who is gay.

The problem is that few hetero males are self-confident sexually. Many fear their own quite normal homosexual impulses; their role stereotypes, being few and difficult to live up to, inspire self-doubts and anxiety. Thus gay men become useful to them as scapegoats and also to highlight their masculinity: "Maybe I'm not Superstud, but at least I'm no goddamned faggot."

All this said, let us point out that *some* heterosexual males will not be bothered by your sexual orientation, so don't write off *all* of them.

Straight female friends are far more likely to take your news without getting upset. You can expect a nasty reaction in only a few cases. The first, again, is the woman who is not confident of her sexuality. This type is a small minority among females. The second is the woman who, although you may not know it, happens to be in love with you. Naturally she is going to be disappointed. Finally, if you've been dating a female merely to pass yourself off as Mr. Macho, she's not going to enjoy learning that she has been used.

Coming out to your family

For the young man, these are the most usual reactions:

• Your parents will accept you as you are. This is not common, and with the best intentions in the world they may take a long time to come to terms with your situation.

• Your parents will try to understand, but the news will make them feel guilty, as if your gayness is their fault. They probably will think your life is headed for ruin if you persist in your homosexuality, and therefore will pressure you to change.

• Your parents will not react. They will refuse to believe you, and the subject will never be brought up again.

• Your parents will reject you. Melodramatic as this may seem, gay people do get thrown out of their family home, disowned, and told never to come back.

If you are an older man, living on your own and perhaps located at some distance from your parents, you don't have the problems a younger man has — it is easier to leave well enough alone.

At any age, the parents you tell may want you to keep your gayness a dark secret. Remember, that is for you alone to decide; it's your life and nobody else's.

Brothers and sisters can be very unpredictable at any time. Homophobia, often in the form of exaggerated fears for their children's safety in your presence, or sibling rivalry, or the fear that if you are, maybe they could be, can affect their reaction.

On all sides the potential for hurt is great. Whatever you decide to do, tread very carefully and consider what is to be gained by your revelation and what lost.

Where to come out

Valuing the friendship and warmth of straight friends and family but not wanting to live in the closet, many gay men leave their community and settle in some usually distant city that has a large gay population. New York, Chicago, New Orleans, Los Angeles, and San Francisco are common choices, and each of them has one or more gay neighborhoods or districts.

For some men this works well and gives a sense of freedom. For others, especially those with close attachments to family and straight friends, this alternative is more an exile than a liberation.

The etiquette of coming out

There are gay men that everybody can spot, that nobody can spot, and that only other gay men can spot. Some of us are up-front all the time by choice, some of us are deeply closeted, and a lot of us range somewhere in between. Every gay man has the right to decide for himself just how open he will be about his gayness, and this may vary with time, place, and situation.

Do not identify anybody as homosexual to any person who is heterosexual. This may sound like a needless warning, but it is easy to screw up — uncloseting a man who will not appreciate the favor.

Just how open you want to be is a decision to make only after carefully considering your own feelings and personal circumstances. Some men choose the closet, others refuse to hide at all, still others don't want to make a big fuss about it, and effeminate men may feel they have no choice in the matter.

Certainly for most men, the less strain and play-acting, the better. And on a larger scale, the more men who come out publicly as gay, the greater the benefit to all gay men. However many of us there are, we can't defend ourselves and maintain our rights if each of us is hiding alone.

———

Wes Muchmore and William Hanson have written two books on the subject of coming out: *Coming Out Right: A handbook for the gay male,* from which this article is excerpted, and *Coming Along Fine: Today's gay man and his world.*

Irene Young

THE LESBIAN EX-LOVER TRANSITION
by Carol Becker

It is our inward journey that leads us through time — forward or back, seldom in a straight line, most often spiraling. Each of us is moving, changing, with respect to others. As we discover, we remember; remembering, we discover; and most intensely do we experience this when our separate journeys converge.
— Eudora Welty

To varying degrees, lesbian ex-lovers retain their ties to one another after their breakup and use these bonds to rebuild their lives. An ex-lover remains an important part of a woman's evolving identity: as a woman, as a lesbian, and as a participant in intimate relationships.

The bond of lesbianism.

Because lesbians are a stigmatized minority group, lesbian ex-lovers are united to one another by a bond of sisterhood. As lovers, they have fought for acceptance and understanding from their nuclear families, their children, their colleagues, and their neighbors. Having grown up in a homophobic environment, they have shared a battle against internalized homophobia as well.

When both women remain lesbian-identified after their breakup, they share the cultural experience of recovering from the ending of a stigmatized relationship. Despite the unresolvable differences that resulted in their breakup, lesbian ex-lovers remain connected by an overriding common cause — that of combating negative stereotypes of themselves, their relationships, and their lifestyle.

When her lover relationship ends, a lesbian loses a major source of validation for her identity as a lesbian — the intimate relationship that was a central expression of her sexual orientation. In leaving or in being left by her lover, a woman's evolving identity as a lesbian is disrupted. To sustain herself in the face of homophobia, it is important for her to strengthen her relationships with other lesbians and non-homophobic family members and friends. Because they had shared a common struggle against society's negations and had validated each other's positive lesbian identities, lesbian ex-lovers remain connected by this bond of sisterhood.

Most often, a woman's family of friends help her through the ending of a partnership and its aftermath. Lesbian friends model and mirror a woman's life choices and give social validity to her personal experiences. Ex-lovers, who have known one another more intimately than other friends, are important sources of validation for one another. Because former partners have lived through many aspects of their lives together, they provide an inclusive reference point in each other's histories.

Relationships between lesbian ex-lovers provide a context within which a woman can weave together the broken pieces of her intimate relationships and her identity. A woman's relationship with an ex-lover provides an important touchstone that adds continuity to her changing life. When a casual or a close friendship with an ex-lover is possible, a woman can integrate the important aspects of her past into her present and future life. When a relationship with an ex-lover is fictitious or absent, a woman has to find other sources of validation with which to mend her lesbian identity.

In addition to the personal support systems that tie lesbian ex-lovers to one another, these women share an involvement in their wider gay and lesbian communities. Extending their support systems into cultural and political realms is an important way they strengthen their lives as a depreciated minority. For many lesbians, building friendships with ex-lovers is an important part of building a wider community. A woman's sense of belonging is cultivated by this legitimating social world; it provides her a realm within which she can celebrate her relationships and her lifestyle.

Breakups as catalysts for growth.

When a woman is ending a lover relationship, she often experiences the breakup as a death: of the relationship, of aspects of her lover, and of parts of herself. She sees her dreams shatter; she feels herself torn from the safe place where she belonged in the world. She witnesses the depths of her disappointment, pain, and longing. At first she can think only of how she might have saved the relationship or of how she or her lover could have been different.

As time passes and her emotional wounds heal she is able to see that she has grown and changed in desired ways by experiencing these losses. As her involvement with a lover is stripped away, she is left facing herself. She becomes aware of aspects of herself that she had forgotten while in the partnership — the hopes behind her disappointments, and the old wounds that were reopened by the new pain.

As a woman recovers from the ending of a relationship, she finds that she has increased her understanding of herself and her interpersonal needs and desires. In sifting through the rubble of the breakup, she has to clarify who she had been in the relationship and who she wants to be in subsequent relationships. She has to decide what she wants to salvage and what she wants to leave behind. In retrospect, she can see the errors she has made: how she had tried to make her lover into who she wished her to be; how she had not known what she wanted when she entered the relationship; how she had been unaware of her ambivalences and fears and dissatisfactions.

A woman acquires a better understanding of her emotional strengths and weaknesses by going through the ex-lover transition. In becoming aware of her own interpersonal habits and problems, she improves her ability to realistically assess her own, and her partner's, limitations and capabilities. A woman also gains knowledge of some of the fundamental issues in intimate relationships and improves her ability to prioritize her needs and preferences. This reconciliation of old issues increases her self-awareness, enriches her life experience, and enables her to develop stronger and more satisfying relationships in the future.

In the resolution of the ex-lover transition, lesbians discover that what they once thought of as a tragedy was an important catalyst for their evolution.

———

Carol Becker practices psychotherapy in San Francisco and Berkeley, and is the author of *Unbroken Ties: Lesbian ex-lovers,* in which she explores various aspects of the breakup of lesbian relationships. This article is excerpted from that book.

HEALTH

There is no such thing as a "gay disease." Lesbians and gay men are subject to infection by the same bacteria, viruses, and parasites as are heterosexuals.

Many sexually-transmitted diseases, however, have been more prevalent among gay men than in the general population. There are several reasons for the difference: Gay men have the opportunity to engage in sex with more people than do most heterosexual men, and some practices that have been common in the gay community — especially rimming (anal-oral contact) and anal intercourse — are highly efficient ways of transmitting disease. In addition, closeted gay people are often reluctant to get prompt medical attention for sexually-transmitted diseases, lest their sexual identity become known. Fortunately, the increasing acceptance of safer sex, as a way of preventing AIDS, has also reduced the spread of other sexually-transmitted diseases.

Lesbians have a lower incidence of most sexually-transmitted diseases than does the general population. But this is a mixed blessing. Many women with AIDS have been diagnosed later than necessary, by doctors who perceived AIDS as primarily a male concern. And some diseases, such as gonorrhea, show symptoms less readily in women than they do in men; women who may have been exposed, then, must make it a point to be tested for it even if they are asymptomatic.

AIDS

What it is: AIDS is a condition which greatly reduces the body's ability to fight off infection. It is believed by most medical specialists to be caused by a virus, known as the Human Immunodeficiency Virus (HIV).

Cause and Prevention: The HIV virus is transmitted through the exchange of bodily fluids, primarily semen and blood. The risk of contracting the virus can be significantly reduced by limiting sexual activity to less risky practices ("safer sex") and by using condoms, latex gloves, or dental dams when engaging in activities that could spread the virus.

Symptoms: The symptoms of AIDS can vary greatly, but generally include one or more of the following: unexplained, prolonged fever; weight loss; diarrhea; swollen glands; and purple lesions known as Kaposi's Sarcoma.

Treatment: There is currently no universally accepted treatment for the HIV virus itself, but the various infections and conditions associated with AIDS have been treated with a number of approved and experimental drugs.

AMEBIASIS

What it is: Amebiasis is caused by a small parasite — an ameba — that lives in the large intestine. Until the 1970s, this ameba was little known in the United States. In the 1970s, however, it began to spread rapidly through sexual contact, and amebiasis is now recognized as a sexually-transmitted disease.

Cause and Prevention: The amebas causing this disease are usually transmitted through oral-anal contact. But any other activity, such as anal intercourse, which allows one person's fecal matter to eventually come into contact with a partner's mouth, can transmit it.

Symptoms: It is possible to have amebiasis for years without showing any symptoms. However, once the amebas begin invading the actual wall of the bowel, symptoms are likely to appear. These may include a change in bowel habits; bloody diarrhea; and abdominal cramps.

Treatment: Amebiasis is difficult to diagnose. Usually several stool specimens are examined under a microscope for signs of infection; however, this method does not always detect infections. Nor is the treatment sure to be successful; none of the drugs available for amebiasis is always effective, and frequently two or three treatments are required.

CHLAMYDIA

What it is: Chlamydia is a family of organisms that cause several different diseases, including lymphogranuloma venereum (LGV), nongonococcal urethritis, and trachoma eye infections.

Cause and prevention: The various diseases associated with the chlamydia organisms are usually contracted through sexual contact. The best means of prevention is to avoid contact with sexual partners who are infected. Condoms are protective.

Symptoms: Symptoms can be quite varied, but men usually experience burning on urination and a discharge from the penis. Women often have no symptoms at all until PID (Pelvic Inflammatory Disease), when the organism has spread interiorly through the fallopian tubes. Many contagious people, both men and women, show no symptoms of the disease.

Treatment: Testing and treatment with antibiotics are necessary.

CRAB LICE

What it is: Known as "crabs," pubic lice are closely related to head and body lice, but they cannot infect the scalp, because their living habits require hairs that are relatively far apart.

Cause and Prevention: Crabs are almost always caught from sexual partners and are said to be the most highly contagious sexually-transmitted disease.

Symptoms: The main symptom of crabs is itching in the anogenital region. It is often possible to see the lice and their eggs (nits) in the pubic hair.

Treatment: The main prescription medication is gamma benzene hexachloride (sold under the name Kwell), which is available as a shampoo, cream, or lotion. The nits may have to be removed with a fine-tooth comb. Over-the-counter remedies are also available, but are not always as effective.

CYSTITIS

What it is: Cystitis is an inflammation of the female urinary tract which can lead to a more serious kidney infection if not treated.

Cause and Prevention: Cystitis is most often caused by friction from intercourse, and is more common in heterosexual women than in lesbians. However, it can be caused by any continuous irritation to the urinary opening, and women with a low resistance due to poor health are more susceptible to it.

Symptoms: A frequent desire to urinate, and a burning sensation while urinating, are the usual symptons of cystitis.

Treatment: Some women have reported successful home treatment by drinking large quantities of cranberry juice and water, taking vitamin C supplements, and avoiding caffeine and alcohol. Sulfa drugs and antibiotics are the usual medical treatments. Before using sulfa drugs, black women must be sure they are tested for an inherited blood deficiency of the enzyme G6PD; this occurs in about one-eighth of the black population in the U.S., and for anyone with this deficiency, use of sulfa drugs can be fatal.

GIARDIASIS

What it is: Giardiasis is similar to amebiasis, but is caused by a protozoan — *Giardia lamblia* — which lives in the small intestine. It is responsible for what is often known as "traveler's diarrhea," and in the past decade, has become common in gay men as well.

Cause and Prevention: The same anal-oral contact that transmits amebas (see *Amebiasis*) will transmit giardia.

Symptoms: Symptoms are often not present. Diarrhea (without blood present), nausea, and cramps are among the most common symptoms.

Treatment: Giardia, like amebas, is usually detected through a stool examination, although even then the disease is not always detectable. Several relatively effective drugs have been found for it.

GONORRHEA

What it is: Gonorrhea, known colloquially as the "clap," the "drip," or "GC," is caused by a bacterium that can infect the urethra, the rectum, the throat, or the eye. It can also appear as a generalized infection.

Cause and Prevention: Sexual contact with an infected partner is the usual cause of gonorrhea. It can also be contracted by infants as they pass through the birth canal. The only way to avoid gonorrhea is by avoiding sexual contact

with someone who is infected. Urinating after sexual contact may decrease the likelihood of developing urethral gonorrhea.

Symptoms: Because the bacterium can infect many different parts of the body, the symptoms can be quite varied. In men, the primary symptoms are a burning sensation when urinating, and sometimes a sore throat or diarrhea. In women, there are often no symptoms until pelvic inflammatory disease (PID) develops. Many people never develop symptoms, though they are still infected and contagious, especially when gonorrhea occurs in the throat or rectum.

Treatment: Patients must be treated with the appropriate antibiotic, depending on where the infection is located.

HEPATITIS-A

What it is: Hepatitis-A is caused by a virus that multiplies within the liver and causes inflammation of that organ. Hepatitis-A is considered the least harmful type of hepatitis because it does not cause permanent damage to the liver. A person who has had hepatitis-A will develop an immunity to future exposure, and will not be contagious after the initial bout is over.

Cause and Prevention: The hepatitis-A virus is found in fecal matter, and is commonly transmitted when even a small amount of feces is ingested. Oral-anal sex is a common route of transmission, as is anal intercourse. (The use of a condom does not necessarily protect against this disease, since a person's hands may come into contact with fecal matter on the rubber while removing it, and it can then be easily transmitted to his partner's mouth.) Hepatitis-A is also sometimes caught from drinking contaminated water, from eating food that is not prepared under sanitary conditions, or from eating contaminated raw shellfish.

Symptoms: In its early stages, hepatitis-A can cause symptoms such as fever, headache, loss of appetite. Then come the more distinctive symptoms: jaundice (a yellow tint to the eyes and skin); dark urine; and light, chalk-colored stools.

Treatment: Only in rare cases does hepatitis-A require hospitalization. Usually bed rest at home is adequate, and some people are able to continue their usual daily routines while recovering from hepatitis-A. A person who suffers from hepatitis should not drink alcohol, as it will place a further burden on an already-strained liver. Drugs or medications should be used only after consulting with a doctor.

HEPATITIS-B

What it is: Like hepatitis-A, hepatitis-B is an inflammation of the liver. However, it is much more serious. It sometimes causes permanent liver damage and cancer, and it is possible for persons infected with this virus to become permanent carriers of it, able to infect others for the rest of their lives. It is estimated that about five percent of gay men are chronic carriers.

Cause and Prevention: The hepatitis-B virus, like the AIDS virus, is carried in many bodily fluids, most notably blood and semen, and it is transmitted in many of the same ways that the AIDS virus is transmitted. Anal intercourse and needle-sharing are especially effective ways to transmit hepatitis-B. However, hepatitis-B is transmitted much more easily than the AIDS virus; you can become infected with hepatitis-B by sharing a toothbrush or drinking glass; through oral sex; or any other activity in which you are exposed to the blood, semen, saliva, or urine of another person.

If you believe you have recently been infected with hepatitis-B, you can get an inexpensive gamma globulin shot, which helps your body's short-term defenses against the disease. For the longer term, a hepatitis-B vaccine is now available. Although relatively expensive ($100 to $200), most doctors recommend it for sexually active gay men who have not yet been infected. Many gay men are already immune.

Symptoms: About half of the people with hepatitis-B don't show any visible symptoms. When symptoms do appear, they may include fever or headache, joint aches, loss of appetite, or a rash. As with hepatitis-A, the best-known symptoms, which take slightly longer to appear, are jaundice (a yellow tint to the eyes and skin), dark urine, and light stools.

Treatment: Hepatitis-B is best diagnosed through blood tests. It usually does not require hospitalization, but adequate rest at home is important in fighting off the infection. Anyone still infected after about six months is considered to have chronic hepatitis.

HERPES SIMPLEX

What it is: Herpes Simplex is a virus that causes cold sores and genital infections. It belongs to a family of four DNA viruses that cannot be completely eradicated by the immune system. Once infection occurs, the virus remains in the body, even if no symptoms are present.

Cause and Prevention: Herpes is spread only through close physical contact. It is transmitted through the mucous membranes of the mouth, genitals, rectum, or eye. As with other sexually-transmitted diseases, the best prevention is to avoid sexual contact with infected persons. Although it is possible to get herpes from asymptomatic partners, most people catch herpes from partners with visible lesions.

Symptoms: The primary symptoms are clusters of painful blisters or ulcers in the mouth or throat or vagina, on the penis, near or in the rectum, or on the buttocks. There may be itching or burning in the genital or rectal area. Generalized symptoms such as fever, headache, and vomiting may also be present.

Treatment: Acyclovir, an anti-viral drug, has been helpful in diminishing the severity and duration of outbreaks in some cases. However, it cannot prevent the virus from recurring unless it is taken daily.

NGU/NSU

What it is: Nongonococcal urethritis (NGU) or nonspecific urethritis (NSU) is an infection caused by two bacteria-like organisms, *Chlamydia trachomatis* and *Ureaplasma urealyticum*.

Cause and Prevention: NGU/NSU is transmitted primarily through sexual contact.

Symptoms: The primary symptoms are burning upon urination and more frequent urination. A penile discharge often accompanies NGU as well.

Treatment: NGU is usually treated after diagnosis with tetracycline. If NGU is accompanied by gonorrhea, other drugs may also be required.

SCABIES

What it is: Scabies is caused by a mite too small to be seen with the naked eye. It belongs to the Arachnida class of insects, along with spiders and scorpions. While crabs stay on the surface of the skin, the female mite burrows under the skin, where she lays her eggs.

Cause and Prevention: Scabies is transmitted primarily through close physical contact. Since the mite can survive on sheets and towels for two to three days, it is also possible to catch it from them.

Symptoms: Itching begins about a month or two after infestation.

Treatment: Like crabs, scabies is treated with Kwell. The cream or lotion must be applied to the entire body from the neck down, left on for eight to twenty-four hours, and then washed off. A second application is necessary a week to ten days later to kill newly hatched organisms. Itching may persist for weeks, even after successful therapy.

SHIGELLOSIS

What it is: The Shigella bacteria, like other sexually transmitted intestinal diseases, has spread rapidly in the last couple of decades.

Cause and Prevention: The same anal-oral contact that transmits amebas (see *Amebiasis*) will transmit Shigella.

Symptoms: Shigellosis may be asymptomatic. Often, however, it is characterized by a violent and sudden onset of cramps, diarrhea, and fever within three days of exposure.

Treatment: A stool culture can detect the presence of Shigella; however, this process takes one to two days. Although drugs are available for the disease, most people with Shigellosis recover on their own after about a week. During this period, it is important to drink enough fluids to replace those being lost because of the diarrhea. Anti-diarrheal medications are generally not advisable unless recommended by a doctor.

SYPHILIS

What it is: Syphilis is caused by an organism known as a spirochete. In

1983, gay and bisexual men accounted for fifty percent of new cases.

Cause and Prevention: The vast majority of syphilis cases are sexually transmitted. The spirochete enters the body through broken skin or mucous membranes. The only way to prevent syphilis is by avoiding sexual contact with infected partners.

Symptoms: The symptoms of syphilis vary according to how long a person has been infected. In the primary stage, there is often a painless ulcer at the point of contact, usually the penile shaft or anus for men, and around the vaginal opening for women. In the secondary stage, a rash may develop, and lymph nodes may become swollen.

Treatment: Persons infected with syphilis must be treated with antibiotics, usually penicillin.

TRICHOMONIASIS

What it is: Often just called trich, trichomoniasis is a vaginal infection caused by a one-celled protozoan called a trichomonad. If not treated, it sometimes leads to more serious problems.

Cause and Prevention: The parasite which causes trich is common, and easily spread. Women can pass it to one another through sexual contact, and by sharing clothing, towels, or toilet seats. Heterosexual and bisexual women can get it through vaginal intercourse with a man. (Men can carry the infection, though they do not show symptoms.)

Symptoms: Trich is characterized by a foul-smelling greenish or greenish-yellow vaginal discharge. Vaginal itching and irritation may also occur.

Treatment: The most effective treatment for this persistent infection is a potent drug called Flagyl, which must be used under a doctor's supervision.

VENEREAL WARTS

What it is: Warts are skin tumors caused by a virus.

Cause and Prevention: Venereal warts are almost always sexually transmitted, and the only way to avoid getting them is by avoiding sexual contact with infected partners.

Symptoms: Warts are painless growths usually around the vaginal opening, the anus, or on the shaft of the penis. They may make their first appearance several months after exposure. Anal warts can cause itching and bleeding with anal intercourse or after bowel movements.

Treatment: Several forms of treatment are possible. Podophyllin is the most common form of treatment. It is applied directly to the warts and washed off several hours later. Other treatments include liquid nitrogen, lasers, and surgery. Repeated treatments are often necessary; if left untreated, genital warts may progress into cancer.

YEAST INFECTION

What it is: Also called monilia or candiasis, a yeast infection is a vaginal infection usually caused by the body's reaction to an unwelcome change in a woman's diet, medication, or clothing. When it appears in the throat, the infection is called thrush.

Cause and Prevention: This infection may be triggered by such diverse factors as too much sugar in the diet; wearing tight or non-cotton underwear; high stress; pregnancy; vaginal deodorants; frequent douching; and certain medications. It may be spread from one woman to another through sexual contact, and by sharing clothing, or towels; it can also be transmitted via toilet seats.

Symptoms: Yeast infections are characterized by a thick white discharge from the vagina, which resembles cottage cheese and smells like yeast. Vaginal itching may also occur.

Treatment: A common home treatment for yeast infection consists of inserting several spoonfuls of unflavored, unsweetened yogurt into the vagina twice a day. This will not work in all cases, and medical treatments, involving vaginal suppositories, are also available.

For more reading:
A number of books are available which discuss lesbian and gay health in greater detail. We suggest:

Fenwick, R.D. *The Advocate Guide to Gay Health.* Boston: Alyson Publications, Inc., 1982.

Hepburn, Cuca and Bonnie Gutierrez. *Alive and Well: A lesbian health guide.* Freedom, Calif.: The Crossing Press, 1988.

Kassler, Jeanne. *Gay Men's Health.* New York: Harper & Row, Publishers, 1983.

SAFER SEX

As soon as it became clear that AIDS could be transmitted sexually, advice about "safe sex" began to appear. The usual warning was to "avoid the exchange of body fluids" — a phrase so euphemistic as to be meaningless to anyone who didn't already understand what was being communicated. The message was further garbled by a tendency, on the part of the mass media, to confuse promiscuity with unsafe sex.

Here are a few points about AIDS that should be understood by anyone who is sexually active today. Knowledge of AIDS is changing daily; read your local gay paper, or a national publication like *The Advocate*, to stay abreast of these changes.

AIDS is caused by what you do, not by who you are. At first, AIDS was called "the gay plague" or "the gay disease." It still is, by some people. But you don't get AIDS because you are gay; you get it because you engage in certain activities. High-risk sexual practices and sharing infected needles are

the main such activities, and they'll put you in danger whether you're gay, straight, or undecided.

It's what you do, not how many people you do it with, that puts you at risk. If you're in a monogamous relationship with just one other person and you engage in risky activities, you can still get AIDS if your partner is infected. You can have sex with dozens of people, whether they have AIDS or not, and you'll be safe as long as you restrict yourself to safe practices.

You'll often hear that "having fewer sex partners will reduce your chances of getting AIDS." That's misleading. It's good advice for anyone who's ignoring safer-sex guidelines. But far better advice would be to understand what practices can transmit AIDS, and avoid them.

It's not easy to be sure that someone is free of the virus that causes AIDS. If you are certain that neither you nor your partner is infected with AIDS, then you can have "high-risk sex" with-

Many organizations have responded to the need for educational materials that promote safer sex. *Gay Chicago* magazine's "Safe Sex is Great Sex..." calendar uses erotic images to get the message across.

out putting one another at danger. But it's not easy to be certain of that.

Obviously, you want to know someone well and have complete trust in them before you accept at face value the statement that "I could never have been exposed to AIDS" or "I've been tested and I was negative." Even with that trust, you need to be careful. Your partner may not fully understand the ways the virus can be passed on. And test results have to be used with great care. It's now believed that a person can be infected with AIDS for several years before developing the antibodies which these tests detect.

The use of drugs or alcohol can weaken a person's judgment about what activities are safe, especially with a new sex partner. Thus the advice to "avoid heavy use of drugs and alcohol" is sound.

AIDS isn't the only possible hazard associated with sex. Safer sex guidelines generally focus on avoiding practices that can transmit AIDS. But if you're sexually active, make sure you're familiar with other sexually-transmitted diseases, as well. Most experts believe that oral sex carries little or no risk of transmitting the HIV virus that causes AIDS — but syphilis and gonorrhea infections *can* be transmitted that way. Such infections are bad news for anybody, and can be especially hazardous for someone whose immune system may already be weakened by HIV infection.

Different sexual practices involve different degrees of danger. The warning to "avoid the exchange of body fluids" was coined by people who are uncomfortable using words like semen and menstrual fluid. Unfortunately, that warning blurs some important distinctions. Here is what experts believe are the relative risks of various activities, as far as spreading AIDS. Knowledge of AIDS is changing rapidly. Keep abreast of these changes by reading local gay papers or a national publication like *The Advocate,* which has an excellent AIDS column in every issue.

HIGHEST RISK:

• Anal or vaginal intercourse (fucking) without a condom.
• Watersports, if urine comes into contact with the mouth or open cuts or sores on the skin.
• Sharing dildoes or other sex toys that come into contact with feces, blood, urine, or semen.
• Sharing IV-drug needles.
• Oral-anal contact (rimming) and fisting.

SOME RISK:

• Anal or vaginal intercourse with a condom.
• Fellatio (cock-sucking) when there are open sores in the mouth.

LOWER RISK:

[AIDS is not known to ever have been been transmitted by the following activities. However, the theoretical possibility of transmission exists, and health experts disagree as to whether these should be considered risk-free.]
• French (wet) kissing.
• Oral-genital contact, if there are no open sores or cuts in the mouth. No cases of AIDS have been traced to the swallowing of semen, although most authorities believe that doing so could increase the risk. Oral-genital contact between lesbians seems to involve little or no risk.

CONSIDERED TO BE SAFE:

• Dry kissing.
• Massage.
• Mutual masturbation, of yourself or your partner, provided that semen does not come into contact with an open cut or sore.
• Body-rubbing, including rubbing to the point of orgasm.
• Watersports, provided urine comes into contact only with unbroken skin, and not with any mucous membranes (i.e. the mouth, eyes, and genitals).
• Light S/M activities which do not involve bleeding or penetration.
• Use of sex toys, if they are not shared.

PENPALS FOR GAY TEENAGERS

Alyson Publications, a gay-owned publisher of literature for lesbians and gay men, runs a letter exchange service to help gay teenagers get in touch with others who would like to correspond. If you'd like to participate in this, here is the procedure to follow:

1. Get an address where you can receive this mail. If you can use your home address, fine. Otherwise, some possibilities are: (a) ask at the Post Office how much it costs to rent a box there, or whether you can have mail addressed to you at General Delivery in the town where you live, and pick it up at the Post Office; (b) find a friend, perhaps an older gay person, who will let you use their address.

2. Write a letter introducing yourself, and be sure your address is on the letter. Put it in an envelope with a first class postage stamp but without an address; do not seal the envelope. Then put *that* letter and envelope along with a cover letter into a larger envelope and mail it to us:

Alyson Publications
(letter exchange)
40 Plympton Street
Boston, Mass. 02118

We'll seal this letter and forward it to someone else who has expressed interest in exchanging correspondence.

In the cover letter, which will be for our confidential files, you should (a) give your name, address, age and sex; (b) state that you are under 21; (c) give us permission to have mail sent to you; and (d) sign your name at the bottom.

3. When we get your letter, we'll forward it on to someone else who has expressed interest in corresponding. We'll also keep your name on file to get someone else's letter eventually. Once you've established correspondence with someone you should mail letters directly to them; you'll only go through us to get that initial contact.

4. Be patient. It may take a while to get a first response. If no one replies, it could be that someone has received your letter but is having problems at home or for some other reason isn't able to write back; in that case, try again.

5. There's no charge for this service, but we do ask that it be used only by gays and lesbians under 21 years of age.

WE'RE NOT ALL ALIKE: FACTS ABOUT COUPLES

In the mid-1970s, with support from two major foundations, Philip Blumstein and Pepper Schwartz undertook a major study of how people relate as couples. Several thousand couples were interviewed and, unlike so many other researchers, Blumstein and Schwartz included not only married heterosexuals in their study, but also unmarried heterosexuals, gay male couples, and lesbian couples. They broke down their results according to these four categories, often finding significant differences between them. Some of these findings, revealed in 1983 in their book *American Couples,* are summarized here.

In general, the partner with the greater income has more power within the relationship. In only one category was this not the general rule. For lesbians, the division of money and the division of power in a relationship were usually unconnected. The connection between power and income was stronger for gay male couples than for heterosexual couples.

Gay men enjoy their jobs more if they can be out at work. For lesbians, being out at work does not seem to make a difference in job satisfaction. This, the researchers speculate, may be because single women are not assumed to be lesbian as readily as single men are assumed to be gay.

During the first two years of a relationship, gay men have sex together more often than any other category of couple. After ten years, they have sex together much less often than do married couples. This reflects a common pattern by which gay male relationships turn into more of a friendship than a sexual relationship after a period of years, often with both partners having sex outside of the relationship. *[Since this study was completed long before the full impact of the AIDS epidemic was felt, these figures might be different today.]*

Lesbians generally have sex less frequently than do other types of couples. This study, however, only covered genital sexuality, and thus did not include what some participants would have considered to be fully satisfying but non-genital sexual experiences. After being together ten years or more, the percentage of couples who said that they had sex together no more than once a month was:

Lesbians: 47%
Gay men: 33%
Married couples: 15%

The importance of kissing varies among types of couples. The percentage who said that they always kissed when they had sex ranged as follows:

Lesbians: 95%
Heterosexuals: 80%
Gay men: 71%

People who were disappointed with the amount of money they had, as a couple, were also less satisfied with the relationship — except for lesbians. The authors note that many lesbians are all too aware of the tendency in heterosexual relationships for differences in income to translate into differences in power. Lesbians, they speculate, "bend over backward to avoid letting money have that kind of control over their lives."

In general, men are more likely to approve of sex without love than are women. But lesbians are more likely to approve of it than are married men. Those who said they approved of sex without love broke down as follows, by category:

Gay men: 79%
Male co-habitors: 72%
Female co-habitors: 67%
Lesbians: 57%
Married men: 52%
Married women: 37%

Gay men are much less sexually possessive than are any of the other categories studied. When asked if they would be bothered were their partners to have sex with someone else, the percentage who said "Yes" in each category were:

Wives: 84%
Husbands: 79%
Lesbians: 74%
Female co-habitors: 72%
Male co-habitors: 68%
Gay men: 35%

...But when it came to "meaningful outside affairs," the differences were less dramatic. At least three-quarters of people in every category said that would bother them. The actual percentages were:

Wives: 93%
Female co-habitors: 89%
Husbands: 87%
Lesbians: 86%
Male co-habitors: 80%
Gay men: 76%

Gay men were far less monogamous than other couples. When asked if they had engaged in sex with someone other than their partner since that relationship started, the percentage who said "Yes" for each category was:

Gay men: 82%
Male co-habitors: 33%
Female co-habitors: 30%
Lesbians: 28%
Husbands: 26%
Wives: 21%

A DICTIONARY OF SLANG AND HISTORICAL TERMS

This glossary contains a variety of words and phrases that have been used in the gay and lesbian community of the past or present. Most of the listings are slang, but some are considered standard usage, or represent past attempts to coin scientific or technical terms relevant to gay people.

-A-

AC-DC. Bi-sexual.

ACCORDION. A penis which becomes dramatically longer when erect.

ADAM'S PAJAMAS. A state of full nudity. ("There I was in Adam's pajamas.")

ANDROTROPE. A gay male. Kurt Hiller suggested this term in 1946 (and *gynaecotrope* for lesbians), because of what he considered the negative connotations of "homosexual." It never caught on.

ANGEL FOOD. A gay man in the Air Force.

AUNTIE. An older gay man. This term is generally pejorative, and includes a sense of being dainty and engaging in gossip.

-B-

B&D. Bondage and discipline. B&D enthusiasts find erotic satisfaction in sex that involves one person being tied up by the other and being disciplined. Similar to, but by no means synonymous with, *S&M*.

BABY-BUTCH. A young, masculine-acting lesbian.

BALL-BEARING OIL. Semen, especially when used to lubricate a partner's penis.

BALLS. Testicles.

BAMBI-SEXUALITY. Physical interaction centered more about touching, kissing, and caressing than around genital sexuality. Not to be confused with *bestiality,* a very different concept.

BASKET. Male genitals, usually as emphasized by tight-fitting clothes.

BEAN QUEEN. A non-Hispanic man who is attracted to Hispanic men.

BEAT OFF. To masturbate.

BEAT THE TOM-TOM. To masturbate.

BENT. *[British slang]* Homosexual.

BERDACHE. A member of an American Indian tribe who lived with, dressed as, or identified with the opposite sex. Berdaches often occupied a revered and unusual position within their tribes. The term comes from the French word meaning *slave boy.*

BILITIS. From *Chansons de Bilitis,* a collection of lesbian love poems published in 1894 by Pierre Louys and supposedly based on those by Sappho. The word is best known as part of the name of the Daughters of Bilitis (DOB), a lesbian organization founded in 1955 by Del Martin and Phyllis Lyon.

BIRD'S NEST. Pubic hair.

BISEXUAL. Attracted to people of both sexes.

BLIND MEAT. An uncircumcised penis.

BJ. Abbreviation for *blow job,* or fellatio.

BLINDS. The foreskin on an uncircumcised penis.

BONER. An erect penis.

BOSTON MARRIAGE. A living-together relationship involving two women. This term was mainly used in nineteenth-century New England, and could refer both to actual lesbian relationships, and to situations where two women chose to live independent of men, often while they pursued their own careers.

BOTTOM. The receptive partner in anal intercourse (for gay men) or in vaginal intercourse with a dildo (for lesbians).

BROWN FAMILY, THE. Bruce Rodgers traces this term to the 1940s, when it referred to the homosexual subculture.

BRUSH YOUR TEETH. To perform fellatio on a man.

BUGGERY. Anal sex, usually between two men. The term is derived from *Bulgaria,* where an eleventh-century religious philosophy arose which permitted sex but forbade its members to have children; an increase in homosexuality and heterosexual anal intercourse were the natural consequences. As this philosophy spread into Germany, Italy, and France, its proponents were known as *Bulgars* or *Boulgars*; in France, this became corrupted into *bougre,* and ultimately the English word *bugger.*

BULL DYKE. A lesbian who dresses and behaves in a masculine style.

BUM BOY. *[British slang]* A man who prefers the receptive role in anal intercourse.

BUMPER TO BUMPER. Vagina-to-vagina. Generally used in reference to two lesbians engaging in sex, or dancing, etc. Occasionally used in referring to gay men or heterosexual couples.

BUNS. Buttocks.

BUTCH. Strong or tough; displaying traits considered masculine. The term is used to describe both physical build and personality, and is used with reference to both sexes.

-C-

CAMP. An ironic, often gay-identified, approach to life, dress, and speech. The term gained popularity with Susan Sontag's essay "Notes Toward a Definition of Camp" in the *Parisian Review* in 1964.

CANTONESE GROIN. A dildo. The term appears in a medieval novel, describing a plant used in China for this purpose.

CATAMITE. A boy kept for sexual purposes, from "Catamitus," the cupbearer for the Roman god Jupiter. The term came into use in the seventeenth century. *See also Ganymede.*

CATCHER. The passive partner in anal intercourse.

CHEEKS. Buttocks.

CHEESE. The accumulated smegma beneath the foreskin on an unwashed, uncircumcised penis.

CHICKEN. A young gay male, usually in his teens or very early twenties.

CHICKEN HAWK. An older gay man who pursues boys or very young men.

CHUBBY CHASER. A man attracted to obese men.

CIAO. [pronounced *chow.*] Good-bye. In Italian, the term can mean "hello" or "good-bye." As American slang, it has come to mean "good-bye for now; see you again soon."

CLONE. A gay man of a certain somewhat standardized appearance. The term arose in the early 1970s (often interchangeably with *Castro clone,* referring to the main street in the heart of San Francisco's gay male community). The classic clone look consists of short-cropped hair and a trim moustache, a flannel shirt, and 501 brand jeans — all on a relatively well-sculpted body.

CLOSET. The place where gay men or lesbians hide, figuratively speaking, if they do not want their homosexuality to be known. "In the closet" means "not open about being gay." A *closet case* or *closet queen* is someone who is in the closet.

COCK. Penis.

COCK RING. A ring, usually made of leather or metal, secured around the base of the penis and testicles (or just of the penis) to increase an erection.

COLOR IN THE COLORING BOOK. To masturbate while looking at an erotic magazine.

COME, also **CUM.** To reach orgasm. As a noun, this is also the most common slang term for semen. Some writers use the spellings *cum* for the noun and *come* (which thus lends itself to the past tense *came*) for the verb.

COME OUT. To acknowledge one's homosexuality, either to oneself or to others.

CORNHOLE. To be the insertive partner in anal intercourse.

COUCH AUDITION. A job interview that includes sex with the prospective employer.

CREAM. Semen.

CRUISE. To actively look for a sex partner, generally in an area where others are likely to be found engaged in the same pursuit.

CRUSH HOUR. The period late at night, just before a bar closes.

CUM. *See Come.*

CUNT. Vagina. The word is derived from *cunnus,* the Latin word for the female genitals. According to etymologist Eric Partridge, the Old English term *cwithe,* for *womb,* also influenced the term's pronunciation, giving it the final *t.*

CUPCAKES. Buttocks, especially when small and well-rounded.

CURE THE BLIND. To perform fellatio on an uncircumcised penis.

CURTAIN(S). The foreskin on an uncircumcised penis.

CUT. Circumcised.

CUT SLEEVES. A Chinese phrase for male homosexuality. The term, *tuan hsiu* in Chinese, comes from a story about Emperor Ai-ti (6 B.C. to A.D. 2). When a favored young man fell asleep on the sleeve of the emperor's robe, the emperor cut off the sleeve rather than disturb his rest. According to Wayne Dynes, who relates this story in *Homolexis,* many Chinese rulers from the third century onward kept minions

(*luan-tung*), and Buddhist monks and nuns often interpreted their vows of chastity as barring heterosexual affairs, but not homosexual ones.

-D-

DADDLE. To engage in lesbian sex, in a face-to-face position.

DAISY CHAIN. Three or more men engaged in simultaneous anal intercourse.

DAISY DUCK. A man who prefers the receptive role in anal intercourse.

DANGLER or **DANGLE QUEEN.** A male exhibitionist.

DASH. Open to experimenting with homosexuality, though not self-defined as gay.

DESPERATION NUMBER. A sex partner found just before closing time at the bar.

DICK. Penis. The term probably derives from *dirk,* an early English term for a short dagger.

DICK IT UP. To engage in gay male sex.

DIESEL DYKE. A lesbian who dresses and behaves in a masculine style.

DILDO. A device shaped somewhat like a penis and used as a sex toy.

DINGE QUEEN. A non-black gay man who is attracted to black men. Often considered racist.

DIONING. The heterosexual apple of a gay man's eye. This term was coined by Karl Heinrich Ulrichs in the 1860s, to describe the object of a homosexual man's attraction. *See also Urning.*

DISHONORABLE DISCHARGE. To masturbate at home after unsuccessfully going out in search of a sex partner.

DONG. Penis.

DOUBLE RIBS. A euphemism for male homosexuality, used in ancient China.

DRAG. Dressed in a way usually identified with the opposite sex. Drag differs from *transvestism* in that *drag* usually refers to a specific act of cross-dressing, while *transvestism* refers to a general enjoyment of the act. In the movie *Some Like It Hot,* Jack Lemmon dresses in drag, but the character he played was not intended to be a transvestite.

DRAG QUEEN. A man who dresses like a woman.

DROP A HAIRPIN. To give a clue that one is homosexual.

DUTCH GIRL. A lesbian.

DYKE. A lesbian. The term derives from the nineteenth-century slang word *dike,* which referred to male clothing, and when it was first used to refer to women, it carried a derogatory connotation of masculine appearance or behavior. The masculine connotation is often still present, but many lesbians have adopted the word as their term of preference.

-E-

EONISM. Transvestism. Havelock Ellis coined this term from the cross-dressing Frenchman, the Chevalier d'Eon, but it never gained acceptance.

-F-

FACE-FUCKING. Engaging in oral-genital sex.

FAG HAG. A heterosexual woman who socializes extensively with gay men. Sometimes, but not always, pejorative.

FAGGOT. Also **FAG.** A male homosexual. Like *dyke,* this term was originally used as an epithet, but has been adopted by many of the people to whom it refers. There is no general agreement about the origin of the term. In the early years of the gay liberation movement, some activists proposed that it derived from *fagot,* the sticks used as kindling during the Inquisition when heretics, homosexuals, and others were burned at the stake, but the evidence for this is weak. Others have suggested it comes from *fag,* the younger boy required in British boy's schools to do menial tasks for an older student.

FAIRY. A male homosexual, especially one who acts or dresses in an effeminate manner. This was a common derogatory term for homosexuals during much of the twentieth century. Like *dyke* and *faggot,* it has been reclaimed by gay people, and a sizeable number of gay men now identify themselves as *radical fairies,* thus asserting pride in their refusal to accept the traditional male roles expected of them.

FEMME. A lesbian or gay man who acts and dresses effeminately.

FINGER, also **FINGER-FUCK.** Using a finger to manipulate the clitoris or anus of a partner.

FINOCCHIO. An Italian slang term for homosexual, sometimes carrying a connotation of effeminacy. In Italian, the term refers to the plant fennel, and the origins of its slang meaning are not known.

FIST, or **FIST-FUCK.** To insert part or all of one's hand into the anus or vagina of a sex partner.

FRENCH. To engage in fellatio. In its more common usage as an adjective, the term refers to a preference for oral-genital sex. *See also Greek.*

FRENCH EMBASSY. Any location, especially a gym or Y, where gay sex is readily available.

FRIG. Sex between two women, often involving one rubbing the genitals of the other with her fingers; probably derived from *friction.*

FROG QUEEN. A French-Canadian gay man; also a gay man attracted to Frenchmen.

FUCK. To engage in sexual intercourse. The term is most often used for anal or vaginal intercourse. The origins of the term are uncertain. According to one theory, it was first used as an acronym for "For Unlawful Carnal Knowledge." Other etymologists believe it derives from the word *firk,* which means "a sharp thrust."

FUNCH. A quick sexual encounter performed at lunchtime.

-G-

GANYMEDE. A boy or youth kept for sexual purposes. In Greek myth, Ganymede was the Trojan youth whom Zeus made his cupbearer and bedmate. The term was used in this sense as early as 1603 by the writer Philemon Holland, and seems to have dropped from general use a few centuries later. In Roman mythology, Zeus is known as Jupiter and his cupbearer, Catamitus, is the equivalent of Ganymede. *See also Catamite.*

GAY. Homosexual. In the seventeenth century, *gay* expanded from its earlier meaning of cheerful and came also to refer to men with a reputation for being playboys; the phrase *gay Lothario* appears in 1703. By the early 1800s, it had further expanded to refer to women with a reputation for sexual promiscuity. It seems to have been adopted as a slang term by gay people as a way of referring to themselves early in the twentieth century. According to historian John Boswell, the first public use of the term in the U.S., outside of pornography, was probably in the 1939 film *Bringing Up Baby*, in which Cary Grant, appearing in a dress, exclaimed that he had "gone gay." Only since 1970 has it gradually gained acceptance as a standard, non-slang synonym for homosexual. In the late 1980s, one of the last barriers to widespread usage of the term was broken when the New York *Times* began using it as an adjective in their reporting.

GILLETTE BLADE. A bisexual woman.

GISM. Semen.

GIVE HEAD. To perform fellatio.

GLORY HOLE. A hole carved in the partition between stalls in a men's room, and used for sexual liaisons.

GO DOWN ON. To perform fellatio on.

GOATSKIN. The foreskin of the penis.

GOAT'S MILK. Bitter-tasting semen.

GOLDEN SHOWER. A stream of urine, when used in a sexual context.

GOVERNMENT-INSPECTED MEAT. A gay man in the armed forces.

GREEK. To engage in anal intercourse. In its more common usage as an adjective, the term refers to a preference for anal sex. *See also French.*

GUNSEL. One who is or is destined to be a catamite. From the German/Yiddish word for little goose.

GYNAEOTROPE. A lesbian. Kurt Hiller suggested this term in 1946 (and *androtrope* for a gay male), because of what he considered the negative connotations of "homosexual." Neither term caught on.

-H-

HETEROSEXUAL. Primarily attracted to people of the opposite sex. Today this term is considered to be the opposite of *homosexual.* However, it was not coined until after that term, and when first used in the late nineteenth century, *heterosexual* referred to people attracted to both sexes — those we now refer to as *bisexual.*

HOLD A BOWLING BALL. To sexually stimulate another woman by rubbing the thumb and forefinger, simultaneously, on her clitoris and anus.

HOLLYWOOD UTERUS. Anus. Bruce Rodgers reports this term being used in southern California in the late 1960s.

HOMOGENIC. Homosexual. Over the years, many synonyms for *homosexual* have been suggested; this one was proposed by Edward Carpenter, who objected to the fact that *homosexual* combined Greek and Latin roots. Others, such as Havelock Ellis, also objected to the coinage, but the objections never took hold, and Carpenter's creation died a natural death.

HOMOPHILE. Homosexual. *Philos* is the Greek word for love. This alternative to *homosexual* gained currency in the U.S. in the 1950s, when some early gay leaders began using it because they felt that *homosexual* put too much emphasis on the sexual aspect of their feelings. It was widely used for several decades, but gradually fell from favor when gay activists of the early 1970s felt it was euphemistic.

HOMOPHOBIA. Irrational fear of gay people and of homosexuality. George Weinberg, author of *Society and the Healthy Homosexual*, coined this word in the early 1970s. It filled a need for gay people at that time because, in one word, it eloquently conveyed the idea that it was gay-bashers, not gays themselves, who had a problem. Unlike so many other consciously-created words, *homophobia* filled a clear need and has gained widespread usage, even outside the gay community. *Homophobic* (adj.) and *homophobe* (n.) are related forms.

HOMOSEXUAL. Attracted physically to people of the same sex. The term was coined in 1869 by Karl Maria Kertbeny, who used it in a pamphlet (which he published anonymously) arguing for the repeal of Prussia's anti-homosexual laws. The term first appeared in U.S. medical journals in the 1890s, and began appearing in general usage in the 1920s.

HOT-DOGGING. Having anal intercourse.

HUNDRED-AND-SEVENTY-FIVER. A homosexual. Paragraph 175 of the German Penal Code of 1871 outlawed homosexual practices; thus a 175er *(hundert-funf-und-siebziger)* in Germany was someone violating this paragraph.

HUNG. Well-endowed; having a large penis. The term can also be used more generally: "He was hung like a mouse" means "he had a small penis."

HUSTLER. A male prostitute.

-I-

IN-SISTERS. Two men, usually both effeminate, who have a close but not necessarily sexual relationship.

IN THE LIFE. Gay. Most common within the black community.

INTERMEDIATE SEX. Homosexual. The term was used by Edward Carpenter and others around the turn of the century, but soon fell into disfavor.

INVERSION. Homosexuality. This term, which seems to have first appeared in Italian (as *inversione*) in 1878, encompassed a philosophy of homosexuality as well as providing a new term for it, and for its practitioners *(inverts)*. There is a natural order of things, this philosophy suggested — and it is to be contrasted with the unnatural state of homosexuality. The term first appeared in English late in that century; in 1897 Havelock Ellis wrote that "Caesar was proud of his physical beauty, and like many modern inverts he was accustomed carefully to shave his skin." Despite its judgmental connotations, the term was often used by gay people even in the early 1900s.

IRISH CONFETTI. Semen.

-J-

JACK OFF. To masturbate.

JANEY. Vagina.

JERK OFF. To masturbate.

JIZZ, JIZZUM. *See Gism.*

JOHNSON BAR. A dildo.

JOY-STICK. Erect penis.

-K-

KIKI. 1940s slang for a lesbian comfortable with either a passive or aggressive partner.

KINSEY SIX. A person who is completely homosexual, as opposed to one with some bisexual inclinations. The term comes from Alfred Kinsey, who developed a scale from 0 to 6 to indicate a subject's sexual orientation. Someone with no homosexual feelings was rated as zero, and someone who was exclusively homosexual was a six.

KISSING FISH. Lesbians.

KNITTING. Masturbating. (Gay male)

KOSHER. Circumcised.

KY. A brand of water-soluble lubricant often used for sex.

-L-

LESBIAN. A gay woman. The ancient Greek poet Sappho lived on the island of Lesbos. As Sappho became known for her poems celebrating love between women, the term *lesbian* changed its primary meaning from "one who lives on Lesbos" to "a woman like Sappho and her followers."

LILIES OF THE VALLEY. Hemorrhoids.

LOLLIPOP STOP. A highway rest stop used by gay men for cruising.

LOVE JUICE. Semen.

LUCKY PIERRE. The middle man in three-way sex.

LUKE. The coital fluid in a woman.

-M-

MAKE A MILK RUN. To cruise a men's room.

MAKE SCISSORS OF SOMEONE. To masturbate a woman by simultaneously rubbing her clitoris with the thumb and her anus with the forefinger.

MARICÓN. A gay man. This is the Spanish equivalent of *faggot*.

MARIPOSA. This Spanish word for *butterfly* has come to also refer to a male homosexual.

MEAT RACK. A gay male cruising area.

MILKING MACHINE. A vibratory device used by men to masturbate.

MISSIONARY WORK. An attempt by a gay man or lesbian to seduce a straight person of the same sex.

MOLLY DYKE. The more passive woman in a lesbian relationship or liaison.

MONKEY. Vagina.

MUFF, or **MUFF-DIVE.** To lick a partner's vagina and clitoris. *Muff* and *muffet* can also refer to the vagina itself, in an erotic context.

MUFFER. A woman who muffs.

-N-

NANCE. *[British slang]* Effeminate.

NAPKIN RING. A cock ring.

NUMBER. A trick; a casual sex partner.

-O-

OLD FACEFUL. An erect penis, especially when it is ejaculating.

ONE-EYED CYCLOPS. *[French]* The head of the penis.

-P-

PANSY. An effeminate gay man, usually used derogatorily. The term has been in use at least since the 1920s.

PANSY WITHOUT A STEM. Bruce Rodgers identifies this as a 1960s camp term for a lesbian.

PENIS BUTTER. Pre-ejaculate lubricatory fluid; pre-cum.

PICK UP THE SOAP. To be fucked.

PITCHER. The active partner in anal intercourse.

PLAY LEAP FROG. To engage in anal intercourse.

PLAY BUGLE BOY. To perform fellatio on another man.

POCKET POOL. Male masturbation.

POOF. A gay man. This word, generally derogatory, is common in Australia and England. Sometimes also *poofter*.

PRINCETON RUB. Intercourse between two men in which one's penis rubs between the other's thighs, or between the two men's abdomens. Usually used humorously, this term is of unclear origins. It may have been coined in pride by Princeton undergraduates who thought they had discovered something new — or it could be strictly of Yale origins.

PUSSY. Female genitals. The first documented appearance of the term was in 1662, spelled *pusse*.

-Q-

QUEEN. An effeminate gay man. Gay men who aspire to royalty will be disappointed to learn that this usage of the word *queen* is only a distant relative of the queen who sits on a throne. It is linguistically closer to *quean* — a disparaging word for an unpleasant or promiscuous woman, dating to the sixteenth century. Because of its pejorative tone and implication of effeminacy, it was later applied to gay men.

QUEER. Homosexual, usually with reference to men. Originally meaning "odd," the term seems to have taken on this meaning early in the twentieth century. Oddly, the same people who complain that "We shouldn't call homosexuals 'gay' because that confuses the meaning of a perfectly good word" have never made the same complaint with regard to usage of *queer*.

-R-

RAINCOAT. A condom.

RICE PUDDING. Semen, esp. the semen of an Asian man.

RIM. To lick or suck the anus of a sex partner.

RUBBER QUEEN. Someone with a fetish for rubber or latex sheets or other items.

RUBIES. Lips.

-S-

S&M. Sadism and masochism. S&M enthusiasts derive part of their pleasure from inflicting pain or humiliation (the sadist) or having pain inflicted upon them (the masochist) — but always within defined and mutually agreed limits.

SAPPHISTRY. Lesbian love; derived from *Sappho,* the lesbian poet of ancient Greece. *See also Lesbian.*

SEAFOOD. A gay sailor.

SEWING CIRCLE. A circle-jerk.

SKIN FLUTE. Penis.

SIGNIFICANT OTHER. A partner in a serious relationship. In the early 1970s, unhappy with terms such as *lover, girlfriend,* and *boyfriend* for describing their same-sex partners, some gay men and lesbians began using the term *significant other,* occasionally shortened to *sother.* It is now used by unmarried heterosexuals as well.

SIX. *See Kinsey Six.*

SIXTY-NINE. Mutual and simultaneous fellatio or cunnilingus. The term comes from the resemblance of the numerals 69, and is sometimes expressed in French: *soixante-neuf.* If only one partner reaches orgasm, the position has variously been called 68 or 34-½.

SIZE QUEEN. A gay man who is especially interested in partners with large penises.

SLACKS. A lesbian. The term is now considered obsolete.

SNOW QUEEN. A non-white gay man who is attracted to white men.

SODOMY. Sexual acts deemed unnatural by the person defining the term. People have been harassed, imprisoned, and burned at the stake for the crime of sodomy, yet its opponents have never agreed on just what it is. The word is derived from the city of Sodom, on the Dead Sea; Sodom and Gomorrah are described in the Book of Genesis as being destroyed because of their inhabitants' evil ways, which according to some interpretations included homosexual practices.

Sodomy is variously used to mean any sex between two men; anal intercourse involving a man and a partner of either sex; or sexual acts involving a human and an animal. In the seventeenth century, the precise definition of the word gave rise to heated debate among jurists and clergy, as they sought to decide who should be punished under the sodomy laws of the time; Jonathan Katz explores this debate in his *Gay/Lesbian Almanac.* One influential lawmaker defined sodomy as any penetrative act involving two men, or a male animal and a human partner of either sex. Another, smaller, faction defined it as any act of male ejaculation that did not include the possibility of procreation;

masturbation was thus considered sodomy.

SOTHER. *See Significant Other.*

SOUL SAUCE. The semen of a black man.

SPITTER. A penis (referring to moment of ejaculation.)

SPLIT. The vagina.

SPUNK. Semen.

SUGAR DADDY. An older man who provides funds to a younger sex partner or lover.

SWAFFONDER. Mutual oral sex. This term, sometimes used in the British navy, has a circuitous history. It began as "69" — a number which, by the shape of its digits, suggests two people engaging in mutual oral sex. This was sometimes sweetened up by being expressed in French, as *soixante-neuf*, a phrase which eventually was changed back into English as *swaffonder* or *swassonder*.

SWASSONDER. *See Swaffonder.*

SWORD SWALLOWER. A man who enjoys, or is good at, performing oral sex on other men.

-T-

TAKING CARE OF BUSINESS. *[Black slang.]* Masturbating.

TEAROOM. A public lavatory that is often cruised by gay men.

TEMPERAMENTAL. A euphemism for homosexual, documented by Jonathan Katz as being in use as early as 1927.

TIT KING. A lesbian attracted to women with large breasts.

TRADE. A man, frequently straight-identified, who allows fellatio to be performed on him by another man, but does not reciprocate. Often used to describe hustlers.

TRANSSEXUALITY. A deep-seated identification with the opposite sex, usually including a desire to actually be the opposite sex. Although transsexual feelings are not new (see "Heliogabalus" in the *People* chapter), the medical knowledge and surgical skills to actually perform a sex-change operation have existed only since the 1930s. Different from, though often confused with, *transvestism.*

TRANSVESTISM. Dressing in clothes generally identified with the opposite sex. Although transvestism and homosexuality have often been lumped together as synonymous by ignorant writers, they are quite different. Many heterosexuals are transvestites, and many lesbians and homosexual men are not; the difference is that cross-dressing is more accepted in the gay culture. *See also Drag; Transsexuality.*

TRIBADISM. Lesbianism; sometimes used specifically to describe sexual activity in which one woman rubs another's pudenda with her thigh or with a dildo. The term originated with the ancient Greeks.

TRICK. A sex partner with whom there is no long-term or emotional involvement.

TROLL. To cruise; to look for a sex partner.

TS. A transsexual.

TURTLENECK SWEATER. The foreskin on an uncircumcised penis.

TV. A transvestite.

TWILIGHT. *[Obsolete.]* Homosexual. This adjective gained prominence in the 1920s, producing such terms as *twilight men, twilight women,* and *twilight world.*

TWINKLE-TOES. An effeminate gay man, esp. one who is young.

TUNA. A young gay sailor. The term is extrapolated from the tuna fish brand "Chicken of the Sea."

-U-

UNCUT. Uncircumcised.

URANIAN. *See Urning.*

URNING. A homosexual male. This term was introduced by Karl Heinrich Ulrichs in 1864 as part of his theory of homosexuality. Ulrichs, who was himself homosexual (see listing in the *People* chapter), was attempting to explain homosexuality in a positive light, but his work was done in a near-vacuum — few other scholars were even discussing the subject, much less trying to do so from a perspective free of prejudice. Extrapolating heavily from his own experience and feelings, Ulrichs hypothesized that only a female psyche could be attracted to a male body. Homosexuals, therefore, constituted a third sex — that of female souls in male bodies. He referred to such persons as Urnings. (In English, the term is often translated as *Uranian*.) Ulrichs later also recognized the existence of a counterpart in the opposite sex; his term for lesbians was *Urningin*. Ulrichs's theory is now discredited, and his terminology has not endured, but he laid the groundwork for much of the research that was done in the following decades.

In 1916, when the New York *Times* first used a word to refer to homosexuality, *Uranian* was the term it chose.

-V-

VANILLA SEX. Relatively conventional forms of sexual activity, usually used in contrast to S&M sex.

VEGETARIAN. A gay man who does not perform fellatio (and thus who does not "eat meat.")

VICE ALLEMAND. A nineteenth-century French term for homosexuality. It translates as "the German vice."

-W-

WANK. *[British slang]* To masturbate.

WARM BRUDER. A German expression, literally translated as *warm brother,* referring to a male homosexual.

WARME SCHWESTER. German for *warm sister* — a lesbian.

WATER CHESTNUT. A gay Japanese man.

WEAR BOXER SHORTS. To be the active partner in a lesbian relationship.

WINK. To be uncircumcised.

For more reading:

Readers interested in gay language will find the following books, which were used as a source for many of these listings, to be of interest:

Dynes, Wayne. *Homolexis: A Historical and Cultural Lexicon of Homosexuality.* New York: Gai Saber, 1985.

Grahn, Judy. *Another Mother Tongue: Gay Words, Gay Worlds.* Boston: Beacon Press, 1984.

Rodgers, Bruce. *The Queen's Vernacular* (later reprinted as *Gay Talk*). San Francisco: Straight Arrow Books, 1972.

GAY SYMBOL
THROUGH THE A

Today, the lambda and the pink triangle are widely recognized symbols within the gay community. But over the centuries, a number of other symbols have also served to represent gayness in one way or another. Here are a few of them.

CALAMUS. Walt Whitman took the calamus plant as a symbol of homoerotic love, and one section of his book *Leaves of Grass* is titled "Calamus."

DOUBLE-AXE. *See Labrys.*

GREEN. According to historian Wayne Dynes, the color green was associated with homosexuality both in ancient Rome, and again in late nineteenth-century England. Poet and writer Judy Grahn recalls that at her high school in the 1950s, anyone who wore the color green on Thursday was promptly labeled as "queer."

In 1894, a satirical novel by Robert Hichens, titled *The Green Carnation,* included malicious attacks on Oscar Wilde's homosexuality, furthering the gay connotations of both the color green, and of the carnation.

HARE. In his book *Christianity, Social Tolerance, and Homosexuality,* John Boswell documents an early association of the hare with male homosexuality. It apparently began in the first century with the Epistle of Barnabus, which cited various prohibitions supposedly set forth by Moses. Eating a hare, the author said, would make one a pederast because the hare grows a new anal opening each year.

In the same vein of logic, this text forbade eating hyenas "because this animal changes its gender annually." It

further condemned the weasels, "who we hear commit uncleanness with their mouths . . . For this animal conceives through its mouth."

All three animals, Boswell shows, continued to be associated with homosexuality even into the Middle Ages.

HYENA. *See Hare.*

LABRYS. The double-bladed ax known as a *labrys* appears in art dating as far back as ancient Crete. In modern times, it has come to be a symbol of lesbianism, and often appears in the form of jewelry.

Barbara G. Walker, in her *Woman's Encyclopedia of Myths and Secrets*, traces the labrys back to mythological times when it was used as a scepter by the ancient Amazon goddess Demeter (also known as Gaea or Artemis). Walker speculates that it may originally have been used as a battle-axe by female Scythian warriors, who adopted it as a symbol when the goddess's shrine at Delphi was taken over by a male priesthood.

LADSLOVE. In the nineteenth century, the plant ladslove was sometimes used by poets as a symbol of homosexuality. The name of the plant was itself certainly part of the reason; in addition, some said it had an odor like that of a man's semen.

LAMBDA. The Greek letter *lambda* was chosen by the Gay Activists Alliance in 1970 to become a symbol of the gay movement. Its original militant associations have softened, and the symbol often appears on jewelry, as a sign that will go unrecognized by the uninitiated. The word has also been useful for

organizations such as Lambda Legal Defense and Education Fund, as a way of expressing the concept "lesbian and gay male" in a minimum of syllables.

LAVENDER. Today, lavender is the color most often identified with gayness. The association goes back to ancient times, and has been strengthened by the fact that lavender or purple is the combination of red and blue — traditional male and female colors. The gemstone amethyst, because of its purple color, has acquired the same connotations.

PINK TRIANGLE. The Nazis required known homosexuals to wear an inverted pink triangle (with one tip pointing down) on their clothing, so that they could be quickly picked out for special abuse. In the 1970s, gay activists began using this symbol as a way of identifying themselves, and at the same time calling attention to this long-forgotten chapter of gay history.

RAINBOW FLAG. Since at least 1979, a flag with six stripes representing the six colors of the rainbow has been used as a symbol of gay and lesbian community pride.

RING ON LITTLE FINGER. Wearing a ring on the little finger, especially the little finger of the left hand, has come to be a discreet way of indicating gayness. There is evidence that this tradi-

tion goes back many centuries, but its origins have been lost to antiquity. In her groundbreaking book *Another Mother Tongue,* Judy Grahn notes that the occult sciences gave the color purple the same attributes as it did to the little finger: spiritual knowledge and transformation. This connection may have given rise to the little finger ring tradition.

VIOLETS. One of the earliest major plays to include a lesbian theme was Edouard Bourdet's *La Prisonnière,* which was translated and produced on Broadway as *The Captive* in 1926. In the play, a bouquet of violets is used to symbolize lesbian love, and theater historian Kaier Curtin writes that "As a result of the success of *The Captive,* French florists experienced a devastating drop in the violet market. The same thing happened in those sections of America familiar with the drama's lesbian love notoriety."

Curtin speculates that Bourdet, who was familiar with Sappho's lesbian love poems, selected this particular flower for his play because Sappho describes herself and her lover, in one poem, as wearing tiaras made of violets when they were happy together. Perhaps he also knew of the tradition in sixteenth-century England, reported by Judy Grahn, of violets being worn by men and women who did not plan to marry.

WEASEL. *See Hare.*

TRAVEL DESTINATIONS

What are the favorite travel destinations for gay and lesbian travelers? Here are the most popular spots named in a survey by the board of directors of the International Gay Travel Association:

DOMESTIC TRAVEL

1. Key West
2. San Francisco area
3. Provincetown
4. New York City area
5. Southern California
6. Miami/Ft. Lauderdale area
7. Hawaii
8. Washington, D.C.
9. New Orleans
10. Phoenix

(Other vote getters: St. Thomas; Puerto Rico; Chicago)

INTERNATIONAL TRAVEL

1. London
2. Paris
3. Mexico
4. Amsterdam
5. Caribbean Islands
6. Toronto
7. South Pacific Islands
8. Australia
9. Rio de Janeiro
10. Berlin

(Other vote getters: Munich; Montreal; Spain; Hong Kong; Greece; Italy)

The International Gay Travel Association is a non-profit association of gay travel professionals. For further information about the IGTA, write them at PO Box 18247, Denver, CO 80218.

Photos courtesy Hanns Ebensten Travel, Inc.

The ruins of Machu Picchu in the Peruvian Andes provided this group of travelers with a memorable vacation.

OFF THE BEATEN TRACK: UNUSUAL VACATIONS

ADVENTURE BOUND EXPEDITIONS, 711 Walnut St., Boulder, CO 80302; (303) 449-0990. Run by David L. Johnson, this new tour agency organizes trips for gay men and women. Includes ski trips, backpacking, and river expeditions in the Colorado area, as well as more far-reaching trips of two weeks or more to the Himalayas, Machu Picchu, and other destinations worldwide.

ASPEN GAY SKI WEEK. Once a year, several hundred gay skiers assemble at Aspen for a week of daytime skiing and weekend partying. For dates and details, call the Aspen Gay Center, (303) 925-1725; or write or call Ron Erickson, Hillcrest Travel, 431 Robinson Ave., San Diego, CA 92103; (619) 291-0758.

CAMP CAMP-IT-UP. Kalani Honua is a retreat center in the beautiful Kalapana/Black Sand Beach area of Hawaii; it holds workshops year-round in spirituality, dance, massage, and yoga. The founder, Richard Koob, is a gay man, and once a year, the center hosts Camp Camp-It-Up, a gathering of about 100 gay people. For information, contact Kalani Honua, Box 4500, Kalapana Beach, HI 96778; (808) 965-7828. (When telephoning, remember that it's five hours earlier in Hawaii than it is on the east coast, and two hours earlier than the west coast.) For reservations, call (800) 367-8047, ext. 669.

HANNS EBENSTEN TRAVEL, INC. This gay-owned travel agency specializes in tours for gay men. It offers tours of small groups, with skilled tour guides, to such destinations as the Amazon, the Himalayas, Venice, and Morocco. Although more expensive than a typical charter tour, Ebensten's trips have a reputation among travelers looking for more cultural and intellectual experiences on their vacations. For information, contact Hanns Ebensten Travel, Inc., 513 Fleming St., Key West, FL 33040; (305) 294-8174.

HOTLANTA RIVER EXPO, PO Box 8528, Atlanta, GA 30306; (404) 874-EXPO. This weekend celebration takes place once a year, on the first weekend in August. It combines night-life in Atlanta with a raft trip on the Chattahoochee River. The event has been taking place for over a decade now, and attracts thousands of people each year.

RSVP CRUISES. Several times each year, this travel group offers Caribbean and Mediterranean cruises for gay men. Most are a week long, but their Halloween cruise is a three-day affair, docking in Key West. Information is available through your local travel agent.

WOMANTREK. Tours of Tanzania, the Galapagos Islands, and Nepal, and a bicycle tour through China are just a few of the trips that have been sponsored by Womantrek over the past several years. These trips are limited to women only. For information, contact Womantrek, 1411 E. Olive Way, PO Box 20643, Seattle, WA 98102; (206) 325-4772.

And don't forget... An increasing number of cities have local organizations that organize trips for gay and lesbian members. Usually these are run on a volunteer basis, and are very inexpensive. Call your nearest gay hotline, or check a local gay or lesbian paper, to find out if there's such an organization near you.

GETTING AROUND THE MAJOR CITIES

We asked gay publications in 30 of the largest metropolitan areas of the country to tell us about lesbian and gay life in their area; in some cases we added information from our own mailing lists. What they told us will be helpful for anyone interested in traveling, or even relocating, to one of these cities. Among the information here is:

Information: A hotline or other phone number you can call for general information about gay and lesbian organizations and activities.

Neighborhoods: Areas of the city where gay people are especially visible, or even in the majority.

Bookstores: Stores listed here will generally specialize in books for lesbians and gay men. Some feminist or general bookstores with strong lesbian or gay sections will also be listed, and will be noted as such.

Bars: Bars and clubs with a predominantly lesbian or gay male clientele are included in these figures.

Organizations: Some of the other types of special-interest organizations that exist are noted. We especially asked about neighborhood groups and those focused around gay youth; older people; sports; leather; and political action.

Other publications: In addition to the publication supplying this information (named at the top), other publications directed at the gay community are listed.

Arts: The existence of a gay chorus, band, theater, or other arts group is noted here.

Religion: Some of the more active gay religious groups are listed. Among the most common are Dignity (Catholics), Integrity (Episcopalians), and MCC (Metropolitan Community Church). Denominational affiliations of others are given, if not obvious from their names.

Health: If one or two major health centers are associated with the gay and lesbian community, they are listed.

AIDS: One or two major AIDS-related organizations are listed, when they exist.

Civil rights: Local and state laws protecting the civil rights of gay people are noted, if they exist.

Space limitations make it impossible to give a more comprehensive listing of businesses and organizations in each city, or to list smaller metropolitan areas. To do that would require a book in itself — and in fact, there is such a book: *The Gayellow Pages*, updated annually and published by the Renaissance House in New York. It's available in gay bookstores. To learn more about a particular city, call the number listed under **Information**, or look through one of the papers listed.

ATLANTA
as reported by *Etcetera*
Population: 2.5 million
Information: Gay Helpline, (404) 892-0661, 6 p.m. to 11 p.m., every day.
Neighborhoods: Mid-town; Grant Park

Bookstores: Charis (feminist); Oxford (general)
Bars: about 20
Organizations: Lesbian Feminist Alliance; leather; sports; political action
Other publications: *Guide Magazine; Southern Voice*
Arts: Chorus
Religion: Dignity; Integrity; MCC; and others
AIDS: AID Atlanta
Civil rights: Protection within Atlanta against housing discrimination

BALTIMORE
as reported by the *Baltimore Gay Paper*
Population: 2.3 million
Information: Gay and lesbian switchboard, (301) 837-8888, 7:30 p.m. to 10:30 p.m., every day. A recorded message offers information 24 hours a day.
Neighborhoods: Mt. Vernon; Waverly; Govans
Bookstores: Lambda Rising; Thirtyfirst Street Bookstore (feminist/gay)
Bars: about 15
Organizations: Community center; neighborhood groups; leather; older people; sports; political action; Women's Growth Center
Other publications: *The Alternative*
Arts: Chorus; band; theater
Religion: Dignity; Integrity; MCC
Health: Chase-Brexton Clinic
AIDS: Chase-Brexton Clinic
Civil rights: City anti-discrimination ordinance

BOSTON
as reported by *Gay Community News*
Population: 2.8 million
Information: Gay and lesbian helpline, (617) 426-9371, 6 p.m. to 11 p.m. weekdays.
Neighborhoods: South End; Jamaica Plain; Fenway
Bookstores: Glad Day; New Words (feminist)

Bars: about 20
Organizations: Neighborhood groups; gay youth; leather; older people; sports; political action; Cambridge Women's Center
Other publications: *Bay Windows; Next; The Mirror; The Guide to the Gay Northeast*
Arts: Chorus; band; theater
Religion: Dignity; MCC; Am Tikva; and others
Health: Fenway Community Health Center
AIDS: AIDS Action Committee
Civil rights: Local laws provide protection in Boston and some surrounding communities.

CHICAGO
as reported by *Windy City Times*
Population: 6.1 million
Information: Gay and lesbian switchboard, (312) 929-4357, 7 p.m. to 11 p.m., every day.
Neighborhoods: Lakeview (New Town)
Bookstores: People Like Us; Unabridged (general); Women and Children First (feminist)
Bars: about 70
Organizations: Community center; businessmen's league; gay youth; leather; older people; sports; political action; Kinheart Women's Center
Other publications: *Gay Chicago magazine; Outlines*
Arts: Chorus; theater
Religion: Dignity; Integrity; MCC; Havurat Achayot; and many others
Health: Howard Brown Memorial Clinic
AIDS: AIDS Alternative Health Project; Chicago House; and others
Civil rights: None

CINCINNATI
as reported by *Gaybeat*
Population: 1.4 million
Information: Gay and lesbian community switchboard, (513)

221-7800. Lesbian Line, (513)
381-5610, weekdays.
Neighborhoods: None
Bookstore: Crazy Ladies
(feminist/gay)
Bars: about 10
Organizations: Gay youth; sports;
political action; Gabriel's Corner
(feminist cultural space)
Other publications: *To The Roots*
Arts: Chorus; theater
Religion: Dignity; Integrity; MCC;
All Saints Chapel (Protestant);
Unitarian
Health: STD Clinic
AIDS: STD Clinic
Civil rights: None

CLEVELAND
as reported by Lesbian/Gay
Community Service Center
Population: 1.8 million
Information: Lesbian & Gay Hotline,
(216) 781-6736, 7:00 p.m. to 11:00
p.m., Monday to Friday; 3:00 p.m. to
11:00 p.m., Saturday and Sunday.
Neighborhoods: Lakewood
Bookstore: Another State of Mind
Bars: about 25
Organizations: Community center;
gay youth; leather; sports
Publications: *What She Wants; The Gay
People's Chronicle; Now Cleveland*
Arts: Chorus; band; square dancing
Religion: Dignity; MCC; Chevrei
Tikva
AIDS: Health Issues Taskforce
Civil rights: Employment protection
for state employees only

COLUMBUS
as reported by *Stonewall Union*
Population: 1.3 million
Information: Stonewall Union, (614)
299-7764, Monday to Friday, 9:00
a.m. to 5:00 p.m.
Neighborhoods: German Village,
Victorian Village, Clintonville, Olde
Towne East
Bookstore: Fan the Flames (feminist)

Bars: about 12
Organizations: gay youth; leather;
older people; sports; political action
Publications: *Gaybeat; New Voice; News
of Columbus*
Arts: Theater; Columbus Gay Writers
Guild; Women's Music Union
Religion: Integrity; MCC; Catholic
Men's Support Group; Unitarian;
Spiritualist Association; Chavarah
(Jewish); Lutherans Concerned;
Friends for Lesbian & Gay Concerns;
United Church; Evangelicals
Concerned; Christ United Evangelical
Church; Neo-pagan group
AIDS: Columbus AIDS Task Force
Civil rights: Anti-discrimination for
housing and accommodation

DALLAS/FT. WORTH
as reported by *Dallas Voice*
Population: 3.5 million
Information: Gayline, (214)
368-6283, 7:30 p.m. to midnight.
Neighborhoods: Oak Lawn
Bookstores: Community Bookstore
Bars: about 35
Organizations: Community center;
neighborhood groups; gay youth;
leather; older people; sports; political
action; Among Friends (lesbian educa-
tional organization)
Other publications: *This Week in Texas*
Arts: Chorus; band; theater
Religion: Dignity; Integrity; MCC;
Affirmation; Evangelicals Concerned;
Grace Fellowship; Holy Trinity;
Lutherans Concerned; Affirmation;
United Church of Christ; Beth El
Binah
Health: Oak Lawn Physicians Group
AIDS: AIDS Resource Center/Oak
Lawn Counseling Center
Civil rights: None

DENVER
as reported by *Out Front*
Population: 1.6 million
Information: Gay and Lesbian
Community Center, (303) 831-6268,

10:00 a.m. to 10:00 p.m. weekdays;
4:00 p.m. to 10:00 p.m. Saturdays.
Neighborhoods: Capitol Hill,
Broadway Terrace
Bookstore: Category Six; The Book
Garden (feminist)
Bars: about 20
Organizations: Community center;
gay youth; sports; political action;
Forum (monthly lesbian forum)
Other publications: *Quest* (formerly
The Guide)
Arts: Chorus; band; theater
Religion: Dignity; MCC; United
Faith Ministries
AIDS: Colorado AIDS Project
Civil rights: None

DETROIT
as reported by *Metra Magazine*
Population: 4.3 million
Information: Gay & Lesbian
Community Information Center
(sponsored by Chosen Books), (313)
345-2722, noon to midnight daily.
Neighborhoods: Palmer Park
Bookstore: Chosen Books
Bars: about 40
Organizations: Gay youth; leather;
older people; sports; political action;
many others
Other publications: *Cruise Magazine*
Arts: Chorus; dance groups
Religion: Dignity; Integrity; MCC;
Lutherans Concerned
Health: Henry Ford Hospital
AIDS: Wellness Networks
Civil rights: Anti-discrimination
protection in Detroit

HOUSTON
as reported by *Montrose Voice*
Population: 3.2 million
Information: Gay and Lesbian
Switchboard, (713) 529-3211, 4:00
p.m. to midnight every day.
Neighborhoods: Montrose
Bookstore: Lobo
Bars: about 35

Organizations: Neighborhood groups;
gay youth; leather; sports; political
action
Other publications: *This Week in Texas*
Arts: Band; theater; chamber singers
Religion: Dignity; Integrity; MCC;
Houston Mission Church; Kingdom
Community Church
Health: Montrose Clinic
AIDS: Counseling Center
Civil rights: None

INDIANAPOLIS
as reported by *New Works News*
Population: 1.2 million
Information: Gay & Lesbian Switch-
board, (317) 253-4297, 7:00 p.m. to
11:00 p.m. daily.
Neighborhoods: None
Bookstore: Dreams and Swords
(feminist)
Bars: about 12
Organizations: Sports; political action
Other publications: *The Mirror*
Arts: None
Religion: Dignity; Integrity; MCC
Health: Bell Flower STD Clinic
AIDS: AIDS Task Force
Civil rights: Anti-discrimination law
in Indianapolis

KANSAS CITY, MO.
as reported by *Alternate News*
Population: 1.5 million
Information: Gay Talk, (816)
931-4470, 6:00 p.m. to 5:00 a.m.
every day.
Neighborhoods: Mid-town (31st to
47th Streets)
Bars: about 15
Organizations: Leather; older people;
sports; political action; Lavender
Umbrella (women's group)
Arts: Chorus; band
Religion: Dignity; Integrity; MCC;
L'Cha dogi (Jewish); Atheist; Buddhist
Health: KC Free Health Clinic
AIDS: Good Samaritan Project
Civil rights: None

LOS ANGELES/LONG BEACH

as reported by *L.A. Dispatch*
Population: 8.3 million
Information: Gay and Lesbian
Community Center, (213) 464-7400,
9:00 a.m. to 10:00 p.m. Monday
through Saturday.
Neighborhoods: West Hollywood,
Silver Lake, Hollywood, Studio City
Bookstores: A Different Light;
Unicorn; Sisterhood (feminist)
Bars: about 95
Organizations: Community center;
neighborhood groups; gay youth;
leather; older people; sports; political
action; several women's centers
Other publications: *Edge, Frontiers,
The News, Reactions, Update, Compass,
The Directory, Community Yellow Pages,
Lesbian News, Nightline*
Arts: Chorus; band; theater
Religion: Dignity; Integrity; MCC;
Beth Chayim Chadashim (First gay
Jewish temple in U.S.); many others
Health: Edelman Health Center;
Connexxus
AIDS: AIDS Project LA; AID for
AIDS; AIDS Services Foundation;
Shanti Project; Being Alive
Civil rights: Anti-discrimination laws
in Los Angeles, West Hollywood, and
Laguna Beach

MIAMI/FT. LAUDERDALE

as reported by *The Weekly News*
Population: 2.8 million
Information: Gay Community
Hotline, (305) 759-3661, 7:00 to 9:00
p.m. Monday through Thursday.
Neighborhoods: Miami: Coconut
Grove, Coral Gables, Belle Meade;
Ft. Lauderdale: Riverside, Victoria
Park
Bookstore: Lambda Passages
Bars: about 30
Organizations: Gay youth; sports;
political action; businessman's associa-
tion; women's group
Other publications: *David Magazine*
Arts: Chorus; band; square dancing

Religion: Dignity; Integrity; MCC;
Synagogue Etz-Chaim
Health: TheraFirst (Ft. Lauderdale)
AIDS: Health Crisis Network, PWA
Coalition, Center One, Body Positive
Civil rights: None

MILWAUKEE

as reported by *Wisconsin Light*
Population: 1.3 million
Information: Gay People's Union
Hotline, (414) 562-7010, 7:00 to 10:00
p.m. daily.
Neighborhoods: East Side, Walker's
Point
Bookstores: Harry Schwartz
(general); Websters (general); People's
(progressive)
Bars: about 25
Organizations: Community center;
gay youth; leather; older people;
sports; political action; business
association; Women's Coalition
Other publications: *InStep*
Arts: Chorus; theater
Religion: Dignity; Integrity; MCC;
Lutherans Concerned
Health: Brady St. East Clinic
AIDS: Milwaukee AIDS Project
Civil rights: Statewide anti-
discrimination law

MINNEAPOLIS/ST. PAUL

as reported by *Twin Cities GAZE*
Population: 2.3 million
Information: Gay and Lesbian
Community Action Council Helpline,
(612) 379-6390, 4:00 p.m. to mid-
night, Monday through Saturday.
Neighborhoods: Loring, Kenwood,
Whittier, Powderhorn Park
Bookstores: A Brothers Touch;
Amazon (feminist)
Bars: about 8
Organizations: Gay youth; leather;
older people; sports; political action;
women's center
Other publications: *Equal Time, GLC
Voice, James White Review, Evergreen
Chronicles,* GAZE-TV (cable channel)

Arts: Chorus; band; theater; Quatrefoil Library
Religion: Dignity; Integrity; MCC; Beyt G'Vurah (Jewish); Ecumenical Community Church; many others
AIDS: Minnesota AIDS Project
Civil rights: Anti-discrimination law in Minneapolis; none in St. Paul

NEW ORLEANS

as reported by *Impact*
Population: 1.3 million
Information: There is no switchboard or hotline.
Neighborhoods: French Quarter, Marigny
Bookstore: Faubourg-Marigny
Bars: about 40
Organizations: Leather; sports; political action
Other publications: *Ambush, The Rooster, The Big Easy Times*
Arts: Chorus; theater
Religion: Dignity; MCC; Grace Fellowship; Charismatic; Unitarian
AIDS: New Orleans AIDS Task Force
Civil rights: None

NEW YORK CITY

as reported by *New York Native*
Population: 8.5 million
Information: Lesbian Switchboard, (212) 741-2610, 6:00 p.m. to 10:00 p.m. Monday through Friday. Gay Switchboard, (212) 777-1800, noon to midnight daily.
Neighborhoods: East Village, Upper West Side
Bookstores: A Different Light; Oscar Wilde Memorial
Bars: about 40 in Manhattan; hundreds in greater metropolitan area
Organizations: Community center; neighborhood groups; gay youth; leather; older people; sports; political action
Arts: Chorus; band; theater
Religious: Dignity; Integrity; MCC; Temple Beth Simchat Torah; Lutherans Concerned; Methodists;

many others
Health: Gay Men's Health Crisis; Community Health Project
AIDS: Gay Men's Health Crisis; PWA Coalition
Civil rights: City anti-discrimination ordinance

NORFOLK/VIRGINIA BEACH

as reported by *Our Own Community Press*
Population: 1.3 million
Information: Gay Information Line, (804) 423-0933, 7:00 to 10:00 p.m. most evenings.
Neighborhoods: Ghent (Norfolk)
Bookstores: None with particularly strong gay selection.
Bars: about 10
Organizations: Gay youth; sports; political action
Religion: Dignity; MCC; Unitarian Church
AIDS: Tidewater AIDS Crisis Task Force
Civil rights: None

PHILADELPHIA

as reported by *Philadelphia Gay News*
Population: 4.8 million
Information: Gay Switchboard, (215) 546-7100, 6:00 p.m. to 11:00 p.m. daily. Lesbian Hotline, (215) 222-5110, 6:00 p.m. to 9:00 p.m. Monday and Thursday.
Neighborhoods: Center City
Bookstore: Giovanni's Room
Bars: about 25
Organizations: Community center; gay youth; leather; older people; sports; political action; Sisterspace
Other publications: *Au Courant, Labyrinth*
Arts: Chorus; theater; poetry group
Religion: Dignity; Integrity; MCC; Atheist group
AIDS: Action AIDS; AIDS Task Force; BEBASI
Civil rights: The Human Rights

Ordinance in Philadelphia covers gay rights.

PHOENIX
as reported by *Western Express*
Population: 1.9 million
Information: Lesbian/Gay Community Switchboard, (602) 234-2752, 10:00 a.m. to 10:00 p.m. every day.
Neighborhoods: None.
Bookstore: Humanspace (feminist/gay)
Bars: about 25
Businesses: Restaurants; bookstores
Organizations: Gay youth; leather; older people; sports; political action; professional women's group; businessman's association; FLAC (support group for women)
Other publications: *Phoenix Resource, The Transformer*
Arts: Band; theater
Religion: Dignity; Integrity; MCC; Lutherans Concerned; Affirmation (Mormons)
Health: Phoenix Clinic
AIDS: Community AIDS Council; Arizona AIDS Project; Shanti Project
Civil rights: State housing and employment anti-discrimination bill for minorities covers gay men and lesbians.

PITTSBURGH
as reported by *Out Magazine*
Population: 2.1 million
Information: Gay and Lesbian Community Center, (412) 243-4522, 6:00 p.m. to 9:00 p.m. Monday through Friday; 1:00 p.m. to 3:30 p.m. Saturday.
Neighborhoods: Shadyside; Mexican War Streets area; Southside
Bookstore: St. Elmo's (general)
Bars: about 10
Organizations: Community center; gay youth; leather; older people; sports; political action
Other publications: *Metro*

Arts: Chorus
Religion: Dignity; MCC; Beth Ahava (Jewish)
AIDS: Pitt Men's Study; Pittsburgh AIDS Task Force
Civil rights: None.

SACRAMENTO
as reported by *Mom . . . Guess What*
Population: 1.3 million
Information: Lambda Community Center, (916) 442-0185, 10:00 a.m. to 6:00 p.m. Monday through Friday.
Neighborhoods: Downtown
Bookstore: Lioness (feminist)
Bars: about 10
Organizations: Community center; gay youth; leather; sports; political action; business group; women's center
Other Publications: *Patlar Gazette*
Arts: Chorus; theater; square dancing
Religion: Dignity; Integrity; MCC; Ahvat Zion; Lutherans Concerned
AIDS: Sacramento AIDS Foundation
Civil rights: City anti-discrimination ordinance

SAN DIEGO
as reported by *Update*
Population: 2.2 million
Information: Lesbian and Gay Men's Community Center Information and Counsel Line, (619) 692-4297, 6:00 p.m. to 10:00 p.m. Monday through Saturday.
Neighborhoods: Hillcrest, North Park, Golden Hill
Bookstore: Blue Door (general)
Bars: about 30
Organizations: Community center; gay youth; leather; older people; sports; political action; women's center
Other publications: *Gay Times, Scene, Lesbian Press, Neighbors*
Arts: Chorus; band; theater
Religion: Dignity; MCC; Yachad (Jewish); others
Health: Ciaccio Clinic
AIDS: AIDS Project; Ciaccio Clinic

Civil rights: Anti-discrimination protection in San Diego

SAN FRANCISCO/OAKLAND
as reported by *San Francisco Sentinel*
Population: 3.4 million
Information: Gay and Lesbian Hotline, (415) 841-6224, 10:00 a.m. to 10:00 p.m. Monday through Saturday; Noon to 4:00 p.m. Saturday; 6:00 p.m. to 9:00 p.m. Sunday.
Neighborhoods: Castro, Polk, Noe Valley, Hayes, Valencia
Bookstores: A Different Light; The Love That Dares; Walt Whitman; Old Wives Tales
Bars: about 200
Organizations: Gay youth; leather; older people; sports; political action; women's building
Other publications: *Bay Area Reporter, Coming Up*
Arts: Chorus; band; theater; chamber singers; twirling corps
Religion: Dignity; Integrity; MCC; Congregation Sha'ar Zahav
AIDS: San Francisco AIDS Foundation
Civil rights: City anti-discrimination ordinance

SEATTLE
as reported by *Seattle Gay News*
Population: 1.7 million
Information: There is no hotline. The Gay News, (206) 324-4297, will make referrals and answer brief questions about gay and lesbian businesses and services in Seattle.
Neighborhoods: Capitol Hill; First Hill; Queen Anne; Downtown
Bookstores: Beyond the Closet; Bailey/Coy (general)
Bars: about 30
Organizations: Gay youth; leather; older people; sports; political action; lesbian resource center; businessman's club; antique car club
Other publications: *The Guide Magazine*

Arts: Chorus; band; theater
Religion: Dignity; Integrity; MCC; Congregation Tikvah Chadashah; Affirmation; Pentecostals
Health: Seattle Gay Clinic; Irradia
AIDS: Northwest AIDS Foundation
Civil rights: City anti-discrimination ordinance that covers employment, housing, and public accommodations

ST. LOUIS
as reported by *Gay News-Telegraph*
Population: 2.4 million
Information: Gay and Lesbian Hotline and Action Line, (314) 367-0084, 7:00 to 10:00 p.m. daily.
Neighborhoods: Central West End; Lafayette Square; Soulard; South Grand Area
Bookstore: Our World Too
Bars: about 20
Organizations: Gay youth; older women; leather; sports; political action
Other publications: *Show Me Guide*
Arts: Chorus
Religion: Dignity; MCC; Affirmation (Methodist); others
AIDS: Effort For AIDS
Civil rights: None

TAMPA/ST. PETERSBURG
as reported by *The Weekly News*
Population: 1.9 million
Information: Tampa: Gay Hotline, (813) 229-8839, 7:00 p.m. to 11:00 p.m. daily; St. Petersburg: The Line, (813) 586-4297, 6:00 to 11:00 p.m. most days.
Neighborhoods: Hyde Park (Tampa)
Bookstore: Tomes and Treasures
Bars: about 15
Organizations: Leather; older women; sports; political action; business guild; The Salon (women's group); women's center
Other publications: *Womyn's Words; The Friendly Voice*
Arts: Chorus
Religion: Dignity; MCC

AIDS: Tampa AIDS Network
Civil rights: None

WASHINGTON, D.C.
as reported by *The Washington Blade*
Population: 3.5 million
Information: Gay and Lesbian
Switchboard, (202) 429-4971, 7:30
p.m. to 10:30 p.m.; Lesbian Line,
(202) 387-5525, 7:30 p.m. to 10:30
p.m. daily.
Neighborhoods: Dupont Circle,
Georgetown, Capitol Hill
Bookstores: Lambda Rising; Lammas

(feminist)
Bars: about 30
Organizations: Community center;
neighborhood groups; gay youth;
leather; older people; sports; political
action; women's center
Arts: Chorus; band
Religion: Dignity; Integrity; MCC;
Bet Mishpachah; many others
Health: Whitman Walker Clinic
AIDS: Whitman Walker Clinic
Civil rights: District of Columbia
Human Rights Ordinance covers gay
men and lesbians.

CHURCH POLICIES ON GAY CONCERNS

Church policies on gay issues vary
greatly today. Here's where some of the
major denominations now stand.

Roman Catholic Church
The Catholic Church has consistently condemned all homosexual activity as inherently sinful. It has at the
same time, however, distinguished between a homosexual orientation, which
in itself is considered to be morally neu-
tral, and homosexual practices, which
are considered to be sinful in every case.

In 1976, the Sacred Congregation
of the Faith issued a "Declaration on
Certain Questions Concerning Sexual
Ethics," which addressed a number of
questions related to sexual morality, including homosexuality. The Declaration reaffirmed the Church's traditional
stance on homosexuality, stating that
"homosexual acts are intrinsically disor-
dered and can in no case be approved
of." Further, the Vatican's Congregation for the Doctrine of the Faith issued
a letter on homosexuality in 1986 in
which homosexuality was referred to as

"behavior to which no one has any con-
ceivable right."

Protestant Episcopal Church
Although the Episcopal Church
was the first denomination to ordain a
woman who was openly lesbian, it has
by no means given its unqualified approval to homosexual behavior. At its
Sixty-sixth Triennial General Convention in 1979, the House of Bishops approved a resolution barring the ordination of practicing homosexuals and reaffirmed "the traditional teaching of the
Church on marriage, marital fidelity
and sexual chastity."

In July 1988, the House of Bishops
approved a proposal to forbid discrimination in the church on the grounds of
sexual orientation; however, the House
of Deputies, a body made up of clergy
and laity, voted the proposal down.
Moreover, the Episcopal General Convention's Standing Commission on
Human Affairs and Health declared
that "a homosexual person is someone
whose humanity is considered to be sex-

ually perverted and thus the homosexual person is given to unnatural sexual acts which are immoral in light of Scripture and the Church's teaching."

Presbyterian Church

In 1979, before the merger by which they became the Presbyterian Church (U.S.A.), the northern and southern Presbyterian churches jointly adopted a policy opposing the ordination of gay people. In 1976, the United Presbyterian Church's General Assembly had already voted that it would be "injudicious if not improper" to ordain homosexuals to the ministry. At the same time, the Assembly reaffirmed a previous resolution which stated that the "practice of homosexuality is a sin."

United Methodist Church

In 1972, the Methodist Church issued a "Statement of Social Principles" in which the church declared that homosexuality was "incompatible with Christian teaching," although it supported the civil rights of homosexuals. Three years later, the United Methodist Council of Bishops unanimously approved a statement which declared that the bishops did not "advocate or support ordination for practicing homosexuals."

United Church of Christ

In 1972, the United Church of Christ became the first Christian denomination to ordain an openly gay person to the ministry. Further, in 1975 it affirmed the civil liberties of gay and bisexual persons, stating that the church "must bear a measure of responsibility for the suffering visited upon same-gender-oriented persons."

Unitarian Universalist Association

The Unitarian Universalist Association has perhaps gone further than any other denomination to defend the rights of gay men and lesbians. A series of resolutions from 1970 to 1984 repeatedly upheld the rights of gay men and lesbians. These resolutions include a call to end discrimination against gay and lesbian candidates for the ministry; an affirmation of the practice of conducting services of union for gay and lesbian couples; and the funding of an Office of Gay Concerns.

Southern Baptist Church

Of the mainline denominations, the Southern Baptist Church has probably taken the most conservative view of homosexuality. In 1987, the Southern Baptist Convention condemned homosexuality as "a manifestation of a depraved nature" and "a perversion of divine standards." Furthermore, the Convention linked homosexuality to a general problem of moral decline in modern society. Unlike other churches which, though unbending in their condemnation of homosexual acts, make a distinction between homosexual orientation and homosexual acts, the Southern Baptist Church fails even to make this distinction, declaring that "homosexuals like all sinners can receive forgiveness and victory" through faith in Jesus.

Judaism

Because Jewish congregations vary so widely in questions of doctrine and policy, there is not one definitive Jewish policy regarding homosexuality. Orthodox and Conservative synagogues have generally taken a dim view of the practice of homosexuality. The Union of American Hebrew Congregations, however, which is the main association of Reformed congregations in the United States, adopted a statement in 1979 upholding the human rights of homosexuals. In this statement, it was resolved that homosexual persons were "entitled to equal protection under the law," and congregations were encouraged to "conduct appropriate educational programming . . . to provide greater understanding of the relation of Jewish values to the range of human sexuality."

CONGRESSIONAL REPORT CARD

After Congress adjourned at the end of 1988, the National Gay and Lesbian Task Force prepared a breakdown of how each member of the House and Senate voted during that session on the issues that were of special concern to lesbians and gay men.

Because of the way Congress works, often it was not a particular bill that was being voted on, but an amendment, or a parliamentary motion concerning a bill. Each vote, however, was considered by the NGLTF to be critical to the gay community, and a good indication of how a particular legislator stands on lesbian and gay issues.

The votes for the House of Representatives are different than those for the Senate. Before the chart for each of these bodies is a brief description of the votes being tallied, indicating what the NGLTF considers to be the "correct" vote. The correct votes are shown again, at the top of each page, for easy reference.

The line for each member of Congress indicates whether they voted Yes (Y) or No (N) on each bill or motion; a dash (—) indicates that the member did not vote. The last entry on the line indicates the percentage of the time that member voted with the NGLTF position; a 100% score indicates that every one of their votes cast supported the NGLTF position.

THE HOUSE OF REPRESENTATIVES

1: 1987, DANNEMEYER MOTION TO INSTRUCT — HELMS EDUCATION AMENDMENT

On October 20, 1987, Representative William Dannemeyer (R-CA) introduced a motion to instruct House conferees to agree to the provisions contained in the Helms amendment #963 of HR 3058, Labor, Health and Human Services, and Education Appropriations of 1988.

Amendment #963 prohibits the use of any funds provided under HR 3058 to the Centers for Disease Control from being used to provide AIDS education, information or prevention materials and activities that promote, encourage, or condone homosexual sexual activities or the intravenous use of illegal drugs.

The House approved the Dannemeyer motion by a vote of 368 to 47. A no (N) vote indicates opposition to the motion and the Helms amendment, and is considered the correct vote.

2: 1988, S 557 — THE CIVIL RIGHTS RESTORATION ACT

On March 2, 1988, the House voted 315 to 98 in favor of S 557, the Senate version of the Civil Rights Restoration Act.

The CRRA restores the broad scope of coverage and clarifies the application of Title IX of the Education Amendments Act of 1972, section 504 of the Rehabilitation Act of 1973, the Age Discrimination Act of 1975 and Title VI of the Civil Rights Act of 1964.

Section 504 of the 1973 Rehabilitation Act protects people with contagious or infectious diseases, such as AIDS, from discrimination in employment as long as they do not pose a direct threat to the health and safety of others and are able to perform the duties of the job.

A yes (Y) vote indicates support for the bill, and is considered the correct vote.

3: 1988, S 557 — OVERRIDE OF THE PRESIDENT'S VETO

On March 16, 1988, President Reagan vetoed the Civil Rights Restoration Act. The House voted to override the President's veto by a vote of 292 to 133.

Fearing the House and Senate would vote to override the veto, Jerry Falwell and other right wing leaders rallied their supporters and began a disinformation campaign that members of Congress termed, ". . . unmatched by any other in recent memory." The issue picked to strike fear into the hearts of elected officials was lesbian and gay civil rights. Opponents claimed that the CRRA would create civil rights for homosexuals and called it a gay rights bill in disguise.

In spite of the right-wing effort to kill the legislation, the House voted to override the President's veto.

A yes (Y) vote indicates support for the override, and is considered the correct vote.

4: 1988, HR 3193 — HATE CRIME STATISTICS ACT

On May 18, 1988, the House approved a measure to provide for the collection of statistics on crimes motivated by prejudice based on race, religion, homosexuality, heterosexuality or ethnicity.

The House voted overwhelmingly in favor of the legislation by a vote of 383 to 29.

A yes (Y) vote indicates support for the legislation, and is considered the correct vote.

5: 1988, HR 3193 — MILLER PERFECTING AMENDMENT

During consideration of HR 3193, there was an attempt by Representative George Gekas (R-PA) to strike sexual orientation from the legislation. Representative John Miller (R-WA), in an effort to retain data collection efforts on anti-gay violence, offered a second degree perfecting amendment which deleted the phrase "sexual orientation" and inserted the phrase "homosexuality or heterosexuality."

The House overwhelmingly voted for the retention of anti-lesbian/gay violence data collection efforts by a vote of 384 to 30 for the Miller perfecting amendment.

A yes (Y) vote indicates support for the Miller second degree amendment, and is considered the correct vote.

6: 1988, HR 4783 — DANNEMEYER AMENDMENT TO CUT AIDS FUNDING

During consideration of HR 4783, the Labor, Health and Human Services and Education Appropriations for 1989, Representative William Dannemeyer moved to delete $400 million from the proposed AIDS funding level of $1.35 billion.

A no (N) vote indicates opposition to the reductions, and is considered the correct vote.

7: 1988, HR 1158 — FAIR HOUSING AMENDMENTS ACT

On June 29, 1988, the House overwhelmingly approved the Fair Housing Amendments Act, legislation designed to revise the procedures for enforcement of fair housing. Among other things, HR 1158 would add "handicapped persons" as a protected class under the Fair Housing Law. The bill also provides housing protections for families with children.

The House approved the measure by a vote of 376 to 23. A yes (Y) vote indicates support for the legislation, and is considered the correct vote.

8: 1988, BURTON MOTION TO RECOMMIT HR 1158

Before final approval of the Fair Housing Amendments Act, Representative Dan Burton (R-IN) moved to recommit HR 1158 to the Judiciary Committee with instruction to report the legislation back to the House with the following amendment: the term "handicap" does not include any current infection with the etiological agent for AIDS.

The House rejected the motion to recommit by a vote of 63 to 334.

A no (N) vote indicates opposition to the motion, and is considered the correct vote.

9: 1988, HR 4783, DANNEMEYER MOTION TO RECOMMIT

During consideration of the conference report to HR 4783, Labor, HHS Appropriations, Rep. William Dannemeyer moved to recommit the report back to the conference committee with instructions to agree to Senate amendments — one of which was the Humphrey amendment.

The House rejected the motion to recommit by a vote of 183 to 212.

A no (N) vote indicates opposition to the Dannemeyer motion, and is considered the correct vote.

10: 1988, GREEN MOTION TO INSTRUCT HR 4776, DC APPROPRIATIONS

On September 22, 1988, Rep. Bill Green (R-NY) offered a motion to instruct House conferees to accept a Senate amendment dealing with employee pay raises in the District of Columbia. Rep. Green's motion to instruct was considered before a motion to instruct by Rep. William Dannemeyer (R-CA). Rep. Dannemeyer's motion would have instructed House conferees to accept two Senate amendments — the repeal of the DC AIDS Insurance Bill (offered by Senator Nickles) and the Armstrong amendment dealing with religious exemption in the DC Human Rights Ordinance for discrimination based on sexual orientation.

Rep. Green's motion passed by a vote of 198 to 188. Rep. Dannemeyer's motion was not considered. A yes (Y) vote indicates support for Green's motion, and is considered the correct vote.

11: 1988, HR 5142 — FEDERAL AIDS POLICY ACT

On September 23, 1988, the House passed HR 5142, the Federal AIDS Policy Act by a vote of 367 to 13.

The legislation, sponsored by Rep. Henry Waxman (D-CA), provides $400 million for HIV testing and counseling, provides for confidentiality, and amends the Public Health Service Act with respect to AIDS research programs.

A yes (Y) vote indicates support for the measure, and is considered the correct vote.

12: 1988, HR 5142 — MANDATORY NAME REPORTING

During consideration of HR 5142, Rep. Dannemeyer offered an amendment to mandate the reporting of names for individuals who test positive for HIV infection.

The amendment was defeated by a vote of 70 to 327. A no (N) vote indicates opposition to the Dannemeyer amendment, and is considered the correct vote.

13: 1988, HR 5142 — MANDATORY TESTING MARRIAGE LICENSES

During consideration of HR 5142, Rep. Bill McCollum (R-FL) offered an amendment to mandate HIV testing for applicants of marriage licenses.

The amendment was rejected by a vote of 91 to 304. A no (N) vote indicates opposition to the amendment, and is considered the correct vote.

14: 1988, HR 5142 — HOSPITAL ADMISSION TESTING

During consideration of HR 5142, Rep. Dannemeyer offered an amendment to require hospitals to offer routine HIV testing to persons between the ages of 15 and 49 entering the hospital system for surgery or whose blood will be tested for other purposes.

The amendment was rejected by a vote of 89 to 302. A no (N) vote indicates opposition to the testing amendment, and is considered the correct vote.

15: 1988, HR 5142 — DEMONSTRATION HIV TREATMENT CENTERS

During consideration of HR 5142, Rep. Nancy Pelosi offered an amendment which would establish up to six demonstration HIV monitoring and treatment centers and to provide outpatient monitoring and treatment for research on individuals who are infected with the etiologic agent for AIDS.

The amendment was agreed to by a vote of 322 to 60. A yes (Y) vote indicates support for the Pelosi amendment, and is considered the correct vote.

16: 1988, HR 5142 — McCOLLUM MOTION TO RECOMMIT

During consideration of HR 5142, Rep. Bill McCollum (R-FL) moved to recommit the legislation back to the Committee on Energy and Commerce with instructions to amend the bill to include a measure requiring physicians and counselors to notify spouses of HIV-infected individuals.

The motion to recommit was defeated by a vote of 105 to 279. A no (N) vote indicates opposition to the motion, and is considered the correct vote.

17: 1988, HR 4776, DC APPROPRIATIONS — ARMSTRONG AMENDMENT

During consideration of the conference report to HR 4776, Appropriations for the District of Columbia, the House rejected an attempt by Rep. Julian Dixon (D-CA) to dilute the House's acceptance of an amendment sponsored by Senator Bill Armstrong (R-CO) directing the District of Columbia to alter its Human Rights Ordinance and allow religious institutions to discriminate on the basis of sexual orientation without losing their funding. Rep. Dixon's language would have allowed religious institutions to disavow homosexuality but not to refuse funds, services or use of facilities to people on the grounds of their sexual orientation.

The House rejected the Dixon amendment on September 30, 1988 by a vote of 134 to 201. A yes (Y) vote indicates support for the Dixon amendment, and is considered the correct vote.

representative	1	2	3	4	5	6	7	8	9	10	11	12	13	14	15	16	17	
correct vote	N	Y	Y	Y	Y	N	Y	N	N	Y	Y	N	N	N	Y	N	Y	
ALABAMA																		
Callahan (R-1)	Y	N	N	Y	Y	Y	Y	Y	Y	N	Y	N	Y	Y	N	Y	N	41%
Dickinson (R-2)	Y	N	N	Y	Y	N	Y	Y	Y	N	Y	N	Y	Y	Y	Y	N	41%
Nichols (D-3)	Y	Y	Y	Y	Y	N	Y	N	–	N	–	–	–	–	–	–	–	78%
Bevill (D-4)	Y	Y	Y	Y	Y	N	Y	N	Y	N	Y	N	N	N	Y	N	N	76%
Flippo (D-5)	Y	Y	Y	Y	Y	N	Y	N	Y	N	–	N	N	N	–	–	N	71%
Erdreich (D-6)	Y	Y	Y	Y	Y	N	Y	N	Y	N	Y	N	N	N	Y	N	N	76%
Harris (D-7)	Y	Y	Y	Y	Y	N	Y	N	Y	N	Y	N	N	N	Y	N	N	76%
ALASKA																		
Young (R)	Y	Y	Y	Y	Y	N	Y	N	Y	N	Y	N	N	N	Y	N	N	76%
ARIZONA																		
Rhodes (R-1)	Y	N	N	Y	Y	N	Y	N	Y	N	Y	N	N	N	Y	Y	N	53%
Udall (D-2)	Y	Y	Y	Y	Y	N	Y	N	N	N	Y	Y	N	N	N	Y	N	94%
Stump (R-3)	Y	N	N	N	N	Y	N	Y	Y	N	N	Y	Y	Y	N	Y	N	0%
Kyl (R-4)	Y	N	N	N	N	Y	Y	Y	Y	N	Y	Y	N	Y	N	Y	–	19%
Kolbe (R-5)	Y	Y	Y	Y	Y	N	Y	N	N	Y	Y	N	N	N	Y	N	N	88%
ARKANSAS																		
Alexander (D-1)	Y	Y	Y	Y	Y	N	Y	N	–	Y	Y	N	N	N	Y	N	–	93%
Robinson (D-2)	Y	Y	Y	Y	Y	N	Y	N	Y	N	Y	N	N	N	Y	N	N	76%
Hammerschmidt (R-3)	Y	N	N	N	Y	N	Y	N	Y	N	–	N	Y	N	–	–	N	43%
Anthony (D-4)	Y	–	Y	Y	Y	N	Y	N	N	Y	–	N	N	N	–	–	N	85%
CALIFORNIA																		
Bosco (D-1)	Y	Y	Y	Y	Y	N	Y	N	N	Y	Y	N	N	N	Y	N	Y	94%
Herger (R-2)	Y	N	N	N	Y	N	Y	Y	Y	N	Y	Y	Y	Y	N	Y	N	24%
Matsui (D-3)	–	Y	Y	Y	Y	N	Y	N	N	–	–	N	N	N	–	–	–	100%
Fazio (D-4)	N	Y	Y	Y	Y	N	Y	N	N	Y	Y	N	N	N	Y	N	Y	100%
Pelosi (D-5)	N	Y	Y	Y	Y	N	Y	N	N	Y	Y	N	N	N	Y	N	Y	100%
Boxer (D-6)	N	Y	Y	Y	Y	N	Y	N	N	Y	Y	N	N	N	Y	N	–	100%
Miller (D-7)	N	Y	Y	Y	Y	N	Y	N	N	–	Y	N	N	N	Y	N	–	100%
Dellums (D-8)	N	Y	Y	Y	Y	N	Y	N	N	Y	Y	N	N	N	Y	N	Y	100%
Stark (D-9)	N	Y	Y	Y	Y	N	Y	N	–	Y	Y	N	N	N	Y	N	Y	100%
Edwards (D-10)	N	Y	Y	Y	Y	N	Y	N	N	Y	Y	N	N	N	Y	N	Y	100%
Lantos (D-11)	Y	Y	Y	Y	Y	N	Y	N	N	Y	Y	N	N	N	Y	N	Y	94%
Konnyu (R-12)	Y	N	N	Y	Y	Y	–	–	N	N	Y	Y	Y	Y	N	Y	N	27%
Mineta (D-13)	Y	Y	Y	Y	Y	N	Y	N	N	Y	Y	N	N	N	Y	N	Y	94%
Shumway (R-14)	Y	N	N	N	N	N	N	Y	Y	N	N	Y	Y	Y	N	Y	N	6%
Coelho (D-15)	Y	Y	Y	Y	Y	N	Y	N	N	–	Y	N	N	N	Y	N	Y	94%
Panetta (D-16)	Y	Y	Y	Y	Y	N	Y	N	N	Y	Y	N	N	N	Y	N	–	94%
Pashayan (R-17)	Y	Y	Y	Y	Y	N	Y	N	Y	N	Y	N	N	N	Y	N	Y	82%
Lehman (D-18)	Y	Y	Y	Y	Y	N	Y	N	N	Y	Y	N	N	N	Y	N	Y	94%

representative	1	2	3	4	5	6	7	8	9	10	11	12	13	14	15	16	17	
correct vote	N	Y	Y	Y	Y	N	Y	N	N	Y	Y	N	N	N	Y	N	Y	
Lagomarsino (R-19)	Y	N	N	Y	Y	N	Y	N	Y	N	Y	N	Y	Y	Y	Y	N	47%
Thomas (R-20)	Y	N	N	Y	Y	N	Y	N	Y	–	Y	N	N	N	Y	Y	Y	63%
Gallegly (R-21)	Y	N	N	Y	Y	N	Y	Y	Y	N	Y	Y	Y	Y	Y	Y	N	35%
Moorhead (R-22)	Y	N	N	Y	Y	N	Y	N	Y	N	Y	N	Y	Y	N	Y	–	44%
Beilenson (D-23)	N	Y	Y	Y	Y	N	Y	N	N	Y	Y	N	N	N	Y	N	Y	100%
Waxman (D-24)	N	Y	Y	Y	Y	N	Y	N	–	Y	Y	N	N	N	Y	N	Y	100%
Roybal (D-25)	N	Y	Y	Y	Y	N	Y	N	N	Y	Y	N	N	N	Y	N	Y	100%
Berman (D-26)	N	Y	Y	Y	Y	N	Y	N	N	Y	Y	N	N	N	Y	N	Y	100%
Levine (D-27)	N	Y	Y	Y	Y	N	Y	N	N	Y	Y	N	N	N	Y	N	–	100%
Dixon (D-28)	N	Y	Y	Y	Y	N	–	–	N	Y	Y	N	N	N	Y	N	Y	100%
Hawkins (D-29)	N	Y	Y	Y	Y	N	Y	N	N	Y	–	–	–	–	–	–	Y	100%
Martinez (D-30)	Y	Y	–	Y	Y	N	Y	N	N	Y	Y	N	N	N	Y	N	Y	94%
Dymally (D-31)	N	Y	Y	Y	Y	N	Y	N	–	–	Y	–	–	–	Y	N	Y	100%
Anderson (D-32)	Y	Y	Y	Y	Y	N	–	–	N	Y	Y	N	N	N	Y	N	Y	94%
Dreier (R-33)	Y	N	N	Y	Y	N	N	Y	Y	–	–	–	–	–	–	–	N	30%
Torres (D-34)	Y	Y	Y	Y	Y	N	Y	N	N	Y	Y	N	N	N	Y	N	Y	94%
Lewis (R-35)	Y	Y	N	–	–	N	–	–	Y	N	Y	N	N	N	Y	N	N	62%
Brown (D-36)	N	Y	Y	Y	Y	N	Y	N	N	–	–	–	–	–	–	–	–	100%
McCandless (R-37)	Y	N	N	Y	Y	N	N	Y	Y	N	Y	Y	Y	Y	N	Y	–	25%
Dornan (R-38)	Y	N	N	–	–	Y	Y	N	Y	N	N	Y	Y	Y	Y	Y	N	20%
Dannemeyer (R-39)	Y	N	N	N	N	Y	N	Y	Y	N	N	Y	Y	Y	N	Y	N	0%
Badham (R-40)	Y	N	N	N	Y	Y	–	–	–	N	–	–	–	–	–	–	–	14%
Lowery (R-41)	Y	N	N	Y	Y	–	Y	Y	N	–	Y	N	Y	Y	Y	Y	–	50%
Lungren (R-42)	Y	Y	Y	N	Y	N	Y	N	Y	N	Y	Y	Y	Y	Y	Y	–	50%
Packard (R-43)	Y	N	N	Y	Y	–	Y	Y	–	N	–	Y	Y	Y	–	–	N	25%
Bates (D-44)	–	Y	Y	Y	Y	N	Y	N	N	Y	Y	N	N	N	Y	Y	Y	94%
Hunter (R-45)	Y	N	N	N	N	Y	N	Y	Y	N	N	Y	Y	Y	N	Y	N	0%

COLORADO

Schroeder (D-1)	Y	Y	Y	Y	Y	N	Y	N	–	Y	Y	N	N	N	Y	N	–	93%
Skaggs (D-2)	Y	Y	Y	Y	Y	N	Y	N	N	N	Y	Y	N	N	N	Y	N	Y	94%
Campbell (D-3)	Y	Y	Y	Y	Y	N	Y	N	N	N	Y	Y	N	N	N	Y	N	–	94%
Brown (R-4)	Y	Y	Y	Y	N	N	Y	Y	Y	N	Y	Y	Y	Y	Y	Y	N	41%
Hefley (R-5)	Y	N	N	Y	Y	N	Y	Y	Y	Y	Y	Y	Y	N	Y	Y	N	47%
Schaefer (R-6)	Y	N	N	Y	Y	N	Y	Y	Y	N	Y	Y	N	Y	Y	–	50%

CONNECTICUT

Kennelly (D-1)	Y	Y	Y	Y	Y	N	Y	N	N	Y	Y	Y	N	N	N	Y	N	Y	94%
Gejdenson (D-2)	Y	Y	Y	Y	Y	N	–	–	N	Y	Y	Y	N	N	N	Y	N	Y	93%
Morrison (D-3)	N	Y	Y	Y	Y	N	Y	N	N	Y	Y	Y	N	N	N	Y	N	Y	100%
Shays (R-4)	Y	Y	Y	Y	Y	N	Y	N	N	Y	Y	Y	N	N	N	Y	N	Y	94%
Rowland (R-5)	Y	Y	Y	Y	Y	N	Y	N	Y	N	Y	N	N	N	Y	N	N	76%
Johnson (R-6)	Y	Y	Y	Y	Y	N	Y	N	N	N	Y	N	N	Y	N	Y	N	N	76%

representative	1	2	3	4	5	6	7	8	9	10	11	12	13	14	15	16	17	
correct vote	N	Y	Y	Y	Y	N	Y	N	N	Y	Y	N	N	N	Y	N	Y	

DELAWARE

Carper (D)	Y	Y	Y	Y	Y	N	Y	N	N	N	Y	N	N	N	Y	N	N	82%

FLORIDA

	1	2	3	4	5	6	7	8	9	10	11	12	13	14	15	16	17	
Hutto (D-1)	Y	Y	N	Y	Y	N	Y	N	Y	N	Y	N	N	N	Y	Y	N	65%
Grant (D-2)	Y	Y	Y	Y	Y	N	Y	N	N	–	Y	N	N	N	Y	N	–	93%
Bennett (D-3)	Y	Y	Y	Y	Y	N	Y	N	Y	N	Y	N	N	N	Y	N	N	82%
Chappell (D-4)	Y	Y	Y	Y	Y	N	Y	N	N	N	Y	N	N	N	Y	N	N	88%
McCollum (R-5)	Y	Y	N	N	Y	N	–	–	Y	N	N	Y	Y	Y	N	Y	N	20%
MacKay (D-6)	Y	Y	Y	Y	Y	N	–	–	–	–	–	–	–	–	–	–	–	83%
Gibbons (D-7)	Y	Y	Y	Y	Y	N	Y	N	N	N	Y	N	N	Y	Y	Y	–	75%
Young (R-8)	Y	Y	N	Y	Y	N	Y	Y	Y	N	Y	Y	Y	N	Y	Y	Y	53%
Bilirakis (R-9)	Y	N	Y	Y	N	N	Y	N	Y	N	Y	Y	Y	N	Y	Y	N	41%
Ireland (R-10)	Y	N	Y	Y	N	Y	N	Y	N	Y	Y	Y	–	N	Y	N	38%
Nelson (D-11)	Y	Y	Y	Y	Y	N	Y	N	N	N	Y	Y	Y	Y	Y	Y	N	53%
Lewis (R-12)	Y	N	Y	Y	N	Y	N	Y	N	Y	Y	Y	Y	N	Y	N	35%
Mack (D-13)	Y	–	N	–	–	–	–	–	Y	N	–	–	–	–	–	–	–	0%
Mica (D-14)	–	Y	Y	Y	Y	–	–	–	–	Y	Y	–	–	–	Y	N	–	100%
Shaw (R-15)	Y	N	N	Y	Y	N	Y	N	Y	N	Y	–	Y	–	Y	Y	N	47%
Smith (D-16)	Y	Y	Y	Y	Y	N	Y	N	N	Y	Y	N	N	N	Y	N	–	94%
Lehman (D-17)	N	Y	Y	Y	Y	N	Y	N	N	Y	Y	N	N	N	Y	N	Y	100%
Pepper (D-18)	Y	Y	Y	Y	Y	N	Y	N	N	–	–	–	N	–	–	–	Y	91%
Fascell (D-19)	Y	Y	Y	Y	Y	N	Y	N	N	Y	Y	N	N	N	Y	N	–	94%

GEORGIA

	1	2	3	4	5	6	7	8	9	10	11	12	13	14	15	16	17	
Thomas (D-1)	Y	Y	Y	Y	Y	N	Y	N	N	Y	Y	N	N	N	Y	N	N	88%
Hatcher (D-2)	Y	Y	Y	Y	Y	N	Y	N	N	Y	Y	N	N	N	Y	N	N	88%
Ray (D-3)	Y	Y	N	Y	Y	–	–	–	Y	N	Y	N	N	N	Y	N	–	69%
Swindall (R-4)	Y	N	N	Y	Y	N	N	Y	Y	N	Y	Y	Y	Y	Y	Y	–	29%
Lewis (D-5)	N	Y	Y	Y	Y	N	Y	N	N	Y	Y	N	N	N	Y	N	Y	100%
Gingrich (R-6)	Y	N	Y	Y	Y	Y	Y	Y	Y	N	N	Y	Y	Y	Y	Y	–	31%
Darden (D-7)	Y	Y	Y	Y	Y	N	Y	N	N	Y	Y	N	N	N	Y	N	–	96%
Rowland (D-8)	Y	Y	N	Y	Y	N	Y	N	N	Y	Y	N	N	N	Y	N	–	88%
Jenkins (D-9)	Y	Y	Y	Y	Y	N	Y	N	Y	N	Y	N	N	N	Y	N	–	81%
Barnard (D-10)	Y	N	N	Y	Y	N	Y	N	Y	–	–	–	N	–	–	–	–	56%

HAWAII

	1	2	3	4	5	6	7	8	9	10	11	12	13	14	15	16	17	
Saiki (R-1)	Y	Y	Y	Y	Y	Y	N	–	–	N	N	Y	N	N	N	Y	N	N	80%
Akaka (D-2)	Y	Y	Y	–	–	N	Y	N	N	Y	Y	N	N	N	Y	N	Y	93%

IDAHO

	1	2	3	4	5	6	7	8	9	10	11	12	13	14	15	16	17	
Craig (R-1)	Y	N	N	Y	N	N	Y	Y	Y	N	Y	Y	Y	Y	Y	Y	N	29%
Stallings (D-2)	Y	Y	Y	Y	Y	N	Y	N	Y	N	–	N	N	N	Y	–	N	73%

representative	1	2	3	4	5	6	7	8	9	10	11	12	13	14	15	16	17	
correct vote	N	Y	Y	Y	Y	N	Y	N	N	Y	Y	N	N	N	Y	N	Y	

ILLINOIS

representative	1	2	3	4	5	6	7	8	9	10	11	12	13	14	15	16	17	
Hayes (D-1)	N	Y	Y	Y	Y	–	–	–	N	Y	Y	N	N	N	Y	N	Y	100%
Savage (D-2)	Y	Y	Y	Y	Y	Y	–	Y	N	N	Y	Y	N	N	N	Y	N	Y	94%
Russo (D-3)	Y	Y	N	Y	Y	N	Y	N	Y	N	–	N	–	–	–	–	N	58%
Davis (R-4)	Y	N	N	N	N	Y	Y	N	Y	N	–	N	N	Y	Y	–	–	36%
Lipinski (D-5)	Y	Y	Y	Y	Y	N	Y	N	–	N	–	N	N	N	Y	–	N	79%
Hyde (R-6)	Y	N	N	Y	Y	N	Y	N	Y	N	Y	N	Y	N	Y	N	N	59%
Collins (D-7)	–	Y	Y	–	–	N	Y	N	–	Y	Y	N	N	N	Y	N	Y	100%
Rostenkowski (D-8)	Y	–	Y	Y	Y	N	Y	N	N	Y	Y	N	N	N	Y	N	–	93%
Yates (D-9)	N	Y	Y	Y	Y	N	Y	N	N	–	Y	N	N	N	Y	N	Y	100%
Porter (R-10)	Y	–	Y	Y	Y	N	Y	N	Y	N	Y	N	–	N	Y	N	N	75%
Annunzio (D-11)	Y	Y	Y	Y	Y	N	Y	N	N	Y	Y	N	N	N	Y	N	N	88%
Crane (R-12)	Y	N	N	N	Y	N	Y	Y	N	N	Y	Y	Y	N	Y	N	0%
Fawell (R-13)	Y	Y	N	Y	Y	Y	Y	Y	Y	N	–	N	Y	Y	Y	–	N	40%
Hastert (R-14)	Y	N	N	Y	N	Y	Y	Y	Y	N	Y	N	Y	N	N	Y	N	29%
Madigan (R-15)	Y	N	–	Y	Y	N	–	–	Y	N	Y	N	N	N	Y	N	N	64%
Martin (R-16)	Y	Y	Y	Y	Y	N	Y	N	–	N	Y	N	N	N	Y	Y	–	80%
Evans (D-17)	Y	Y	Y	Y	Y	N	Y	N	N	Y	Y	N	N	N	Y	N	Y	94%
Michel (R-18)	Y	N	N	Y	Y	N	Y	N	–	N	–	Y	Y	N	–	–	N	46%
Bruce (D-19)	Y	Y	Y	Y	Y	N	Y	N	N	Y	Y	N	N	N	Y	N	N	88%
Durbin (D-20)	Y	Y	Y	Y	Y	N	Y	N	N	Y	Y	N	N	N	Y	N	Y	94%
Costello (D-21)	–	–	–	–	–	–	–	–	–	–	Y	Y	N	N	N	Y	N	N	88%
Gray (D-22)	Y	Y	–	Y	Y	N	Y	N	N	–	–	–	–	–	–	–	Y	89%

INDIANA

representative	1	2	3	4	5	6	7	8	9	10	11	12	13	14	15	16	17	
Visclosky (D-1)	N	Y	Y	Y	Y	N	Y	N	N	Y	Y	N	N	N	Y	N	Y	100%
Sharp (D-2)	Y	Y	Y	Y	Y	N	Y	N	Y	N	Y	N	N	N	Y	N	N	76%
Hiler (R-3)	Y	N	N	Y	Y	N	Y	N	Y	N	Y	Y	N	Y	Y	Y	N	47%
Coats (R-4)	Y	N	N	Y	N	N	Y	N	Y	N	Y	Y	Y	Y	Y	Y	–	44%
Jontz (D-5)	Y	Y	Y	Y	Y	N	Y	N	N	Y	Y	N	N	N	Y	N	Y	94%
Burton (R-6)	Y	N	N	N	N	Y	N	Y	Y	N	N	Y	Y	N	Y	N	0%
Myers (R-7)	Y	N	N	Y	Y	N	–	–	Y	N	Y	N	Y	N	N	Y	N	40%
McCloskey (D-8)	Y	Y	Y	Y	Y	N	Y	N	N	Y	Y	N	N	N	Y	N	N	88%
Hamilton (D-9)	Y	Y	Y	Y	Y	N	Y	N	Y	N	Y	N	N	N	N	Y	N	–	81%
Jacobs (D-10)	Y	Y	Y	Y	Y	N	Y	N	N	N	Y	N	N	N	Y	N	N	82%

IOWA

representative	1	2	3	4	5	6	7	8	9	10	11	12	13	14	15	16	17	
Leach (R-1)	Y	Y	Y	Y	Y	N	Y	N	N	Y	Y	N	N	N	Y	N	N	88%
Tauke (R-2)	Y	Y	N	Y	Y	N	Y	N	Y	N	Y	N	N	N	Y	N	Y	N	53%
Nagle (D-3)	Y	Y	Y	Y	Y	N	–	–	N	Y	Y	N	N	N	Y	N	N	87%
Smith (D-4)	Y	Y	Y	–	–	N	Y	N	–	Y	Y	N	N	N	Y	N	N	86%
Lightfoot (R-5)	Y	–	–	Y	Y	N	Y	N	Y	N	Y	N	N	N	Y	N	N	60%
Grandy (R-6)	Y	Y	N	Y	Y	N	Y	N	Y	N	Y	N	N	N	Y	Y	N	65%

representative	1	2	3	4	5	6	7	8	9	10	11	12	13	14	15	16	17	
correct vote	N	Y	Y	Y	Y	N	Y	N	N	Y	Y	N	N	N	Y	N	Y	

KANSAS

Roberts (R-1)	Y	N	N	Y	Y	N	Y	N	Y	N	–	N	N	N	–	–	–	62%
Slattery (D-2)	Y	Y	Y	Y	Y	N	Y	N	Y	N	Y	N	N	N	Y	N	N	76%
Meyers (R-3)	Y	Y	Y	Y	Y	N	Y	Y	Y	N	Y	N	N	N	Y	Y	N	65%
Glickman (D-4)	Y	Y	Y	Y	Y	N	Y	N	Y	N	Y	N	N	N	N	N	N	71%
Whittaker (R-5)	Y	N	N	Y	Y	N	Y	N	Y	N	Y	Y	Y	Y	Y	N	Y	N	41%

KENTUCKY

Hubbard (D-1)	Y	Y	N	Y	Y	N	Y	N	Y	N	Y	N	N	N	Y	Y	Y	71%
Natcher (D-2)	Y	Y	Y	Y	Y	N	Y	N	N	Y	Y	N	N	N	Y	N	Y	94%
Mazzoli (D-3)	Y	Y	Y	Y	Y	N	Y	N	N	Y	Y	N	N	N	Y	N	Y	94%
Bunning (R-4)	Y	N	N	N	Y	N	Y	N	Y	N	Y	Y	Y	Y	N	Y	–	31%
Rogers (R-5)	Y	N	N	Y	Y	N	Y	N	Y	N	Y	Y	Y	Y	–	Y	N	38%
Hopkins (R-6)	Y	Y	Y	N	Y	N	Y	N	Y	N	Y	N	N	N	Y	N	N	59%
Perkins (D-7)	Y	Y	Y	Y	Y	N	Y	N	N	N	Y	N	N	N	Y	N	Y	88%

LOUISIANA

Livingston (R-1)	–	N	N	Y	N	N	N	Y	Y	N	–	Y	Y	N	Y	–	N	27%
Boggs (D-2)	Y	Y	Y	Y	Y	N	Y	N	Y	N	Y	N	N	N	Y	N	Y	88%
Tauzin (D-3)	–	Y	Y	Y	Y	N	Y	N	Y	N	Y	N	N	N	Y	N	N	81%
McCrery (R-4)	–	–	–	–	–	–	–	–	–	N	Y	N	N	Y	Y	N	–	63%
Huckaby (D-5)	Y	–	Y	Y	Y	N	Y	N	Y	N	–	N	N	N	N	–	–	69%
Baker (R-6)	Y	–	N	Y	Y	N	Y	N	Y	–	Y	Y	N	N	N	Y	N	53%
Hayes (D-7)	Y	Y	Y	Y	Y	N	Y	N	Y	Y	Y	N	N	N	Y	N	N	82%
Holloway (R-8)	Y	–	N	N	N	Y	Y	Y	Y	–	N	Y	Y	Y	N	Y	–	14%

MAINE

Brennan (D-1)	Y	Y	Y	Y	Y	N	Y	N	N	Y	Y	N	N	N	Y	N	N	88%
Snowe (R-2)	Y	Y	Y	Y	Y	N	Y	N	Y	N	Y	N	N	N	Y	N	N	76%

MARYLAND

Dyson (D-1)	Y	Y	Y	Y	Y	N	Y	N	Y	–	Y	N	N	N	Y	N	N	81%
Bentley (R-2)	Y	Y	N	Y	Y	N	Y	Y	Y	N	Y	–	N	Y	N	N	N	50%
Cardin (D-3)	Y	Y	Y	Y	Y	N	Y	N	N	Y	Y	N	N	N	Y	N	–	94%
McMillen (D-4)	Y	Y	Y	Y	Y	N	Y	N	N	Y	Y	N	N	N	Y	N	N	88%
Hoyer (D-5)	N	Y	Y	Y	Y	N	Y	N	N	Y	Y	N	N	N	Y	N	Y	100%
Byron (R-6)	Y	Y	Y	Y	Y	N	Y	N	Y	–	Y	–	–	–	–	N	N	75%
Mfume (D-7)	Y	Y	Y	Y	Y	N	Y	N	N	Y	Y	N	N	N	Y	N	Y	94%
Morella (R-8)	Y	Y	Y	Y	Y	N	Y	N	N	Y	Y	N	N	N	Y	N	Y	94%

MASSACHUSETTS

Conte (R-1)	Y	Y	Y	Y	Y	N	Y	N	N	N	Y	N	N	N	Y	N	Y	88%
Boland (D-2)	Y	Y	Y	Y	Y	N	Y	N	–	Y	Y	N	N	N	Y	N	–	94%
Early (D-3)	N	Y	Y	Y	Y	N	Y	N	N	Y	Y	N	N	N	Y	N	–	100%
Frank (D-4)	N	Y	Y	Y	Y	N	Y	N	N	Y	Y	N	N	N	Y	N	Y	100%

representative	1	2	3	4	5	6	7	8	9	10	11	12	13	14	15	16	17	
correct vote	N	Y	Y	Y	Y	N	Y	N	N	Y	Y	N	N	N	Y	N	Y	
Atkins (D-5)	Y	Y	Y	Y	Y	N	Y	N	N	Y	Y	N	N	N	Y	N	Y	94%
Mavroules (D-6)	Y	Y	Y	Y	Y	N	Y	N	N	Y	Y	N	N	N	Y	N	Y	94%
Markey (D-7)	N	Y	Y	Y	Y	N	Y	N	N	Y	Y	N	N	N	Y	N	Y	100%
Kennedy (D-8)	N	Y	Y	Y	Y	N	Y	N	N	Y	Y	N	N	N	Y	N	Y	100%
Moakley (D-9)	Y	Y	Y	Y	Y	N	Y	N	N	Y	Y	N	N	N	Y	N	Y	94%
Studds (D-10)	N	Y	Y	Y	Y	N	Y	N	N	Y	Y	N	N	N	Y	N	Y	100%
Donnelly (D-11)	Y	Y	Y	Y	Y	N	Y	N	Y	Y	Y	N	N	N	Y	N	Y	88%

MICHIGAN

representative	1	2	3	4	5	6	7	8	9	10	11	12	13	14	15	16	17	
Conyers (D-1)	N	Y	Y	Y	Y	N	Y	N	N	Y	Y	–	–	–	Y	N	–	100%
Pursell (R-2)	Y	Y	N	–	Y	N	Y	N	N	N	Y	N	N	N	Y	Y	–	80%
Wolpe (D-3)	N	Y	Y	Y	Y	N	Y	N	N	Y	Y	N	N	N	Y	N	Y	100%
Upton (R-4)	Y	Y	N	Y	Y	N	Y	N	Y	N	Y	N	N	Y	Y	Y	N	59%
Henry (R-5)	Y	N	N	Y	Y	N	Y	N	Y	N	Y	N	Y	Y	Y	Y	N	47%
Carr (D-6)	Y	Y	Y	Y	Y	N	Y	N	N	Y	Y	N	N	N	N	N	Y	88%
Kildee (D-7)	Y	Y	Y	Y	Y	N	Y	N	N	Y	Y	N	N	N	Y	N	Y	94%
Traxler (D-8)	Y	Y	Y	Y	Y	N	Y	N	N	–	Y	N	N	N	Y	N	–	93%
Vander Jagt (R-9)	Y	N	N	Y	Y	N	Y	N	Y	–	Y	N	Y	Y	Y	N	N	56%
Schuette (R-10)	Y	Y	Y	Y	Y	N	Y	N	Y	N	Y	N	Y	Y	Y	Y	–	63%
Davis (R-11)	–	Y	Y	Y	Y	Y	Y	N	N	N	Y	N	N	N	Y	N	–	87%
Bonior (D-12)	N	Y	Y	Y	Y	N	Y	N	N	–	Y	N	N	N	Y	N	Y	100%
Crockett (D-13)	N	Y	Y	Y	Y	N	Y	N	Y	Y	Y	N	N	N	Y	N	–	94%
Hertel (D-14)	Y	Y	Y	Y	Y	N	Y	N	N	Y	Y	N	N	N	Y	N	Y	94%
Ford (D-15)	N	Y	Y	Y	Y	N	Y	N	N	Y	Y	N	N	N	Y	N	Y	100%
Dingell (D-16)	Y	Y	Y	Y	Y	N	Y	N	N	Y	Y	N	N	N	Y	N	N	88%
Levin (D-17)	Y	Y	Y	Y	Y	N	Y	N	N	Y	Y	N	N	N	Y	N	Y	94%
Broomfield (R-18)	Y	Y	N	Y	Y	N	Y	N	Y	N	Y	N	Y	N	Y	Y	N	71%

MINNESOTA

representative	1	2	3	4	5	6	7	8	9	10	11	12	13	14	15	16	17	
Penny (D-1)	Y	Y	Y	Y	Y	N	Y	N	Y	N	Y	Y	N	Y	Y	N	N	64%
Weber (R-2)	Y	Y	N	Y	Y	N	Y	Y	Y	N	Y	Y	Y	–	N	N	N	47%
Frenzel (R-3)	Y	Y	Y	Y	Y	N	Y	N	N	N	Y	N	N	Y	Y	N	–	81%
Vento (D-4)	Y	Y	Y	Y	Y	N	Y	N	–	Y	Y	N	N	N	Y	N	Y	93%
Sabo (D-5)	N	Y	Y	Y	Y	N	Y	N	N	Y	Y	N	N	N	Y	N	Y	100%
Sikorski (D-6)	Y	Y	Y	Y	Y	N	Y	N	N	Y	Y	N	N	N	Y	N	Y	94%
Strangeland (R-7)	Y	N	N	Y	Y	N	Y	N	Y	N	Y	Y	Y	Y	Y	N	N	47%
Oberstar (D-8)	Y	Y	Y	Y	Y	N	Y	N	N	Y	Y	N	N	N	Y	N	Y	94%

MISSISSIPPI

representative	1	2	3	4	5	6	7	8	9	10	11	12	13	14	15	16	17	
Whitten (D-1)	Y	Y	Y	Y	Y	N	Y	N	N	Y	Y	N	N	N	Y	N	N	88%
Espy (D-2)	Y	Y	Y	Y	Y	N	Y	N	N	–	Y	N	N	N	Y	N	Y	94%
Montgomery (D-3)	Y	Y	Y	Y	Y	N	Y	N	Y	–	Y	N	N	N	Y	N	–	87%
Dowdy (D-4)	–	–	Y	Y	Y	N	Y	N	–	–	–	–	–	–	–	–	–	100%
Lott (R-5)	Y	N	N	Y	Y	Y	Y	Y	Y	Y	–	–	–	–	–	–	–	33%

representative	1	2	3	4	5	6	7	8	9	10	11	12	13	14	15	16	17	
correct vote	N	Y	Y	Y	Y	N	Y	N	N	Y	Y	N	N	N	Y	N	Y	
MISSOURI																		
Clay (D-1)	N	Y	Y	Y	Y	N	Y	N	N	Y	Y	N	N	–	Y	N	–	100%
Buechner (R-2)	Y	Y	N	Y	Y	N	Y	N	Y	N	Y	N	N	N	Y	N	N	71%
Gephardt (D-3)	–	–	–	Y	Y	N	Y	N	Y	Y	–	N	N	N	–	–	Y	91%
Skelton (D-4)	Y	Y	Y	Y	N	N	Y	N	Y	Y	Y	N	N	N	Y	N	N	76%
Wheat (D-5)	Y	Y	Y	Y	Y	N	Y	N	N	Y	Y	N	N	N	Y	N	Y	94%
Coleman (R-6)	Y	Y	N	Y	Y	N	Y	N	Y	N	Y	N	N	Y	Y	Y	N	59%
Taylor (R-7)	Y	N	N	Y	Y	N	Y	N	Y	–	–	–	–	–	–	–	–	56%
Emerson (R-8)	Y	N	N	Y	N	N	Y	Y	Y	N	Y	Y	Y	Y	N	Y	N	24%
Volkmer (D-9)	Y	Y	Y	Y	N	N	Y	N	Y	N	Y	N	N	N	Y	N	N	71%
MONTANA																		
Williams (D-1)	Y	Y	Y	Y	Y	Y	N	Y	N	N	Y	Y	N	N	N	Y	Y	88%
Marlenee (R-2)	Y	N	N	N	Y	N	Y	N	Y	N	Y	Y	Y	Y	N	Y	N	29%
NEBRASKA																		
Bereuter (R-1)	Y	Y	Y	Y	Y	N	Y	N	Y	N	Y	N	N	Y	N	N	N	65%
Daub (R-2)	Y	Y	N	Y	Y	–	Y	Y	–	–	–	–	–	–	–	–	–	57%
Smith (R-3)	Y	Y	N	Y	Y	N	Y	N	Y	N	Y	N	N	N	N	Y	N	59%
NEVADA																		
Bilbray (D-1)	Y	Y	Y	Y	Y	Y	N	Y	N	N	Y	Y	N	N	N	Y	N	88%
Vucanovich (R-2)	Y	N	N	Y	Y	N	Y	N	Y	N	Y	N	N	Y	N	Y	N	53%
NEW HAMPSHIRE																		
Smith (R-1)	Y	N	N	Y	Y	N	Y	Y	Y	N	Y	Y	Y	Y	N	Y	N	29%
Gregg (R-2)	Y	Y	N	Y	Y	N	Y	N	Y	N	–	–	–	–	–	–	–	60%
NEW JERSEY																		
Florio (D-1)	Y	Y	Y	Y	Y	N	Y	N	N	Y	Y	N	N	N	Y	N	–	94%
Hughes (D-2)	Y	Y	Y	Y	Y	N	Y	N	N	Y	Y	N	N	N	Y	N	Y	94%
vacant																		
Smith (R-4)	Y	Y	Y	Y	Y	N	Y	Y	Y	Y	N	Y	N	Y	Y	N	N	59%
Roukema (R-5)	Y	Y	Y	Y	Y	N	Y	N	Y	N	Y	–	–	–	Y	Y	N	64%
Dwyer (D-6)	Y	Y	Y	Y	Y	N	Y	N	N	Y	Y	N	N	N	Y	N	N	88%
Rinaldo (R-7)	Y	Y	Y	Y	Y	N	Y	N	Y	N	Y	N	Y	Y	Y	N	N	65%
Roe (D-8)	Y	Y	Y	Y	Y	N	Y	–	N	Y	Y	N	N	–	Y	N	N	87%
Torricelli (D-9)	Y	Y	Y	Y	Y	N	Y	N	N	Y	Y	N	N	N	Y	N	Y	94%
Rodino (D-10)	N	Y	Y	Y	Y	N	Y	N	N	Y	Y	N	N	N	Y	N	Y	100%
Gallo (R-11)	Y	Y	Y	Y	Y	N	Y	N	Y	N	Y	N	Y	N	N	N	N	65%
Courter (R-12)	Y	–	Y	Y	Y	N	Y	N	Y	N	–	–	–	–	–	–	–	67%
Saxton (R-13)	Y	Y	Y	Y	Y	N	Y	N	Y	N	Y	N	Y	N	N	N	N	65%
Guarini (D-14)	Y	Y	Y	Y	Y	N	Y	N	N	Y	Y	N	N	N	Y	N	–	94%

representative	1	2	3	4	5	6	7	8	9	10	11	12	13	14	15	16	17	
correct vote	N	Y	Y	Y	Y	N	Y	N	N	Y	Y	N	N	N	Y	N	Y	

NEW MEXICO

	1	2	3	4	5	6	7	8	9	10	11	12	13	14	15	16	17	
Lujan (R-1)	Y	Y	N	Y	Y	N	Y	N	–	N	Y	Y	Y	N	N	Y	N	50%
Skeen (R-2)	Y	Y	N	Y	Y	N	Y	N	N	N	Y	Y	N	N	Y	N	N	71%
Richardson (D-3)	Y	Y	Y	Y	Y	N	Y	N	N	N	Y	Y	N	N	N	Y	N	Y	94%

NEW YORK

	1	2	3	4	5	6	7	8	9	10	11	12	13	14	15	16	17	
Hochbrueckner (D-1)	Y	Y	Y	Y	Y	N	Y	N	Y	Y	Y	N	N	N	Y	N	N	82%
Downey (D-2)	Y	Y	Y	Y	Y	N	Y	N	N	Y	Y	N	N	N	Y	N	Y	94%
Mrazek (D-3)	Y	Y	Y	Y	Y	N	Y	N	N	Y	Y	N	N	N	Y	N	Y	94%
Lent (R-4)	Y	Y	Y	Y	Y	N	Y	N	Y	N	Y	Y	N	Y	N	N	65%
McGrath (R-5)	Y	–	Y	Y	Y	N	Y	N	Y	N	Y	N	N	N	Y	Y	N	69%
Flake (D-6)	Y	Y	Y	Y	Y	N	Y	N	N	Y	Y	N	N	N	Y	N	Y	94%
Ackerman (D-7)	N	Y	Y	Y	Y	N	Y	N	N	Y	Y	N	N	N	Y	N	Y	100%
Scheuer (D-8)	N	Y	Y	Y	Y	N	Y	N	N	–	–	–	–	–	–	–	Y	100%
Manton (D-9)	Y	Y	Y	Y	Y	N	Y	N	N	N	Y	Y	–	–	–	Y	N	N	86%
Schumer (D-10)	Y	Y	Y	Y	Y	N	Y	N	N	N	Y	Y	N	N	N	Y	N	Y	94%
Towns (D-11)	–	Y	Y	Y	Y	N	Y	N	–	Y	Y	N	N	N	N	Y	N	Y	100%
Owens (D-12)	N	Y	Y	Y	Y	N	Y	N	N	N	Y	Y	N	N	N	Y	N	Y	100%
Solarz (D-13)	Y	Y	Y	Y	Y	N	Y	N	N	N	Y	Y	N	N	N	Y	N	Y	94%
Molinari (R-14)	Y	Y	Y	Y	Y	N	Y	Y	Y	N	Y	N	N	N	N	Y	N	N	71%
Green (R-15)	N	Y	Y	Y	Y	N	Y	N	N	Y	Y	N	N	N	Y	N	Y	100%
Rangel (D-16)	Y	Y	Y	–	Y	N	Y	N	N	Y	Y	–	N	N	Y	N	Y	93%
Weiss (D-17)	N	Y	Y	–	–	N	–	–	N	Y	Y	N	N	N	Y	N	Y	100%
Garcia (D-18)	Y	Y	Y	Y	Y	N	Y	N	–	Y	Y	N	N	N	Y	N	Y	94%
Biaggi (D-19)	–	–	–	–	–	–	–	–	–	–	–	–	–	–	–	–	–	0%
DioGuardi (R-20)	Y	Y	Y	Y	Y	N	Y	N	Y	–	Y	N	Y	N	Y	Y	N	69%
Fish (R-21)	Y	Y	Y	Y	Y	N	Y	N	–	Y	Y	N	N	N	Y	N	Y	94%
Gilman (R-22)	Y	Y	Y	Y	Y	N	Y	N	N	Y	Y	N	N	N	Y	N	Y	94%
Stratton (D-23)	Y	Y	Y	–	–	N	–	–	N	N	Y	N	N	N	N	Y	N	N	69%
Solomon (R-24)	Y	N	N	Y	N	Y	Y	Y	Y	N	Y	Y	Y	Y	N	Y	N	18%
Boehlert (R-25)	Y	Y	Y	Y	Y	N	Y	N	N	N	Y	Y	N	N	N	Y	N	N	88%
Martin (R-26)	Y	Y	Y	Y	Y	N	Y	N	Y	N	–	N	N	N	–	–	N	77%
Wortley (R-27)	Y	Y	N	Y	Y	N	Y	N	Y	–	–	–	–	–	–	–	–	67%
McHugh (D-28)	Y	Y	Y	Y	Y	N	Y	N	N	N	Y	Y	N	N	N	Y	N	Y	94%
Horton (R-29)	Y	Y	Y	Y	Y	N	Y	N	N	N	Y	Y	N	N	N	–	N	–	93%
Slaughter (D-30)	Y	Y	Y	Y	Y	N	Y	N	N	N	Y	Y	N	N	N	Y	Y	Y	88%
Kemp (R-31)	–	–	N	–	–	–	–	–	–	–	N	Y	Y	–	–	Y	Y	–	50%
LaFalce (D-32)	Y	Y	Y	Y	Y	N	Y	N	Y	N	Y	Y	Y	N	N	N	Y	N	N	82%
Nowak (D-33)	Y	Y	Y	Y	Y	N	Y	N	N	Y	–	N	N	N	Y	–	Y	93%
Houghton (R-34)	Y	Y	Y	Y	Y	N	Y	N	–	Y	Y	N	N	N	Y	N	N	88%

NORTH CAROLINA

	1	2	3	4	5	6	7	8	9	10	11	12	13	14	15	16	17	
Jones (D-1)	Y	Y	Y	Y	Y	N	–	–	–	–	Y	Y	N	N	N	Y	N	Y	93%
Valentine (D-2)	Y	Y	Y	Y	Y	N	Y	N	N	Y	Y	N	–	N	Y	N	N	88%
Lancaster (D-3)	Y	Y	Y	Y	Y	Y	N	Y	N	N	Y	Y	N	N	N	Y	N	Y	94%

representative	1	2	3	4	5	6	7	8	9	10	11	12	13	14	15	16	17	
correct vote	N	Y	Y	Y	Y	N	Y	N	N	Y	Y	N	N	N	Y	N	Y	
Price (D-4)	Y	Y	Y	Y	Y	N	Y	N	N	Y	Y	N	N	N	Y	N	Y	94%
Neal (D-5)	Y	Y	Y	Y	Y	N	Y	N	N	Y	Y	N	N	N	Y	N	—	94%
Coble (R-6)	Y	N	N	Y	N	N	Y	Y	Y	N	Y	N	Y	N	N	Y	N	35%
Rose (D-7)	Y	Y	Y	Y	Y	N	Y	N	N	Y	Y	N	N	N	N	N	—	88%
Hefner (D-8)	Y	Y	Y	Y	Y	—	Y	N	N	Y	Y	N	N	N	Y	N	N	88%
McMillan (R-9)	Y	N	N	Y	Y	N	Y	N	N	N	Y	N	Y	N	Y	N	N	71%
Ballenger (R-10)	Y	N	N	Y	N	Y	Y	Y	N	Y	N	Y	N	Y	N	Y	N	35%
Clarke (D-11)	Y	Y	Y	Y	Y	N	Y	N	N	N	Y	N	N	N	Y	N	—	88%

NORTH DAKOTA

	1	2	3	4	5	6	7	8	9	10	11	12	13	14	15	16	17	
Dorgan (D)	Y	Y	Y	Y	Y	N	Y	N	N	—	Y	N	N	N	Y	N	Y	94%

OHIO

	1	2	3	4	5	6	7	8	9	10	11	12	13	14	15	16	17	
Luken (D-1)	Y	Y	Y	Y	Y	N	Y	N	Y	N	Y	N	N	Y	—	N	N	69%
Gradison (R-2)	Y	Y	Y	Y	Y	N	Y	N	N	N	Y	N	N	N	—	Y	—	80%
Hall (D-3)	Y	Y	Y	Y	Y	N	Y	N	N	—	—	—	—	—	—	—	N	80%
Oxley (R-4)	Y	N	N	Y	Y	N	Y	N	Y	N	Y	N	Y	N	—	N	N	60%
Latta (R-5)	Y	N	N	Y	Y	N	Y	Y	Y	N	Y	N	Y	N	—	N	N	50%
McEwen (R-6)	Y	N	N	N	Y	N	N	Y	Y	N	Y	Y	Y	Y	Y	N	—	31%
DeWine (R-7)	Y	N	N	Y	Y	N	Y	N	Y	N	Y	Y	Y	Y	Y	Y	N	41%
Lukens (R-8)	Y	N	N	—	—	Y	N	Y	Y	N	Y	Y	Y	Y	N	Y	N	7%
Kaptur (D-9)	Y	Y	Y	Y	Y	N	Y	N	Y	Y	Y	N	N	N	Y	N	—	88%
Miller (R-10)	Y	N	N	Y	Y	Y	N	N	Y	N	Y	Y	Y	Y	Y	Y	N	29%
Eckart (D-11)	Y	Y	Y	Y	Y	N	Y	N	Y	N	Y	N	N	N	Y	N	N	53%
Kasich (R-12)	Y	Y	N	Y	Y	N	Y	N	Y	N	Y	N	N	Y	N	N	N	65%
Pease (D-13)	Y	Y	Y	Y	Y	—	Y	N	N	Y	Y	N	N	N	Y	N	Y	93%
Sawyer (D-14)	Y	Y	Y	Y	Y	N	Y	N	N	N	Y	N	N	N	Y	N	Y	94%
Wylie (R-15)	Y	N	N	Y	Y	N	Y	N	Y	N	Y	N	Y	Y	Y	Y	N	47%
Regula (R-16)	Y	Y	Y	Y	N	Y	Y	—	N	Y	N	Y	Y	Y	N	N		56%
Traficant (D-17)	Y	Y	Y	Y	Y	N	Y	N	N	N	Y	N	N	N	Y	N	Y	94%
Applegate (D-18)	Y	Y	Y	Y	Y	N	Y	N	Y	N	Y	N	Y	Y	Y	Y	N	59%
Feighan (D-19)	Y	Y	Y	Y	Y	N	Y	N	N	Y	Y	N	N	N	Y	N	Y	94%
Oakar (D-20)	Y	Y	Y	Y	Y	N	—	—	N	Y	Y	N	N	N	Y	N	Y	93%
Stokes (D-21)	—	Y	Y	Y	Y	N	Y	N	N	Y	Y	N	N	N	—	N	—	100%

OKLAHOMA

	1	2	3	4	5	6	7	8	9	10	11	12	13	14	15	16	17	
Inhofe (R-1)	Y	N	N	Y	Y	Y	Y	N	Y	Y	Y	N	N	N	N	Y	N	53%
Synar (D-2)	Y	Y	Y	Y	Y	N	Y	N	N	N	Y	N	N	N	Y	N	Y	94%
Watkins (D-3)	Y	Y	Y	Y	Y	N	Y	N	N	Y	Y	N	N	N	Y	N	N	88%
McCurdy (D-4)	Y	Y	Y	Y	Y	N	Y	N	Y	Y	Y	N	N	N	Y	N	N	82%
Edwards (R-5)	Y	Y	N	Y	Y	N	Y	Y	Y	N	Y	N	N	Y	Y	N	N	59%
English (D-6)	Y	Y	N	Y	Y	N	Y	N	Y	N	Y	N	N	N	Y	N	N	71%

OREGON

	1	2	3	4	5	6	7	8	9	10	11	12	13	14	15	16	17	
AuCoin (D-1)	Y	Y	Y	Y	Y	N	Y	N	N	—	Y	N	N	N	—	N	Y	93%

representative	1	2	3	4	5	6	7	8	9	10	11	12	13	14	15	16	17	
correct vote	N	Y	Y	Y	Y	N	Y	N	N	Y	Y	N	N	N	Y	N	Y	
Smith (R-2)	Y	N	N	N	Y	N	Y	N	Y	N	Y	N	N	N	Y	N	N	59%
Wyden (D-3)	Y	Y	Y	Y	Y	N	Y	N	N	Y	Y	N	N	N	Y	N	Y	94%
DeFazio (D-4)	Y	Y	Y	Y	Y	N	Y	N	N	Y	Y	N	N	N	Y	N	–	94%
Smith (R-5)	Y	N	N	Y	N	Y	Y	Y	Y	N	–	Y	N	N	N	Y	–	25%
PENNSYLVANIA																		
Foglietta (D-1)	N	Y	Y	Y	Y	N	Y	N	N	Y	Y	N	N	N	Y	N	Y	100%
Gray (D-2)	Y	Y	Y	Y	Y	–	Y	–	N	Y	Y	N	N	N	Y	N	–	93%
Borski (D-3)	Y	Y	Y	Y	Y	N	Y	N	N	Y	Y	N	N	N	Y	N	Y	94%
Kolter (D-4)	Y	Y	Y	Y	Y	N	Y	N	N	Y	Y	N	N	N	Y	N	N	88%
Schulze (R-5)	Y	–	Y	Y	Y	N	Y	N	Y	N	Y	N	Y	N	Y	Y	N	63%
Yatron (D-6)	Y	Y	Y	Y	Y	N	Y	N	N	N	Y	N	N	N	Y	N	N	82%
Weldon (R-7)	Y	Y	Y	Y	Y	N	Y	N	Y	N	–	–	–	–	–	–	N	64%
Kostmayer (D-8)	N	Y	Y	Y	Y	N	Y	N	N	Y	Y	N	N	N	Y	N	Y	100%
Shuster (R-9)	Y	N	N	Y	Y	Y	Y	Y	Y	N	N	Y	Y	Y	N	Y	–	19%
McDade (R-7)	Y	Y	N	Y	Y	N	Y	N	N	Y	Y	N	N	N	Y	N	–	88%
Kanjorski (D-11)	Y	Y	Y	Y	Y	N	Y	N	N	Y	Y	N	N	N	Y	N	N	88%
Murtha (D-12)	Y	Y	Y	Y	Y	N	Y	N	N	Y	Y	N	N	N	Y	N	N	88%
Coughlin (R-13)	Y	Y	Y	Y	Y	N	Y	N	N	Y	Y	N	Y	N	Y	Y	N	76%
Coyne (D-14)	Y	Y	Y	Y	Y	N	Y	N	N	Y	Y	N	N	N	Y	N	–	94%
Ritter (R-15)	Y	N	N	Y	Y	N	Y	N	Y	N	Y	Y	N	Y	Y	N	N	53%
Walker (R-16)	Y	N	N	Y	Y	Y	Y	Y	Y	N	Y	Y	Y	Y	Y	Y	N	29%
Gekas (R-17)	Y	N	N	N	N	N	Y	Y	Y	Y	Y	Y	Y	Y	Y	Y	N	24%
Walgren (D-18)	Y	Y	Y	Y	Y	N	Y	N	N	Y	Y	N	N	N	Y	N	Y	94%
Goodling (R-19)	Y	Y	Y	Y	Y	N	Y	N	N	N	Y	N	Y	N	Y	Y	N	71%
Gaydos (D-20)	Y	Y	Y	Y	Y	–	Y	N	N	Y	Y	N	N	N	Y	N	N	88%
Ridge (R-21)	Y	Y	Y	Y	Y	N	Y	N	Y	Y	Y	N	–	–	Y	N	N	80%
Murphy (D-22)	Y	Y	Y	Y	Y	N	Y	N	N	–	Y	N	N	N	Y	N	–	94%
Clinger (R-23)	Y	Y	N	Y	Y	N	Y	N	Y	Y	Y	N	N	N	Y	N	N	76%
RHODE ISLAND																		
St. Germain (D-1)	Y	Y	Y	Y	Y	N	–	–	Y	–	Y	N	N	N	Y	N	–	85%
Schneider (R-2)	Y	Y	Y	Y	Y	Y	N	Y	N	N	Y	–	N	N	N	–	–	Y	93%
SOUTH CAROLINA																		
Ravenel (R-1)	Y	N	N	Y	Y	N	Y	N	N	N	–	N	N	N	–	–	N	64%
Spence (R-2)	Y	N	N	–	–	–	–	–	–	–	N	Y	N	N	N	Y	N	–	60%
Derrick (D-3)	Y	Y	Y	Y	Y	N	Y	N	Y	N	Y	N	N	N	N	N	N	71%
Patterson (D-4)	Y	Y	Y	Y	Y	N	Y	N	Y	N	Y	N	N	N	N	N	N	71%
Spratt (D-5)	Y	Y	Y	Y	Y	–	Y	N	N	N	Y	N	N	N	Y	N	N	81%
Tallon (D-6)	Y	Y	Y	Y	Y	N	Y	N	Y	N	Y	N	N	N	Y	N	Y	76%
SOUTH DAKOTA																		
Johnson (D)	Y	Y	Y	Y	Y	Y	N	Y	N	Y	N	Y	N	N	N	Y	N	N	82%

representative	1	2	3	4	5	6	7	8	9	10	11	12	13	14	15	16	17	
correct vote	N	Y	Y	Y	Y	N	Y	N	N	Y	Y	N	N	N	Y	N	Y	

TENNESSEE

	1	2	3	4	5	6	7	8	9	10	11	12	13	14	15	16	17	
Quillen (R-1)	Y	N	N	Y	Y	N	Y	N	Y	N	–	N	N	N	Y	–	–	64%
vacant																		
Lloyd (D-3)	Y	Y	Y	Y	Y	N	Y	N	Y	N	Y	N	N	N	N	Y	N	65%
Cooper (D-4)	Y	Y	Y	Y	Y	Y	N	Y	N	N	Y	Y	N	N	N	Y	N	88%
Clement (D-5)	–	–	–	–	–	–	–	Y	N	N	Y	Y	N	N	N	Y	N	91%
Gordon (D-6)	Y	Y	Y	Y	Y	Y	N	Y	N	N	Y	–	N	N	N	Y	N	88%
Sundquist (R-7)	Y	N	N	Y	Y	N	Y	Y	Y	N	–	N	Y	Y	–	–	N	36%
Jones (D-8)	Y	Y	Y	–	–	N	–	–	–	–	Y	Y	N	N	N	Y	N	83%
Ford (D-9)	–	–	Y	Y	Y	Y	N	Y	N	N	–	Y	N	–	N	Y	N	Y	100%

TEXAS

	1	2	3	4	5	6	7	8	9	10	11	12	13	14	15	16	17	
Chapman (D-1)	Y	Y	Y	Y	Y	N	Y	N	Y	Y	Y	N	N	N	Y	N	N	82%
Wilson (D-2)	Y	Y	Y	Y	Y	–	–	–	N	N	Y	N	–	–	–	N	–	70%
Bartlett (R-3)	Y	Y	N	Y	Y	Y	N	Y	Y	N	Y	Y	Y	Y	Y	Y	N	35%
Hall (D-4)	Y	N	N	Y	Y	Y	Y	N	Y	N	Y	Y	N	N	Y	Y	N	47%
Bryant (D-5)	Y	Y	Y	Y	Y	N	Y	N	N	Y	Y	N	N	N	Y	N	Y	94%
Barton (R-6)	Y	N	N	N	N	Y	N	Y	Y	N	N	Y	Y	Y	N	Y	N	0%
Archer (R-7)	Y	N	N	N	N	Y	N	Y	Y	N	Y	Y	Y	Y	Y	Y	N	12%
Fields (R-8)	Y	N	N	N	N	Y	N	Y	Y	N	Y	Y	Y	Y	N	Y	N	6%
Brooks (D-9)	Y	Y	Y	Y	Y	N	Y	N	N	Y	Y	N	N	N	Y	N	Y	94%
Pickle (D-10)	Y	Y	Y	Y	Y	N	Y	N	N	Y	Y	N	N	N	Y	N	Y	94%
Leath (D-11)	Y	–	N	N	Y	N	–	–	–	Y	–	–	–	–	–	–	N	43%
Wright (D-12)	*Speaker of the House does not vote.*																	
Boulter (R-13)	Y	–	N	–	–	–	N	Y	–	–	–	–	–	–	–	–	–	0%
Sweeney (R-14)	Y	N	N	Y	Y	Y	–	–	N	–	Y	N	N	N	N	Y	–	46%
De la Garza (D-15)	Y	Y	Y	Y	Y	N	–	–	–	–	Y	N	N	N	Y	N	–	83%
Coleman (D-16)	Y	Y	Y	Y	Y	N	Y	N	N	Y	Y	N	N	N	Y	N	Y	94%
Stenholm (D-17)	Y	N	N	Y	Y	N	Y	N	Y	N	Y	N	N	N	N	N	–	63%
Leland (D-18)	Y	–	Y	Y	Y	–	Y	N	–	Y	Y	N	N	N	Y	N	Y	93%
Combest (R-19)	Y	N	N	N	N	Y	N	Y	Y	N	Y	Y	N	Y	N	N	N	18%
Gonzalez (D-20)	N	Y	Y	Y	Y	N	Y	N	N	Y	Y	N	N	N	Y	N	Y	100%
Smith (R-21)	Y	N	N	Y	Y	Y	Y	Y	Y	N	Y	Y	Y	Y	Y	Y	N	29%
DeLay (R-22)	Y	N	N	N	N	Y	N	Y	Y	N	Y	Y	Y	N	Y	N	Y	12%
Bustamante (D-23)	–	Y	Y	Y	Y	N	Y	N	N	Y	–	N	N	N	–	–	Y	100%
Frost (D-24)	–	Y	Y	Y	Y	N	Y	N	N	Y	–	N	N	N	–	–	Y	100%
Andrews (D-25)	Y	Y	Y	Y	Y	N	Y	N	N	Y	Y	N	N	N	Y	N	–	94%
Armey (R-26)	Y	N	N	N	N	Y	N	Y	Y	N	Y	Y	N	Y	N	Y	N	12%
Ortiz (D-27)	Y	N	Y	Y	Y	N	Y	N	N	Y	Y	N	N	N	Y	N	–	88%

UTAH

	1	2	3	4	5	6	7	8	9	10	11	12	13	14	15	16	17	
Hansen (R-1)	Y	N	N	–	–	N	N	Y	Y	N	Y	Y	N	Y	N	Y	–	21%
Owens (D-2)	Y	Y	Y	Y	Y	N	Y	N	N	Y	Y	N	N	N	Y	N	N	88%
Nielson (R-3)	Y	N	N	N	N	N	N	Y	Y	N	Y	Y	Y	Y	Y	Y	N	12%

representative	1	2	3	4	5	6	7	8	9	10	11	12	13	14	15	16	17	
correct vote	N	Y	Y	Y	Y	N	Y	N	N	Y	Y	N	N	N	Y	N	Y	
VERMONT																		
Jeffords (R)	Y	Y	Y	Y	Y	N	Y	N	N	—	Y	N	N	N	Y	N	—	93%
VIRGINIA																		
Bateman (R-1)	Y	N	N	Y	Y	N	Y	N	Y	N	Y	N	N	N	Y	N	N	65%
Pickett (D-2)	Y	Y	Y	Y	Y	N	Y	N	N	Y	Y	N	N	N	Y	N	N	88%
Blilely (R-3)	Y	N	N	Y	Y	N	Y	N	Y	N	Y	Y	Y	Y	Y	Y	N	41%
Sisisky (D-4)	Y	Y	Y	Y	Y	N	Y	N	N	N	Y	N	N	N	Y	N	N	82%
Payne (D-5)	—	—	—	—	—	—	—	—	—	Y	Y	N	N	N	Y	N	N	88%
Olin (D-6)	Y	Y	Y	Y	Y	N	Y	N	N	N	Y	N	N	N	Y	N	Y	88%
Slaughter (R-7)	Y	N	N	Y	Y	Y	Y	N	Y	N	Y	N	Y	Y	Y	Y	N	41%
Parris (R-8)	Y	N	N	Y	Y	—	Y	N	Y	N	Y	Y	Y	Y	Y	Y	N	38%
Boucher (D-9)	Y	Y	Y	Y	Y	N	—	—	N	—	—	N	N	—	—	—	—	78%
Wolf (R-10)	Y	N	N	Y	Y	N	Y	N	N	Y	N	Y	N	Y	Y	Y	N	53%
WASHINGTON																		
Miller (R-1)	Y	Y	Y	Y	Y	N	Y	N	N	Y	Y	N	N	N	Y	N	Y	94%
Swift (D-2)	N	Y	Y	Y	Y	N	Y	N	N	Y	Y	N	N	N	Y	N	Y	100%
Bonker (D-3)	Y	Y	Y	Y	Y	N	Y	N	N	—	—	—	—	—	—	N	—	89%
Morrison (R-4)	Y	Y	Y	Y	Y	N	Y	N	N	N	Y	N	N	N	Y	N	Y	88%
Foley (D-5)	Y	Y	Y	Y	Y	N	Y	N	N	Y	Y	N	N	N	Y	N	Y	94%
Dicks (D-6)	Y	Y	Y	Y	Y	N	Y	N	N	Y	—	N	N	N	Y	N	Y	94%
Lowry (D-7)	N	Y	Y	Y	Y	N	Y	N	N	—	—	N	N	N	Y	N	Y	100%
Chandler (R-8)	Y	Y	Y	Y	Y	N	Y	N	N	Y	Y	N	N	N	Y	N	Y	94%
WEST VIRGINIA																		
Mollohan (D-1)	Y	Y	Y	Y	Y	N	Y	N	Y	N	Y	N	N	N	—	N	N	75%
Staggers (D-2)	Y	Y	Y	Y	Y	N	Y	N	N	N	Y	N	N	N	Y	N	N	82%
Wise (D-3)	Y	Y	Y	Y	Y	N	Y	N	N	Y	Y	N	N	N	Y	N	N	88%
Rahall (D-4)	Y	Y	Y	Y	Y	N	Y	N	N	N	Y	N	N	N	Y	N	N	82%
WISCONSIN																		
Aspin (D-1)	Y	Y	Y	Y	Y	N	Y	N	N	—	Y	N	N	N	Y	N	Y	88%
Kastenmeier (D-2)	Y	Y	Y	Y	Y	N	Y	N	N	Y	Y	N	N	N	Y	N	Y	94%
Gunderson (R-3)	Y	Y	Y	Y	Y	N	Y	N	Y	N	Y	N	N	N	Y	N	—	81%
Kleczka (D-4)	Y	Y	Y	Y	Y	N	Y	N	Y	N	Y	N	N	N	Y	N	Y	88%
Moody (D-5)	—	Y	Y	—	—	—	—	—	N	Y	Y	N	N	N	Y	N	Y	100%
Petri (R-6)	Y	Y	Y	Y	Y	N	Y	Y	Y	N	Y	N	Y	N	Y	N	N	65%
Obey (D-7)	Y	Y	Y	Y	Y	N	Y	N	N	Y	Y	—	N	N	Y	N	Y	81%
Roth (R-8)	Y	N	N	Y	Y	N	Y	Y	—	N	Y	Y	Y	Y	N	Y	—	33%
Sensenbrenner (R-9)	Y	N	N	Y	Y	N	Y	Y	Y	N	Y	Y	Y	N	Y	Y	N	41%
WYOMING																		
Cheney (R)	Y	Y	N	N	Y	Y	—	—	—	N	N	—	—	—	N	N	—	30%

THE SENATE

1: 1987, DISTRICT OF COLUMBIA AIDS INSURANCE BILL

In 1986, the District of Columbia enacted legislation to prohibit insurers from discriminating against individuals who are HIV positive, perceived to be HIV positive, or perceived to be at risk to HIV infection.

Congress has the power to overturn legislation enacted by the District of Columbia. Senator Jesse Helms has spearheaded the Senate effort to overturn the DC AIDS Insurance Bill.

This home rule motion was defeated, 56 to 43. A yes (Y) vote indicates support for DC Home Rule and the legislation, and is considered the correct vote.

2: 1987, AZT APPROPRIATIONS

The vote was on an amendment to the Supplemental Appropriations Bill for FY 1987 — HR 1827. The amendment would provide $30 million for the emergency provision of the AZT drug and other drugs determined to prolong the life of individuals with AIDS. The amendment passed 74 to 21. A yes (Y) vote indicates support for the appropriations, and is considered the correct vote.

3: 1987, HELMS EDUCATION AMENDMENT #1

On October 14, 1987, Jesse Helms introduced an amendment, #963, to HR 3058, the Labor, Health and Human Services, and Education Appropriations of 1988.

Amendment #963 would prohibit the use of any funds provided under HR 3058 to the Centers for Disease Control from being used to provide AIDS education, information, or prevention materials and activities that promote, encourage, or condone homosexual sexual activity or the intravenous use of illegal drugs.

The amendment passed 94 to 2. A no (N) vote indicates opposition to the amendment, and is considered the correct vote.

4: 1988, S 557 — CIVIL RIGHTS RESTORATION ACT

On January 28, 1988, the Senate voted 75 to 14 in favor of S 557, the Civil Rights Restoration Act. (See House Vote number 2 for a fuller description of this act.)

A yes (Y) vote indicates support for the CRRA, and is considered the correct vote.

5: 1988, S 557 — OVERRIDE OF THE PRESIDENT'S VETO

On March 16, 1988, President Reagan vetoed the Civil Rights Restoration Act. The Senate voted to override the President's veto by a vote of 73 to 24. (See House Vote number 3 for a fuller description of this override.)

In spite of the right-wing effort to kill the legislation, the Senate voted to override the President's veto on March 22. A yes (Y) vote indicates support for the override, and is considered the correct vote.

6: 1988, S 1220 — AIDS RESEARCH AND INFORMATION ACT

On April 28 the Senate approved the AIDS Research and Information Act, legislation designed to provide for a comprehensive program for AIDS information, prevention, care and treatment and research. The measure passed by a vote of 87 to 4.

A yes (Y) vote indicates support for the legislation, and is considered the correct vote.

7: 1988, HELMS EDUCATION AMENDMENT #2

On April 28, during consideration of S 1220, Jesse Helms proposed language to provide that none of the funds under S 1220 be used to provide educational, information, or risk reduction materials or activities to promote or encourage, directly, homosexual sexual activity. The amendment, #1991, passed by a vote of 71 to 18.

A no (N) vote indicates opposition to the amendment, and is considered the correct vote.

8: 1988, KENNEDY MOTION TO TABLE HELMS EDUCATION AMENDMENT #2

On April 28, during consideration of the Helms amendment to S 1220, Senator Edward Kennedy moved to table the amendment. The motion to table was defeated by a vote of 73 to 22.

A yes (Y) vote indicates support for the motion to table, and is considered the correct vote.

9: 1988, ARMSTRONG AMENDMENT TO DC HUMAN RIGHTS ORDINANCE

On July 11, during consideration of HR 4776, the DC Appropriations Bill, William Armstrong offered amendment #2541 to require the District of Columbia to modify its Human Rights Ordinance to allow any educational institution that is affiliated with a religious organization to discriminate on the basis of sexual orientation. (The DC ordinance has banned discrimination based on sexual orientation since 1973.)

The Senate approved the Armstrong amendment by a vote of 58 to 33. A no (N) vote indicates opposition to the amendment, and is considered the correct vote.

10: 1988, HUMPHREY AMENDMENT PROMOTING HOMOSEXUALITY

On July 27, during consideration of HR 4783, the Departments of Labor, Health and Human Services, and Education Appropriations for 1988, Gordon Humphrey proposed an amendment to ensure that funds made available under HR 4783 are not used to promote or encourage homosexuality or to use words stating that homosexuality is normal, natural or healthy. The amendment was adopted by a voice vote.

Senator Edward Kennedy moved to table the amendment and a roll call vote was requested. The motion to table failed by a vote of 15 to 82. A yes (Y) vote indicates support for the motion to table the Humphrey amendment, and is considered the correct vote.

11: 1988, HELMS EDUCATION AMENDMENT #3

On July 27, during consideration of HR 4783, Jesse Helms proposed an amendment to provide that none of the funds made available under this Act shall be obligated or expended if the Secretary of Health and Human Services has not promulgated regulations to prohibit AIDS education, information or prevention materials and activities from promoting or encouraging, directly, homosexual activities.

Senator Lowell Weicker moved to table the amendment. The Senate agreed to table the Helms education amendment by a vote of 47 to 46. A yes (Y) vote indicates support for the motion to table, and is considered the correct vote.

12: 1988, HR 1158 — FAIR HOUS-ING AMENDMENTS ACT

On August 2, the Senate approved the Fair Housing Amendments Act, legislation designed to revise the procedures for enforcement of fair housing. Among other things, HR 1158 would add "handicapped persons" as a protected class under the Fair Housing Law. The bill also provides housing protections for families with children.

The Senate approved the measure by a vote of 94 to 3. A yes (Y) vote indicates support for the legislation, and is considered the correct vote.

13: 1988, HELMS AMENDMENT — TRANSVESTITE

During consideration of the Fair Housing Amendments Act, Jesse Helms proposed an amendment to ensure the term "individual with handicaps" or the term "handicap" does not apply to an individual solely because that individual is a transvestite.

The Helms amendment, #2779, was approved by a vote of 89 to 2. A no (N) vote indicates opposition to the amendment, and is considered the correct vote.

senator	1	2	3	4	5	6	7	8	9	10	11	12	13	
correct vote	Y	Y	N	Y	Y	Y	N	Y	N	Y	Y	Y	N	
ALABAMA														
Heflin (D)	N	Y	Y	Y	Y	Y	Y	N	Y	N	Y	Y	—	42%
Shelby (D)	N	Y	Y	Y	Y	Y	Y	N	Y	N	Y	Y	Y	38%
ALASKA														
Murkowski (R)	N	N	Y	—	Y	Y	Y	N	Y	N	N	Y	Y	33%
Stevens (R)	N	Y	Y	Y	Y	Y	Y	N	Y	N	Y	Y	Y	46%
ARIZONA														
DeConcini (D)	N	Y	Y	Y	Y	Y	Y	N	Y	N	N	Y	Y	38%
McCain (R)	N	Y	Y	Y	Y	Y	Y	N	Y	N	N	Y	Y	38%
ARKANSAS														
Bumpers (D)	Y	Y	Y	Y	Y	Y	Y	N	N	N	Y	—	Y	58%
Pryor (D)	N	Y	Y	Y	Y	Y	Y	N	Y	N	Y	Y	Y	46%
CALIFORNIA														
Cranston (D)	Y	Y	Y	Y	Y	Y	N	Y	N	Y	Y	Y	N	92%
Wilson (R)	N	Y	Y	Y	Y	Y	Y	N	Y	N	Y	Y	Y	38%
COLORADO														
Armstrong (R)	N	N	Y	N	N	N	Y	N	Y	N	N	Y	Y	8%
Wirth (D)	Y	N	Y	Y	Y	Y	N	Y	N	N	Y	Y	Y	69%

senator	1	2	3	4	5	6	7	8	9	10	11	12	13	
correct vote	Y	Y	N	Y	Y	Y	N	Y	N	Y	Y	Y	N	
CONNECTICUT														
Dodd (D)	N	Y	Y	Y	Y	Y	N	Y	N	N	Y	Y	—	75%
Weicker (R)	Y	Y	N	Y	Y	Y	N	Y	N	Y	Y	Y	N	100%
DELAWARE														
Biden (D)	Y	—	Y	—	—	—	—	—	—	—	—	—	—	50%
Roth (R)	N	Y	Y	Y	Y	Y	Y	N	Y	N	N	Y	Y	38%
FLORIDA														
Chiles (D)	N	Y	Y	—	Y	—	—	N	—	N	Y	Y	Y	38%
Graham (D)	Y	Y	Y	Y	Y	Y	Y	N	N	N	Y	Y	Y	62%
GEORGIA														
Fowler (D)	Y	Y	Y	Y	Y	Y	Y	N	Y	N	—	Y	Y	50%
Nunn (D)	N	Y	Y	Y	Y	Y	Y	N	Y	N	Y	Y	Y	46%
HAWAII														
Inouye (D)	Y	Y	Y	—	Y	Y	N	Y	N	Y	Y	Y	Y	83%
Matsunaga (D)	Y	Y	Y	Y	Y	Y	Y	N	N	N	Y	Y	Y	62%
IDAHO														
McClure (R)	N	N	Y	—	N	N	Y	N	Y	N	N	Y	Y	8%
Symms (R)	N	N	Y	N	N	—	—	—	Y	N	N	N	Y	0%
ILLINOIS														
Dixon (D)	N	Y	Y	Y	Y	Y	Y	N	Y	N	N	Y	—	42%
Simon (D)	—	—	—	—	—	—	—	—	Y	—	Y	Y	Y	100%
INDIANA														
Lugar (R)	N	N	Y	N	N	Y	Y	N	Y	N	N	Y	Y	15%
Quayle (R)	N	N	Y	N	N	Y	Y	N	Y	N	N	Y	Y	15%
IOWA														
Grassley (R)	N	Y	Y	Y	N	Y	Y	N	Y	N	N	Y	Y	31%
Harkin (D)	Y	Y	Y	Y	Y	Y	Y	N	N	N	Y	Y	Y	62%
KANSAS														
Dole (R)	N	N	Y	—	—	Y	Y	N	Y	N	N	Y	Y	18%
Kassebaum (R)	N	Y	—	Y	Y	Y	Y	N	Y	N	N	Y	Y	50%
KENTUCKY														
Ford (D)	N	N	Y	—	Y	Y	Y	N	Y	N	N	Y	Y	25%
McConnell (R)	N	Y	Y	N	N	Y	Y	N	Y	N	N	Y	Y	23%

senator	1	2	3	4	5	6	7	8	9	10	11	12	13	
correct vote	Y	Y	N	Y	Y	Y	N	Y	N	Y	Y	Y	N	
LOUISIANA														
Breaux (D)	Y	Y	Y	Y	Y	Y	Y	N	Y	N	N	Y	–	50%
Johnston (D)	Y	Y	Y	Y	Y	Y	Y	N	Y	N	N	Y	Y	46%
MAINE														
Cohen (R)	Y	Y	Y	Y	Y	Y	Y	N	N	N	N	Y	Y	54%
Mitchell (D)	Y	Y	Y	Y	Y	Y	N	N	N	N	Y	Y	Y	62%
MARYLAND														
Mikulski (D)	Y	–	Y	Y	Y	Y	Y	N	N	Y	Y	Y	Y	67%
Sarbanes (D)	Y	Y	Y	Y	Y	Y	Y	N	N	N	Y	Y	Y	62%
MASSACHUSETTS														
Kennedy (D)	Y	Y	Y	Y	Y	Y	N	Y	N	Y	Y	Y	Y	85%
Kerry (D)	Y	Y	Y	Y	Y	Y	N	Y	N	Y	Y	Y	Y	85%
MICHIGAN														
Levin (D)	Y	Y	Y	Y	Y	Y	–	N	N	Y	Y	Y	Y	75%
Riegle (D)	Y	Y	Y	Y	Y	Y	Y	N	N	N	Y	Y	Y	62%
MINNESOTA														
Boschwitz (R)	Y	Y	Y	Y	Y	Y	Y	N	Y	N	Y	Y	Y	54%
Durenberger (R)	Y	Y	Y	Y	Y	Y	Y	N	Y	N	N	Y	Y	46%
MISSISSIPPI														
Cochran (R)	N	Y	Y	Y	N	Y	Y	N	Y	N	N	Y	Y	46%
Stennis (D)	Y	Y	Y	Y	–	–	–	–	N	Y	Y	Y	Y	78%
MISSOURI														
Bond (R)	N	N	Y	Y	N	Y	Y	N	Y	N	N	Y	Y	23%
Danforth (R)	N	N	Y	Y	N	Y	Y	N	Y	N	N	Y	Y	23%
MONTANA														
Baucus (D)	N	Y	Y	Y	Y	Y	Y	N	Y	N	Y	Y	Y	46%
Melcher (D)	Y	Y	Y	Y	Y	Y	Y	N	Y	N	N	Y	Y	46%
NEBRASKA														
Exon (D)	N	N	Y	Y	Y	Y	Y	N	Y	N	Y	Y	Y	38%
Karnes (R)	N	N	Y	N	N	–	–	–	Y	N	N	Y	Y	20%
NEVADA														
Hecht (R)	N	Y	Y	N	N	Y	Y	N	Y	N	N	Y	Y	23%
Reid (D)	Y	Y	Y	Y	Y	Y	Y	N	Y	N	N	–	–	45%

senator	1	2	3	4	5	6	7	8	9	10	11	12	13	
correct vote	Y	Y	N	Y	Y	Y	N	Y	N	Y	Y	Y	N	
NEW HAMPSHIRE														
Humphrey (R)	N	N	Y	N	N	Y	Y	N	–	N	N	N	Y	8%
Rudman (R)	N	Y	Y	–	Y	Y	Y	N	Y	N	Y	Y	Y	42%
NEW JERSEY														
Bradley (D)	Y	–	Y	Y	Y	Y	–	Y	–	Y	Y	Y	Y	70%
Lautenberg (D)	Y	Y	Y	Y	Y	Y	Y	N	N	N	Y	Y	Y	62%
NEW MEXICO														
Bingaman (D)	N	Y	Y	Y	Y	Y	Y	N	Y	N	Y	Y	Y	46%
Domenici (R)	N	Y	Y	Y	Y	Y	Y	N	Y	N	N	Y	Y	38%
NEW YORK														
D'Amato (R)	N	Y	–	Y	Y	Y	Y	N	Y	N	N	Y	–	45%
Moynihan (D)	Y	Y	N	Y	Y	Y	N	Y	N	Y	Y	Y	Y	92%
NORTH CAROLINA														
Helms (R)	N	N	Y	N	N	N	Y	N	–	N	N	N	Y	0%
Sanford (D)	N	Y	Y	Y	Y	Y	N	Y	N	Y	Y	Y	Y	77%
NORTH DAKOTA														
Burdick (D)	Y	Y	Y	Y	Y	Y	Y	N	Y	N	Y	Y	Y	54%
Conrad (D)	Y	Y	Y	Y	Y	Y	Y	N	Y	N	N	Y	Y	46%
OHIO														
Glenn (D)	Y	Y	Y	Y	Y	Y	Y	N	N	N	Y	Y	Y	62%
Metzenbaum (D)	Y	Y	Y	Y	Y	Y	Y	N	N	N	Y	Y	Y	62%
OKLAHOMA														
Boren (D)	N	Y	Y	Y	Y	–	Y	N	Y	N	Y	Y	Y	42%
Nickles (R)	N	N	Y	N	N	Y	Y	N	Y	N	N	Y	Y	15%
OREGON														
Hatfield (R)	N	Y	Y	Y	Y	Y	N	Y	Y	N	N	Y	Y	54%
Packwood (R)	N	Y	Y	Y	Y	Y	N	Y	N	N	Y	Y	Y	69%
PENNSYLVANIA														
Heinz (R)	Y	Y	Y	Y	Y	Y	–	Y	Y	N	N	Y	Y	67%
Specter (R)	Y	Y	Y	Y	Y	Y	N	Y	N	N	Y	Y	Y	77%
RHODE ISLAND														
Chafee (R)	Y	Y	Y	Y	Y	Y	N	Y	N	Y	Y	Y	Y	85%
Pell (D)	Y	Y	Y	Y	Y	Y	N	Y	N	N	Y	Y	Y	77%

senator	1	2	3	4	5	6	7	8	9	10	11	12	13	
correct vote	Y	Y	N	Y	Y	Y	N	Y	N	Y	Y	Y	N	

SOUTH CAROLINA

Hollings (D)	N	Y	Y	Y	Y	Y	Y	N	N	N	N	Y	Y	46%
Thurmond (R)	N	N	Y	N	N	Y	Y	N	Y	N	N	Y	Y	15%

SOUTH DAKOTA

Daschle (D)	N	Y	Y	Y	Y	Y	Y	N	Y	N	–	Y	Y	42%
Pressler (R)	N	Y	Y	Y	N	Y	Y	N	Y	N	N	Y	Y	31%

TENNESSEE

Gore (D)	Y	–	–	–	Y	Y	N	Y	–	Y	Y	Y	Y	89%
Sasser (D)	N	Y	Y	Y	Y	Y	Y	N	–	N	N	Y	Y	42%

TEXAS

Bentsen (D)	N	Y	Y	Y	Y	Y	Y	N	Y	–	–	Y	Y	45%
Gramm (R)	N	N	Y	N	N	Y	Y	N	Y	N	N	Y	Y	15%

UTAH

Garn (R)	N	Y	Y	N	N	Y	Y	N	–	N	N	Y	–	27%
Hatch (R)	N	Y	Y	N	N	Y	Y	N	Y	N	N	Y	Y	23%

VERMONT

Leahy (D)	Y	Y	Y	Y	Y	Y	N	Y	N	Y	–	Y	Y	83%
Stafford (R)	Y	Y	Y	Y	Y	Y	–	Y	N	N	Y	Y	Y	75%

VIRGINIA

Trible (R)	N	N	Y	Y	N	Y	Y	N	Y	N	N	Y	Y	23%
Warner (R)	N	N	Y	Y	N	Y	Y	N	Y	N	–	Y	Y	25%

WASHINGTON

Adams (D)	Y	Y	Y	Y	Y	Y	N	Y	N	–	–	Y	Y	82%
Evans (R)	Y	N	Y	Y	Y	Y	–	–	N	N	Y	Y	Y	64%

WEST VIRGINIA

Byrd (D)	N	Y	Y	Y	Y	Y	Y	N	Y	N	Y	Y	Y	46%
Rockefeller (D)	Y	Y	Y	Y	Y	–	Y	N	Y	N	Y	Y	Y	42%

WISCONSIN

Kasten (R)	N	Y	Y	Y	Y	Y	Y	N	Y	N	N	Y	Y	38%
Proxmire (D)	Y	N	Y	Y	Y	Y	N	Y	N	N	Y	Y	Y	62%

WYOMING

Simpson (R)	N	Y	Y	Y	N	Y	Y	N	Y	N	N	Y	Y	31%
Wallop (R)	N	N	Y	–	N	N	Y	N	Y	N	N	Y	Y	8%

THE OUTLOOK BY STATE

We decided to get a general sense of which states have the best political climate for gay people and gay activism by looking at the overall voting record of their congressional delegation.

The figures below are derived from the preceding section. They show what percentage of the votes cast by senators and representatives from each state were the "correct" vote, as defined by the National Gay and Lesbian Task Force.

1.	Massachusetts	94.29	26.	Florida	66.22
2.	Washington	91.22	27.	Ohio	66.11
3.	Connecticut	88.80	28.	Oklahoma	65.35
4.	Rhode Island	84.91	29.	South Carolina	63.25
5.	Vermont	84.62	30.	Missouri	63.19
6.	New York	84.59	31.	Delaware	62.50
7.	Maryland	81.70	32.	Colorado	62.10
8.	Michigan	81.39	33.	New Mexico	61.84
9.	Hawaii	80.00	34.	Kentucky	60.56
10.	New Jersey	79.04	35.	Virginia	60.45
11.	Pennsylvania	75.63	36.	Alabama	60.15
12.	Mississippi	74.12	37.	Louisiana	58.70
13.	Tennessee	74.07	38.	Indiana	58.33
14.	North Carolina	73.04	39.	Texas	57.38
15.	Minnesota	72.96	40.	Kansas	54.81
16.	Wisconsin	72.62	41.	Nevada	53.45
17.	West Virginia	72.83	42.	Montana	52.54
18.	California	72.73	43.	Alaska	52.38
19.	Maine	71.67	44.	South Dakota	52.38
20.	Illinois	71.01	45.	Nebraska	48.44
21.	Oregon	70.75	46.	Arizona	48.18
22.	Georgia	70.39	47.	Utah	37.50
23.	Arkansas	67.86	48.	New Hampshire	33.33
24.	Iowa	66.94	49.	Idaho	31.48
25.	North Dakota	66.67	50.	Wyoming	22.86

ELECTION '88

The 1988 elections brought more bad news than good news for gay people. In the presidential race, most gay activists backed Michael Dukakis over George Bush, but still felt that a Bush administration would be an improvement over that of Ronald Reagan. On ballot issues specifically dealing with gay and AIDS issues, the results were:

GOOD NEWS

California: Proposition 102, introduced by the notoriously homophobic congressman William Dannemeyer, was defeated. It would have forced doctors to report the names of any of their patients who were infected with the HIV virus. The two-to-one margin of defeat, although a landslide by many standards, was still significantly closer than the margin by which a similar proposition was defeated two years earlier.

San Francisco: A ballot initiative limiting city supervisors to two terms was defeated. The most noticeable effect, had the proposition passed, would have been to force openly gay supervisor Harry Britt to leave the board, of which he had just become president. The vote was 56% to 44%.

BAD NEWS

Oregon: In 1987, Republican governor Neil Goldschmidt issued an executive order protecting gay people from discrimination in state employment and state-provided services. Voters effectively revoked that order by a 53% to 47% margin.

St. Paul, Minnesota: Gay activists here had supported a ballot initiative which would have protected the city's human rights law from being amended by future referenda; they hoped to then have that law extended to include gay civil rights. The initiative was defeated, 56% to 44%.

San Francisco: A proposition forbidding the Navy from engaging in anti-gay discrimination in certain local hiring was defeated, 55% to 45%, despite receiving support from mayor Art Agnos. A related proposition, which supported the Navy's homeporting of a ship in San Francisco while allowing it to discriminate against gays, passed 51% to 49%.

Ft. Collins, Colorado: Gay activists put an initiative on the ballot which would have extended the city's human rights ordinance to cover gay people. It was defeated, 57% to 43%.

California: Proposition 96 was passed by a decisive 62% to 38% majority. It will allow authorities to test prisoners for the HIV antibodies — as well as to test any person accused of committing a sex-related crime.

WORKPLACE POLICIES ABOUT AIDS

As corporations realize that AIDS will be a concern for years to come, many are implementing official policies on AIDS-related issues. The two policies below may be helpful to corporate executives who are considering such a step, and to employees who want to suggest that their firm implement a policy on AIDS.

Actual policy: Pacific Gas and Electric

In 1987, the Allstate Insurance Company's Forum on Public Issues convened in Chicago with the focus on AIDS. The conference and the resulting publication, both titled *AIDS: Corporate America Responds*, looked at the impact of the health crisis from a variety of perspectives — human resources, corporate health services, legislative affairs, to name a few — and also held up several examples of what it felt were model policies for dealing with AIDS in the workplace. With Allstate's permission we have reprinted the guidelines of the Pacific Gas and Electric Company, implemented in July 1987:

PG & E POLICY

In keeping with two of our corporate objectives to ensure a safe, healthy work environment for our employees and the public we serve, and to prohibit all forms of arbitrary discrimination in employment, we have developed the following policy statement and guidelines on how to handle personnel matters related to employees afflicted with AIDS. The policy statement and guidelines are based on the most current medical information on this subject available. If any significant medical developments occur, we will revise the statement and these guidelines accordingly.

Policy Statement

It is PGandE's position that employees afflicted with AIDS do not present a health risk to other employees in the workplace under normal working conditions. Employees with AIDS are subject to the same working conditions and performance requirements as any other employee. However, if there is supervisory concern that an employee with AIDS is not able to perform assigned duties, a medical clarification examination may be required to determine the employee's fitness for work. Lastly, employees with AIDS, provided that they are otherwise eligible, are entitled to coverage under the company's sick leave, medical leave of absence, disability benefits and equal employment opportunity policies.

Guidelines

1. Employees afflicted with AIDS should be treated the same as any other company employee. However, if their medical or physical condition affects their ability to perform their assigned duties, they should be treated as any other employees who have a disability that prevents them from performing the duties of their job.

2. If a supervisor has a reasonable basis to believe that an employee with AIDS

is unable to perform the duties of his/her position, the supervisor must request the employee undergo a medical clarification examination. The results of the medical clarification examination shall guide future personnel decisions affecting the employee.

3. Employees afflicted with AIDS, to the extent they are eligible, are entitled to coverage under the company's sick leave, medical leave of absence, disability benefits and equal employment opportunity policies. When requested, supervisors and personnel department representatives should furnish informa-tion regarding those policies to affected employees.

4. If employees who share the same work environment with an employee with AIDS express concerns over their personal safety and health, supervisors must explain that, based on guidelines issued by the United States Public Health Service and expert medical opinions, casual contact with a co-worker with AIDS poses no threat of transmission. If necessary, supervisors should contact an appropriate EAP counsellor to arrange for more comprehensive education efforts for the work force.

Sample guidelines:
San Francisco Chamber of Commerce

The following guidelines were developed by the San Francisco Chamber of Commerce for use in the business community. These guidelines have been printed as submitted to Allstate's Forum on Public Issues.

GUIDELINES

Epidemics of disease present enormous dilemmas to our society, straining our human, financial and health resources. Like smallpox, cancer and polio before it, Acquired Immune Deficiency Syndrome (AIDS) and its related conditions are approaching pandemic proportions.

The impact of AIDS is and will continue to be devastating. According to the Surgeon General of the United States:

By the end of 1991, an estimated 270,000 cases of AIDS will have occurred with 179,000 deaths within the decade since the disease was first recognized. In the year 1991, an estimated 145,000 patients with AIDS will need health and supportive services at a total cost between $8 billion and $16 billion. However, AIDS is preventable. It is the responsibility of every citizen to be informed about AIDS and to exercise the appropriate prevention measures.

If we are to overcome the obstacles presented by AIDS and its related conditions, it is imperative that we respond immediately as a unified society. A comprehensive and effective approach toward combatting the epidemic only can be realized through a national effort with the full support, understanding and informed decision-making of the business community.

Any sensible and humane response to the epidemic must be based on accurate information, not irrational fear and discrimination. There is an alarming tendency to label people as belonging to AIDS "risk groups." This is not only misleading, it is dangerous. AIDS is not confined to any single community. It is not caused by life-style or sexual orientation. It is caused by a virus — a virus that can be transmitted to anyone who engages in high risk activity. Fortunately, by modifying these high risk behaviors, we can stop virus transmission. Unlike many other life threatening illnesses, AIDS can be prevented.

We are fighting a disease, not people. The business community in America can and must play a major role in creating policies and disseminating accurate information about AIDS and its related conditions.

Any employee with a life threatening and/or catastrophic illness such as AIDS, cancer or multiple sclerosis should be treated in conjunction with the principles outlined below. It is our desire that every business in America adopt and/or incorporate these principles into personnel policies and adhere to the content and spirit of the principles.

1. Employees with any life threatening illness should be offered the right to continue working so long as they are able to continue to perform their job satisfactorily and so long as the best medical evidence indicates that their continual employment does not present a health or safety threat to themselves or others.

2. Employers and co-workers should treat all medical information obtained from employees with strict confidentiality. In the case of an employee with a life threatening illness, confidentiality of employee medical records in accordance with existing legal, medical, ethical and management practices should be maintained.

3. Employees who are affected by any life threatening illness should be treated with compassion and understanding in their personal crisis. Reasonable efforts should be made to accommodate seriously ill patients by providing flexible work areas, hours and assignments whenever possible or appropriate.

4. Employees should be asked to be sensitive to the needs of critically ill colleagues, and to recognize that continual employment for an employee with a life

threatening illness is often life sustaining and can be both physically and mentally beneficial.

5. In regard to the life threatening disease of AIDS and its related conditions, a person carrying the AIDS virus is not a threat to co-workers since AIDS is not spread by common everyday contact. For this reason, the AIDS antibody and/or AIDS virus status of an employee is not relevant information in regard to the health and safety of his/her co-workers.

Therefore, the AIDS antibody test and/or AIDS virus test should not be used as a prerequisite for employment or a condition for continued employment. Knowledge or presumed knowledge of AIDS antibody and/or AIDS virus status should not be used to discriminate against any employee for any reason.

6. Given the irrational fear that AIDS, cancer and other life threatening diseases often inspire, the most effective way to avoid unnecessary disruptions in the workplace is to prepare and educate both management and employees before any employee is affected by a life threatening disease. To this end, employers should implement educational programs based on the best available medical knowledge to understand the disease; what services are locally available to help employees with any medical, psychological or financial hardships caused by the disease; and what policies the company has in place to cover employees with a life threatening illness.

Single copies of *AIDS: Corporate America Responds,* are available free of charge from Allstate Insurance Company, Consumer Information Center, Attn: Public Issues Department 10316, P.O. Box 7660, Mt. Prospect, IL 60056; for additional copies, there is a charge of $4.00 per copy to cover printing and mailing costs.

PEOPLE

The strong distinction between homosexual and heterosexual, which many people now consider to be so important, has not existed in all times and cultures. Some of the individuals listed here would not have considered themselves to be gay, or lesbian, or bisexual — for many, that terminology did not even exist. But in reclaiming a history that has generally been hidden, it's valuable to know how widespread same-sex relationships have been in a variety of eras and cultures.

The gay or bisexual orientation of most individuals listed here is well established. For some, however, the evidence is circumstantial, or based on rumor; these cases are indicated in the text.

Illustrations for this section are by Michael Willhoite, caricaturist for *The Washington Blade.*

ABU NUWAS. (756?-810), *Arabian poet.* Abu Nuwas was born in Persia, and as a young adult moved to Baghdad, where he befriended the great Caliph Harun al-Rashid. In his lifetime, he wrote some five thousand poems, establishing himself as the most widely quoted Arab poet of all time.

The poems of Abu Nuwas celebrate both heterosexual and homosexual love. He was quite open about his own homosexuality, which is graphically illustrated in the Arabian Nights story "Abu Nuwas and the Three Boys."

AGATHON. (450?-400? B.C.), *Athenian dramatist.* None of Agathon's tragedies have survived, but Agathon himself earned a place in literary history when a banquet in his home, in 416 B.C., served as a basis for Plato's famous *Symposium.* He is also noteworthy as history's first recorded example of a stereotypically effeminate homosexual; he was portrayed in that role in Aristophanes' comedy, *The Thesmophoriazusae.*

AKHENATEN. (ruled 1375?-1358? B.C.), *Egyptian Pharoah.* Called by historian James Breasted "the world's first individual," Pharaoh Akhenaten brought fresh and controversial ideas to ancient Egypt — a land which, in the fourteenth century before Christ, already had centuries-old traditions and beliefs. Akhenaten introduced the concept of internationalism to the ancient world. He also introduced monotheism — the idea of a single, omnipotent god, rather than a galaxy of greater and lesser gods, as had been believed by his predecessors. In doing so, he antagonized the powerful priesthood, but set the groundwork for modern religion.

Akhenaten and his lover, Smenkhkare, were also the first historically documented male couple in history. Their homosexuality does not seem to have bothered Akhenaten's contemporaries, but his challenge to the clergy brought his downfall. The priests joined forces with the army and assassinated Akhenaten and Smenkhkare, and Tutankhamen was made Pharaoh.

ALBEE, EDWARD. (1928-), *U.S. playwright.* One of America's most controversial dramatists, Edward Albee is said to have reinvented theater in the United States. A prolific writer, Albee's works include *The Zoo Story, The American Dream,* and *Who's Afraid of Virginia Woolf?* In his plays, Albee portrays a world in which suffering is inevitable, but his vision is not truly pessimistic; although his characters confront pain, they are capable of growth and change. Each is forced to question his or her values and relationships and begin to take a more honest approach to life.

Albee was abandoned at birth by his natural parents and was adopted by millionaires Reed and Frances Albee. He was a rebellious child and was expelled from three prep schools and a military academy before graduating from Choate. He spent his early adulthood working at various odd jobs, and in 1958 he wrote *The Zoo Story* as a "sort of a thirtieth birthday present to myself." It was at that point that his writing career began in earnest. Since then, he has written more than twenty plays and has received a number of awards, including two Pulitzer Prizes.

Albee has consistently avoided discussing his personal life in interviews, preferring to keep the focus on his work, but he has made no secret of his homosexuality. Gay themes and characters find little place in his plays, although many critics feel that his homosexuality has influenced his portrayal of relations between the sexes.

ALCIBIADES. (450?-404 B.C.), *Athenian general.* Born into a wealthy family and endowed with great beauty, Alcibiades gained a reputation early in life for arrogance and unruly behavior. As a teenager, he met Socrates and was captivated by the philosopher's questioning of accepted wisdom. Alcibiades fell in love with Socrates, and attempted to seduce the older man; the seduction scene in Plato's *Symposium* is based on this incident.

In the ensuing years, Alcibiades became active in the political and military affairs of Athens, then switched allegiance to the rival city-state of Sparta. He was run out of Sparta by its king following rumors of an affair between Alcibiades and the queen, and transferred his loyalties to the Persians. A few years later he returned to Athens, where a right-wing coup had replaced his former enemies with allies, and was briefly made general and ruler of the city. He lost this position following a military defeat in 406 B.C., after which the Spartans and Persians, worried about where he might turn up next, had him murdered.

ALEXANDER I. (1777-1825), *Russian czar.* The friendly and handsome Alexander I became czar of Russia in 1801 at the age of twenty-three, following the murder of his father. His early hopes for domestic reform and international peace were quickly thwarted by Napoleon's increasingly aggressive military actions. In June of 1812, Napoleon invaded Russia with half a million soldiers. Rather than fight such an overwhelming force, Alexander's armies retreated, finally giving up Moscow to the French. Whether by genius or luck, this strategy proved sound. Short of supplies, and with a bitter winter approaching, Napoleon had to retreat; when he left Russia, eighty percent of his army had been wiped out.

Alexander's homosexual trysts were the subject of frequent comment during his lifetime. Napoleon referred to him as "the slyest and handsomest of all the Greeks."

ALEXANDER THE GREAT. (356-323 B.C.), *Macedonian king.* Alexander III became king of Macedonia at the age of twenty, and soon thereafter began his campaign to conquer the known world. He quickly subdued Greece, to the south of Macedonia, then began pursuit of the immense Persian army, which he overwhelmed in 330 B.C. By the time of his death seven years later, Alexander had taken his campaign as far as India, deliberately mixing Greek culture with Asian culture, and Greek blood with Asian blood, as he went.

Michael Willhoite

Horatio Alger

For most of his life, Alexander's closest friend and colleague was Hephaestion, although there is no clear proof that their relationship was sexual. Alexander's sexual relationship with the young eunuch Bagoas is more clearly documented, and served as the basis for Mary Renault's novel *The Persian Boy.*

ALGER, HORATIO. (1834-1899), *U.S. writer.* Alger is best known for his novels in which underprivileged boys find great success in life through hard work and virtue. Less known is the fact that as a Unitarian pastor in the Cape Cod town of Brewster, he was run out of town for "the abominable and revolting crime of unnatural familiarity with boys."

Early in 1866 rumors began to fly about young Rev. Alger, particularly in regards to fifteen-year-old John Clark and his thirteen-year-old friend, Thomas Crocker. After the scandal broke, one townsman wrote: "On the sabbath after service, one of these boys called at his room to leave a book . . . [Alger] bolted his door and then committed this unnatural crime, with the poor boy's sister waiting in the carriage in the cold."

Alger's family was able to hush up the scandal, particularly when Horatio left the ministry — thereby ensuring there would not be a repeat of this incident at another church. Alger immediately left New England for New York, where his writing career began in earnest. Later, he "informally" adopted several young boys without any brouhaha.

ANACREON. (572?-488? B.C.), *Greek poet.* Anacreon was a prominent figure in ancient Greece, first in Samos, then in Athens. Little of his love poetry has survived, but it seems to have dealt mainly with boys. One fragment, which survived only because it was used in the Middle Ages to illustrate points of Greek grammar, contains the lines:

I love Cleobulus
I dote on Cleobulus
I gaze at Cleobulus.

The eighteenth century, reports historian Noel I. Garde, saw great interest in English imitations of Anacreon. One result was a popular song, "Anacreon in Heaven," which later supplied the tune for the American national anthem.

ANDERSEN, HANS CHRISTIAN. (1805-1875), *Danish storyteller.* Andersen wrote many plays and novels in his homeland of Denmark, but his international fame rests on his fairy tales, which have been translated into dozens of languages. Toward the end of his life, as he was discussing the music to be used at his funeral with the musician who was to compose it, Andersen put in one request: "Most of those who will walk in my funeral will be small children, so make the beat keep time with little steps." Two sex researchers in the early twentieth century, Magnus Hirschfeld and Edward I. Stevenson, refer to him as being gay.

Queen Anne

Susan B. Anthony

ANNE. (1665-1714), *English queen.* At the age of eighteen, Anne was married to an undistinguished Danish nobleman. They had seventeen children, all of whom died in childhood, and Anne's twelve years as queen, while prosperous ones for Britain, represented the last of the Stuart line that she represented.

The true love of Anne's life, however, was not her husband George, but Sarah Churchill, a duchess known for her intelligence and beauty. Churchill became Anne's attendant, and correspondence between the two women reveals an exceptionally passionate and close relationship.

ANTHONY, SUSAN B. (1820-1906), *U.S. feminist and reformer.* A founder and leading inspiration of the nineteenth-century women's rights movement was Susan B. Anthony, who even as a teenager spoke out vehemently against the inequities of marriage, an institution she would later call "legalized prostitution."

In addition to her work with the women's movement, Anthony supported the abolitionist movement. It

was through anti-slavery work that she met the beautiful Anna Dickinson, with whom she developed a close and probably sexual relationship.

Not all abolitionists saw a connection between their cause and that of women's suffrage. A prominent male abolitionist once told Anthony, "You are not married; you have no business discussing marriage." She replied, "And you are not a slave. Suppose you quit lecturing on slavery."

AUDEN, W.H. (1907-1973), *British poet.* Wystan Hugh Auden was a friend of Christopher Isherwood, and both were influenced by the early 1930s gay movement in Germany. During that period, anti-Nazi cabaret performer Erika Mann asked him to marry her so she could obtain a British passport and escape from Nazi Germany. Auden consented. Soon thereafter, a friend of Mann's found herself in the same predicament, and approached Auden for help. "What else are buggers for?" asked Auden, and he found another gay friend to oblige.

Auden's poem "Lullaby," published after his death in 1973 in a book entitled *Thank You, Fog*, is considered his coming-out poem. One stanza reads:

> The old Greeks got it all wrong:
> Narcissus is an oldie,
> tamed by time, released at last
> from lust for other bodies,
> rational and reconciled.
> For many years you envied
> the hirsute, the he-man type.
> No longer: now you fondle
> your almost feminine flesh
> with mettled satisfaction
> imagining that you are
> sinless and self-sufficient.

AUGUSTINE, SAINT, (354-430), *Roman theologian.* The man who gave us the wonderful epigram, "Lord, grant me chastity — but not yet!" practiced what he preached. Augustine was born in northern Africa; he was raised as a Christian by his mother, then experimented with the gloomy philosophy of Manichaeanism for a time, and finally converted back to Christianity at the age of thirty-three. He is best remembered for his *Confessions,* in which he describes his passionate, youthful attachment to another young man: "I felt that his soul and mine were one soul in two bodies." Most authorities agree that this was a sexual as well as spiritual relationship. But the object of that attachment died young. Augustine went on to become involved with several women, and eventually did become celibate.

BACON, Sir FRANCIS. (1561-1626), *English jurist and scientist.* Born into a well-connected family, Bacon became active in politics early in life, and in 1618 became lord chancellor. Political opponents found evidence that he had accepted bribes while in this post, however, and after only four years Bacon's political career collapsed.

He then turned to scientific pursuits, which had long intrigued him. Bacon was among the first scholars to

Michael Willhoite

Sir Francis Bacon

reject the traditional Aristotelian philosophy of science, preferring a more experimental approach. Although they represented considerable progress for science, Bacon's experiments were not so beneficial to him personally. In the winter of 1626, curious to see whether cold foods would keep longer, Bacon packed a freshly butchered chicken with snow. In doing so, he himself came down with a chill which developed into pneumonia, and he died three days later.

Bacon's homosexuality was commented on by several of his contemporaries, including his mother, who chided him for it. His essay *On Beauty* focuses primarily on male beauty.

BAKKER, JAMES. (1940-), *U.S. evangelist.* In March, 1987, television evangelist James Bakker publicly confessed to having had a fifteen-minute sexual encounter with Jessica Hahn in 1980. What seemed at first like a small scandal quickly snowballed amidst stories of hush money, extravagant and illegal expense accounts, and prostitution. Homosexuality was among the charges.

Chattanooga evangelist John

Ankerberg was one of the accusers, charging that he knew a man who said he had been Bakker's lover. Another accuser was Austin Miles, who had been a guest on Bakker's TV show. One day, Miles reported, he had walked into the steam room "and there was Jim frolicking in the nude with three other men. They were dancing around and taking turns laying on a table, massaging each other. They were so absorbed . . . Then [Bakker] saw me, grabbed a towel, and said, 'That was a great show, you'll have to come back.' I wondered what the heck I had gotten into." Bakker denied these reports. "I am not a homosexual," he said at a press conference. But the next year the charges were back in the press, as former evangelist and fundraiser John Wesley Fletcher described his past sexual escapades with Bakker in *Penthouse* magazine.

BALDWIN, JAMES. (1924-1987), *U.S. writer.* A leader in the black civil rights movement, James Baldwin was also a strong supporter of gay rights, although *The New York Times* and *The Washington Post* scarcely mentioned his homosexuality in their obituaries of him.

After an unhappy childhood in Harlem, Baldwin left New York in 1948 for France, where he spent much of his adult life. A prolific writer, Baldwin left behind a collection of works impressive both for their number and their quality. These include *Go Tell It On The Mountain, Giovanni's Room, Another Country*, and the controversial *The Fire Next Time.*

Baldwin was primarily concerned with American society's need to discard many of its myths. He felt that Americans were "still trapped in a history they do not understand," and that they needed to break out of their false view of reality. The myth of white superiority was in Baldwin's mind the most important, and most destructive, of the many myths which informed American culture, and he saw it as being closely related to the deep-seated homophobia prevalent in America.

BARBER, SAMUEL. (1910-1981), *U.S. composer.* Barber began composing when he was seven, tried writing his first opera when he was ten, and was admitted to the Curtis Institute of Music at the age of thirteen. Throughout a career spanning more than fifty years, he created richly expressive, lyric music, including his Pulitzer Prize-winning opera *Vanessa* and the enormously popular *Adagio for Strings,* written when Barber was twenty-six. He remains today one of the most often performed of American composers in the international symphonic repertoire.

Barber's homosexuality was, throughout most of his adult life, an open secret in the music world. For many years he lived with and maintained a close personal and professional relationship with operatic composer Gian Carlo Menotti, who wrote the libretto for *Vanessa* and collaborated with Barber on a number of other works.

BARNES, DJUNA. (1892-1982), *U.S. novelist.* Said to be the last of the great generation of early twentieth-century modernists in English literature, Djuna Barnes created such literary masterworks as *Nightwood, Ladies Almanack,* and *Ryder.* She specialized in colorful interviews, her subjects including Alfred Stieglitz, Coco Chanel, and James Joyce.

In 1919 or 1920, Barnes moved from Greenwich Village to Paris, where she joined the expatriate literary community. After stays in Berlin and London, she returned to New York at the outbreak of World War II. A period of extreme poverty followed, during which she became highly reclusive. E.E. Cummings lived across from her in Greenwich Village during that time and would occasionally call across to her, "Are you still alive, Djuna?"

Barnes had relationships with both

women and men, but hesitated to call herself a lesbian. She once confided to a close friend, "I'm not a lesbian. I just loved Thelma."

BARNEY, NATALIE. (1876-1972), *Parisian writer and salon hostess.* "My only books/Were women's looks," Barney once wrote of her schoolgirl days. "At twelve I knew exactly what I liked and I firmly decided not to let myself be diverted from my tastes." As a young adult, she fled her upper-class existence in Washington, D.C. to take up residence in Paris, where she became known as *l'Amazone,* and where her affairs with various famous women, including the poet Renée Vivien and the spectacularly beautiful courtesan Liane de Pougy, aroused public curiosity and attention. Her weekly literary salons — held every Friday for more than sixty years — were also renowned as a meeting place for the cultural elite, and regularly attracted such notables as Anatole France, Ezra Pound, Gertrude Stein, and André Gide. Barney wrote numerous epigrams, memoirs, and poetry, but her fame rests primarily on her reputation as the most prominent and candid lesbian of her day.

BARNFIELD, RICHARD. (1574-1627), *British poet.* Considerable mystery still surrounds the life of Shakespeare's friend Richard Barnfield, whose sonnets bear many similarities to those of the Bard. Barnfield's most famous verse appears in his first work, *The Affectionate Shepherd,* published anonymously when he was twenty:

If it be sin to love a lovely lad,
Oh, then sin I.

A year later, Barnfield published further sonnets with a homosexual theme, celebrating his love for a young man whose initials were J.U. — possibly the young actor John Underwood.

BAUMAN, ROBERT. (1937-), *U.S. politician.* Seemingly the quintessential conservative, Robert Bauman, a Republican congressman from Maryland, was a fervent Reaganite who took a strong right-wing stance on virtually every piece of legislation that crossed his desk. A staunch proponent of traditional family values, and himself a family man with a wife and children, Bauman lost his seat in the House after being charged with soliciting sex from a sixteen-year-old boy. In his subsequent autobiography, *The Gentleman from Maryland: Conscience of a Gay Conservative* he suggested that House colleague Barney Frank was also gay.

Since being forced to come out, Bauman has become a supporter of gay rights, although he has chosen not to become a leader in the struggle. As a conservative, he has consistently objected to the liberal, left-wing slant of the gay rights movement.

BEACH, SYLVIA. (1887-1962), *U.S. expatriate literary figure.* Beach moved to Paris permanently from the United States in 1919 and opened her renowned bookstore, Shakespeare and Company, that same year on the Left Bank. The store, which featured English and American literature, became an important meeting place for such expatriate writers as Ernest Hemingway and James Joyce, and for French writers pursuing a new-found passion for American books. In 1922, Beach ventured briefly into publishing: she published the first edition of James Joyce's *Ulysses* after it had been rejected by other publishers because of its sexual content.

For over thirty years, from the start of her permanent residency in Paris, Beach was in a relationship with French writer Adrienne Monnier, who also owned a bookstore, just across the street from Beach's, on the Rue de l'Odéon.

BECKFORD, WILLIAM. (1760-1844), *British writer and politician.* An English novelist of some reputation,

Beckford was unfortunate enough to have the only passionate affair in his life ruined by scandal. At the age of nineteen, he fell in love with eleven-year-old William Courtenay. Five years later they were caught in bed together, and the *Morning Herald* reported the next day on "the rumor concerning a *Grammatical mistake* of Mr. B— and the Hon. Mr. C—, in regard to the genders." It was one of England's first reported gay scandals. Beckford moved to Switzerland and began his career as a novelist. Some of his novels included homosexual episodes. He later returned to England and served in the House of Commons.

Michael Willhoite

Henry Ward Beecher

sought to reconcile Christianity and the theory of evolution, thus inviting attack from many fellow theologians.

Beecher was married, but he described the marriage as "hell on earth." His happiest relationship, he revealed to a biographer in his old age, took place as a student in Amherst. He had fallen in love with Constantine Fondolaik, a Greek student, and the two had drawn up a contract promising eternal devotion to one another. Constantine returned to Greece in 1842, where he died shortly thereafter. Beecher named one of his sons after the friend who had brought him the greatest happiness.

Michael Willhoite

William Beckford

BEECHER, HENRY WARD. (1813-1887), *U.S. lecturer and pastor.* Though not as famous as his sister, Harriet Beecher Stowe, Beecher became known in the nineteenth century for his eloquent and unconventional sermons. His favorite sermons, in the 1840s, dealt with the earthly vices, and his realistic descriptions of such vices often brought crowds of three thousand people to his Brooklyn, N.Y. church. When the Civil War broke out, Beecher put his oratorical skills to work in the cause of emancipation, and after the war he

BEETHOVEN, LUDWIG. (1770-1827), *German composer.* Beethoven's musical training began at the age of five, when his talent became apparent. He was encouraged by his father, an unstable alcoholic who saw the profit potential of having a son who was a child prodigy.

Despite the pressures of this situation, the talents of the young Beethoven flourished. When he was seventeen, he greatly impressed Mozart with his skills, and a few years later, he began a period of study under Haydn. Despite a hearing loss, which began in his late twenties, Beethoven produced nine symphonies, two ballets, and dozens of other works.

Throughout his life, Beethoven developed a reputation for boorish behavior, which was only worsened by his embarrassment about his deafness. There is no evidence that he was ever in a relationship with a woman; his sexual energy seems, rather, to have been focused on a young nephew named Karl, who did not return the affection and may have attempted to blackmail Beethoven by threatening to publicize his homosexuality.

Michael Willhoite

Ludwig Beethoven

BENEDICT IX. (1020-1055?), *Pope.* One of several strong contenders for the title of history's worst pope, Benedict IX was appointed to the papal office in 1032, at the age of twelve, because the council responsible for making such appointments wished to keep the papacy under their control. Benedict is best remembered for the devotion he showed to homosexual orgies while serving as pope, and for his efforts to cash in on his position by selling the rights to the various titles he controlled. Finally, he ran out of lower offices and sold the papacy

itself to his uncle, Johannes Gratianus, in 1044. He subsequently reclaimed the office for two brief periods, but was eventually deposed and run out of Rome. Benedict died in obscurity some years later.

BEZA, THEODORE. (1519-1605), *French theologian.* Theodore Beza was a close friend of theologian John Calvin and an outspoken supporter of Calvinism. He was also, at least in his youth, unmistakably homosexual. In his collection of Latin verse, *Juvenilia,* are love poems addressed to a young man named Audebert. In Beza's later life as a Calvinist, these poems provided considerable ammunition for rival Catholic polemicists, one of whom accused him of having been "tortured by a burning lust for his young Audebert." Another, the Catholic theologian De Sanctis, wrote that "Instead of your Audebert, now you have embraced Calvin, and so have substituted a spiritual male-whore for a carnal one; thus being still what you were — a sodomist."

BONHEUR, ROSA. (1822-1899), *French artist.* By her early twenties, Bonheur had established herself, both in Europe and abroad, as a brilliant painter of animals. Her most famous painting, *The Horse Fair,* was purchased by Cornelius Vanderbilt in 1887 for a then-record sum of $55,000; it now hangs in New York's Metropolitan Museum of Art.

A forceful, strongly unconventional woman, Bonheur had a female lover, Nathalia Micas, for over forty years, and wore men's clothing — at a time when it was considered indecent for women to do so — both for personal pleasure and so that she could more conveniently wander through farms and slaughterhouses to research and sketch animal anatomy. Chided by a male acquaintance one evening for frequenting such places unchaperoned, Bonheur retorted, "Oh my dear sir, if you knew

Michael Willhoite

Rosa Bonheur

how little I care for your sex, you wouldn't get any ideas in your head. The fact is, in the way of males, I like only the bulls I paint."

BOWLES, JANE. (1917-1973), *U.S. writer.* Though in terms of quantity, her literary production was quite limited, Jane Bowles has been called "one of the finest writers of modern fiction in any language." She wrote one novel, *Two Serious Ladies*; one play, *In the Summer House*; and six short stories, all of which she completed by her early thirties.

Bowles was born Jane Auer in New York. She met writer-composer Paul Bowles in 1937 and went to Mexico with him. The following year they were married and spent the next few years traveling in Central America and France. In 1948, they went to Morocco, where Jane Bowles spent much of the rest of her life. In 1957 she suffered a stroke, and her health gradually declined thereafter. She was institutionalized in a psychiatric hospital in Spain in 1967 and died there in 1973.

From her early childhood, Jane Bowles was considered to be different, even odd. When she was twelve, she wrote in a friend's autograph book:

You asked me to write in youre book
I scarcely know how to begin
For there's nothing orriginal about me
But a little orriginal Sin.

As a young, unmarried woman, Jane lived what was thought at the time to be an unconventional and highly adventurous lifestyle for a woman. She associated with bohemians and intellectuals and spent a great deal of time in Greenwich Village bars. On more than one occasion during that period of her life, she was involved sexually with other women.

BOYD, MALCOLM. (1923-), *U.S. Episcopal priest and gay activist.* Boyd gave up a prominent career as a radio-television producer in 1951 to enter seminary and seek ordination as an Episcopal priest. He was ordained in 1955 and became nationally renowned in the 1960s for his bestselling book, *Are You Running With Me, Jesus?*, a collection of deeply personal prayers written in a modern idiom. He was also well known for his civil rights and anti-Vietnam War activism.

In 1976, he publicly acknowledged that he was homosexual. He has since become outspoken as an advocate of gay rights, especially within the context of organized religion.

BRADLEY, DAN. (1940-1988), *U.S. political activist.* In the early years of the Reagan administration, Dan Bradley was president of the Legal Services Corporation, a federal government agency providing legal aid for the poor. In 1982, Bradley publicly announced that he was gay; in so doing, he became the highest-ranking openly gay official in the federal government. Soon thereafter, he resigned from the LSC and became active in the gay rights movement; he served on the boards of many organizations, including the National Gay and Lesbian Task Force, the National Gay Rights Advocates, and the Human Rights Campaign Fund.

When he learned that he was infected with the AIDS virus, Bradley became especially active around that issue. "The fact that many of us are talking about our illness has to be beneficial," he said. "I believe knowledge, information, and awareness are three of the best cures for ignorance, bigotry, and discrimination." He died of AIDS at the age of forty-seven.

BRITTEN, BENJAMIN. (1913-1976), *British composer.* Recognized as perhaps the greatest English composer since Purcell, Britten's reputation rests primarily on his most famous operas — *The Turn of the Screw, Peter Grimes, Death in Venice* — his massive *War Requiem,* and numerous orchestral works, including the popular, often performed *Young Person's Guide to the Orchestra.* He and British tenor Peter Pears were lovers for over forty years; in fact, it was for Pears that Britten wrote most of his solo vocal works and all of his major tenor roles. The two are buried side by side in Aldeburgh, England, the site of a music school and an annual music festival the two men founded in 1947.

BROOKS, ROMAINE. (1874-1970), *U.S. painter.* Brooks lived most of her life in Europe where she gained recognition for her bold, distinctively stylized portraits of various celebrities of her day, including Jean Cocteau, Gabriele D'Annunzio, Ida Rubinstein, and Lady Una Trowbridge. In 1915, she met and became lovers with Parisian writer and salon hostess Natalie Barney. The relationship lasted for more than fifty years. It ended abruptly when both women were well into their nineties: Brooks, in a fit of jealousy and bitter resentment, became incensed over Barney's sexual interest in the 69-year-old wife of a retired Romanian diplomat and vowed never to see Barney or speak to her again. Maintaining her silence to the end, Brooks died a year and a half later; Barney survived her by barely thirteen months.

BUCHANAN, JAMES. (1791-1868), *U.S. president.* As the country's only bachelor president, James Buchanan's sexual orientation has often been the subject of speculation. There is no conclusive evidence on the subject, but writer Carl Sferrazza Anthony fueled the debate with his discovery of two letters to Buchanan by Alabama senator William Rufus de Vane King, with whom Buchanan shared rooms in Washington, D.C. for over two decades. One reads that "I am selfish enough to hope you will not be able to procure an associate who will cause you to feel no regret at our separation."

Buchanan won the presidency as a compromise Democratic candidate, and his single term in office accomplished little, for himself and for the country. When he turned the White House over to his successor, Abraham Lincoln, Buchanan said, "If you are as happy on entering this house as I am in leaving it, you are the happiest man on earth."

BURROUGHS, WILLIAM. (1914-), *U.S. novelist.* Called the "writer and oracle of the Beat Generation," Burroughs rebelled against his upper-class background, depicting it in his novels as dull, lifeless, and oppressive. Throughout his youth and early adulthood, Burroughs sought alternatives to what he saw as the empty existence of the bourgeoisie. He eventually found what he was looking for when he was introduced to morphine in 1944. Burroughs saw in drugs the possibility of breaking free of social conditioning and of expanding his consciousness, and he made addiction a way of life for the next fifteen years.

Since the late 1950s, when he gave up his drug habit, Burroughs has devoted himself to writing. His works include *Naked Lunch,* which a Boston court declared to be obscene in 1965,

Queer, and many others. In his revolt against bourgeois convention, Burroughs created a new novel form known as the pop-art novel, which includes elements of popular culture usually ignored by literary writers.

Although he was married twice, Burroughs has lived in New York since 1974 with James Grauerholz, who acts as his companion, secretary, and agent.

BURTON, Sir RICHARD. (1821-1890), *British explorer and scholar.* Burton was best known during his lifetime for his extensive explorations of Asia, Africa, and South America. He spoke twenty-seven languages, and tried to examine other cultures on their own terms — when he visited Mecca, for example, he disguised himself as a Moslem, even to the point of being circumcised. His fifty books include the first English translation of *The Arabian Nights* to faithfully include its many homoerotic passages.

Despite his marriage, Burton was not secretive about his homosexual activities, and was an early proponent of homosexual equality. After his death, his wife burned his journals and diaries, fearing they would taint his memory.

BYRON, LORD (GEORGE GORDON). (1788-1824), *British poet.* Byron is best remembered as the leading poet of the Romantic period. His epic-satire *Don Juan* is considered his masterpiece; but he is also known for his *Childe Harold,* and *Manfred.*

Byron's life was filled with lovers of both sexes. When he was seventeen and a student at Trinity College, he fell in love with John Eddleston, a choirboy of the same age. Byron wrote that "I certainly love him more than any human being, and neither time nor distance have had the least effect on my (in general) changeable disposition."

Some biographers have dismissed this as a platonic infatuation, but there is less uncertainty surrounding Byron's

Lord Byron

1811 relationship with Nicolo Giraud, a youth of mixed French-Greek blood whom Byron described as "the most beautiful being I have ever beheld." They were inseparable for a time, and Byron is said to have consulted a doctor about a relaxation of the sphincter muscle which was giving Giraud trouble.

Byron's many other liaisons included one with his half-sister Augusta; when this relationship was criticized as incestuous, he explained that "I could love anything on earth that appeared to wish it." He married in 1815 but separated a year later; relationships with a beautiful Italian noblewoman, then with another handsome Greek youth, followed. Parts of Byron's life will remain unknown; although he wrote his memoirs and entrusted them to his friend Thomas Moore, they were considered too scandalous for publication after his death and were burned.

CAESAR, JULIUS. (100?-44 B.C.), *Roman statesman.* Gaius Julius Caesar was born to a great patrician family, but early in life he began adopting the ideology of the democratic leader Marius. In his early adulthood, Caesar studied rhetoric, a skill that would prove to be valuable in his later years; he then became a military tribune, and played a key role in the defeat of the slave uprising organized by Spartacus in 73 B.C. Blessed with great personal charm, as well as military skill and a shrewd political mind, Caesar consolidated his power and in 49 B.C. was appointed dictator for life.

During the final years of his life, as sole consul of Rome, Caesar combined foreign military exploits with internal reform. He began extending Roman citizenship and undertook agrarian reform and codification of the laws. His display of imperial airs and his decision to dissolve the trade unions antagonized many of his former supporters, and on March 15, 44 B.C., he was assassinated by dissatisfied Romans.

Caesar's sex life was varied and busy. He had three wives, as well as his famous relationship with Cleopatra, and several male lovers, thus earning the epithet "Husband to every woman and wife to every man." The best-known of these male lovers was Nicomedes, king of Bithynia. The two young men met during the course of the Second Methridatic War, and their liaison became something of a scandal. When Nicomedes died eight years later, at the age of thirty-six, he left his kingdom to the Romans.

CAMBACÉRÈS, JEAN JACQUES RÉGIS DE. (1753-1824), *French lawmaker.* Born into a family of jurists and trained for the law, Cambacérès put his legal skills to use against the state during the French Revolution in 1789. He survived the feuds and bloodletting that followed the revolution, and served as president of the infamous Committee of Public Safety in 1795. When Napoleon took power in 1799, Cambacérès won his trust and became the primary architect of the new Napoleonic Code.

Cambacérès was apparently discreet, but not secretive, about his homo-

Jean Jacques Régis de Cambacérès

sexuality. It was through his influence that the Napoleonic Code — and the many later laws throughout Europe that were infuenced by it — did not outlaw homosexual acts between adults unless they involved violence or took place in public.

CARPENTER, EDWARD. (1844-1929), *English reformer.* At the age of thirty, Edward Carpenter left his conventional job as a Church of England curator and became active in the working-class movement of the time. He combined Fabian Socialism with his own radical views on sex.

Carpenter's first work on homosexuality, *Homogenic Love and Its Place in a Free Society,* appeared in 1894. Further works followed. In his most widely read book, *Love's Coming of Age* (1897), Carpenter proposed equality between the sexes, and included a gay-positive chapter titled "The Intermediate Sex." This chapter was expanded into a full book a decade later, under the same title, and it became (with Havelock Ellis's *Sexual Inversion*) one of the most widely read books on the subject in the English language.

Even that did not exhaust Carpenter. In 1902 he published *Iolaus: An Anthology of Friendship,* with homoerotic poetry from both ancient and contemporary sources. In 1914, his book *Intermediate Types among Primitive Folk* showed that in primitive societies — held up by anthropologists as reflecting pure human behavior — homosexual behavior was often considered normal, or was even exalted. He himself had at least two male lovers in his lifetime.

CARSWELL, G. HAROLD. (1920-), *U.S. jurist.* In 1970, Carswell was nominated by President Richard Nixon to the U.S. Supreme Court, but his nomination was rejected by the Senate because, among other things, he was regarded as an advocate of racial segregation. In 1976, Carswell was arrested for soliciting a plainclothes police officer outside a shopping mall men's room in Tallahassee, Florida. After his arrest, Carswell checked himself into a local psychiatric hospital.

CASEMENT, Sir ROGER. (1864-1916), *Irish patriot.* Born in Ireland, Roger Casement grew up in a family where the cause of Irish independence was fervently supported. At the age of twenty, his job as a ship's purser took him to the Belgian Congo, where he was horrified at the treatment the native Africans received from European colonists. For the next twenty-six years, Casement fought against these inhuman conditions, and in 1911, he was knighted for his work.

Casement then turned his energies to the Irish nationalist cause. When war broke out between Britain and Germany, Casement urged his Irish compatriots to support the Germans, on the grounds that England was their common enemy. He arranged for Germany to ship arms to Ireland for use against the British. Word of this reached England, and Casement was arrested and tried for treason. He argued that he was Irish, not British, and that his acts were therefore not treasonable, but his reasoning fell on deaf ears and he was sentenced to death by hanging.

Many prominent Americans sympathized with Casement and urged that his sentence be commuted. That probably would have happened except for one twist of fate: the discovery in London of Casement's personal diaries, in which he graphically detailed his numerous homosexual liaisons over the preceding dozen years. Copies of the diaries were distributed by the British government, and sympathy for Casement evaporated. He was executed on August 3, 1916.

Willa Cather

CATHER, WILLA, (1876-1947), *U.S. novelist.* Willa Cather was born in Virginia but grew up in Nebraska. A free spirit from a young age, she wanted at one time to be called William. While at college in Lincoln, Nebraska, she discovered her love of writing, and, upon graduating, moved to Pittsburgh where she thought she would find a more stimulating environment. There she met Isabelle McClung, with whom she developed a close relationship. In 1905 she moved to New York, leaving Isabelle behind in Pittsburgh, and met

Edith Lewish, another Nebraskan who became Cather's lifetime companion. Cather's many works include *My Antonia, Death Comes for the Archbishop,* and *The Song of the Lark.*

Michael Willhoite

Constantine Cavafy

CAVAFY, CONSTANTINE (1863-1933), *Greek poet.* By developing his own individualistic style of poetry, Cavafy became one of the West's most important poets. Most of his best work, however, wasn't written until after he turned forty — and wasn't published until after his death.

Cavafy often visited male houses of prostitution while living in Alexandria. He bribed his servants to ruffle up his sheets at night so his mother would not realize he had not been home.

CHAMBERS, JANE. (1937-1983), *U.S. writer.* Jane Chambers began her professional theatrical career in 1955 as an off-Broadway actress, but by the early sixties she had become a successful free-lance writer and broadcast journalist. She was an ardent supporter of equal rights for minorities, helping to found the New Jersey Women's Political Caucus, and was active in other such organizations, including the East End Gay Organization for Human Rights.

Chambers won her greatest recognition for her stage plays, particularly those set in the lesbian subculture, such as " Last Summer at Bluefish Cove," for which she won a DramaLogue Critics Circle Award, and "A Late Snow." In his anthology, *Gay Plays,* William Hoffman described "A Late Snow" as a "passionate play about a passionate cross-section of lesbians," and a "realistic romantic drama."

Chambers once commented, "I write from my experience and interests. I do not consciously create my characters — I just look up one day and notice that they are standing in front of my typewriter."

CHEEVER, JOHN. (1912-1982), *U.S. writer.* Called "the most graceful American fiction writer after F. Scott Fitzgerald," Cheever was best known for his masterful short stories, which portrayed middle-class, suburban America in an ironic and often comedic light, and for his five novels, including *Bullet Park* and *Falconer,* the latter of which incorporated homosexuality as a central theme. In 1979, a collection of Cheever's short stories won the Pulitzer Prize.

Two years after Cheever's death, his daughter published a memoir in which she disclosed that her father had struggled all his life with homosexual desires. She also revealed — based on material in his private, unpublished journals — that he finally allowed himself to have a love affair with another man.

CHRISTINA. (1626-1689), *Swedish queen.* When Christina was born, the midwives thought she was a boy. Contemporaries often referred to her as having a masculine appearance, and there is speculation that she was a pseudo-hermaphrodite, with superficial male organs. Christina became queen at the age of six, upon the death of her father.

As a young woman, she was rumored to be having love affairs with suitors of both sexes, but it was her open relationship with Ebba Sparre, her lady-in-waiting, that caused the most concern among her advisers. Christina gave little attention to their pleas that she be less open, however, even going so far as to publicly refer to Sparre as her "bedfellow."

Christina encouraged the growth of science and industry in Sweden, but her aloofness from the people, a desire to travel, and the jealousy of her advisers contributed to her frustration with her position as monarch. In 1654 she abdicated and traveled throughout Europe, often dressed as a man. Ultimately, she converted to Catholicism and lived off papal charity in Rome until her death.

Michael Willhoite

Sir Winston Churchill

CHURCHILL, Sir WINSTON.
(1874-1965), *British statesman and author.* Following a successful career as a writer and a mixed career as a politician, Churchill became prime minister of England in 1940, and led the country through World War II. There is no reason to believe Churchill was homo-

sexual, but he is quoted in his biography as saying, "I once went to bed with a man to see what it was like."

CLIFT, MONTGOMERY. (1920-1966), *U.S. actor.* Clift began his professional acting career when he was fourteen and made his screen debut in 1948 in Fred Zinnemann's *The Search,* a performance that earned him the first of his four Oscar nominations. Shortly thereafter, he was arrested in New York City for soliciting sex from a young hustler; his lawyers helped keep the incident out of the newspapers.

After a disfiguring automobile accident in 1957, Clift began to rely heavily on drugs and alcohol; that, along with escalating emotional problems, sent his career into a decline. John Huston, who directed Clift in one of his last films, *The Misfits,* in 1961, later speculated that, "The combination of drugs, drink and being homosexual was a soup that was just too much for him." Clift appeared in only two major films after *The Misfits,* and died of a heart attack at the age of forty-five.

COCTEAU, JEAN. (1889-1963), *French writer, artist, and film director.* Cocteau grew up in Paris and spent most of his life there. In his speech, education, ideas, and habits, he was in many ways the quintessential Parisian.

One of the greatest influences on Cocteau's work was his lover, Raymond Radiguet, whom he met in 1918. Radiguet was then a sixteen-year-old literary prodigy whose writing stressed a simplicity which became characteristic of Cocteau's later work. Radiguet's death in 1923 left Cocteau devastated.

Cocteau's talents extended to a wide variety of areas, including literature, the visual arts, and the cinema. He has been called "the most versatile artist of the twentieth century," and the range and quality of his work attest to the truth of this claim. His works include the play *Orphée,* the novels *Les En-*

fants terribles and *La Machine infernale,* and the film *La Belle et la bête.*

COHN, ROY. (1927-1986), *U.S. attorney.* Well before his thirtieth birthday, Roy Cohn had established his reputation as the flamboyant sidekick of Senator Joseph McCarthy in the 1950s. As the arrogant but incisive inquisitor of McCarthy's communist-hunting congressional committee, Cohn destroyed hundreds of careers and reputations through skillful use of innuendo or guilt by association.

In 1954, Cohn inadvertently triggered McCarthy's downfall when a friend and fellow committee member was drafted into the Army. Cohn tried to get special privileges for his friend; when that failed, he allegedly threatened to wreck the Army with an investigation. In the televised Army-McCarthy hearings that ensued, McCarthy came across as a fulminating demagogue and never recovered his credibility.

Cohn, however, survived the hearings and became a lawyer. Wealthy clients flocked to him, despite his notoriety. "I'd rather have him inside pissing out than outside pissing in," explained one. But even being Cohn's friend wasn't always a successful strategy. Six weeks before his death, Cohn was disbarred in New York after being found guilty of dishonesty, fraud, deceit, and misrepresentation. Among the many accusations upheld by the court was the charge that in 1976, Cohn had gone into the hospital room of a dying friend and tricked him into signing over control of a multi-million-dollar estate.

Only as he died, perhaps, did Cohn's dishonesty catch up with him. His homosexuality, a closely-guarded secret in the fifties, was public knowledge when he finally succumbed to AIDS.

COLETTE (SIDONIE COLETTE GOUDEKET). (1873-1954), *French novelist.* One of the outstanding French woman writers of the twentieth century, Colette wrote novels and short stories largely concerned with the pleasures, pains, and ironies of love. Her work is often remembered for its evocative sensuality — it was said she could describe a vegetable as if it were a love object — and for its unbridled love of life.

Although she married three times, Colette had numerous lesbian affairs; in fact, she left her first husband for another woman. In her life, and in her work, she refused to make what she saw as an artificial distinction between "normal" and "abnormal" sexuality.

CONRADIN. (1252-1268), *Titular king of Jerusalem and Sicily.* Conradin, the son of Hohenstaufen ruler Conrad IV, was born in Bavaria and spent most of his short life there. His father died when he was only two, and while Conradin was still a child, his guardians assumed for him the titles of king of Jerusalem and king of Sicily. At the age of fourteen, he was approached by several Italian cities to help free Italy from its French invaders. Conradin agreed; his army crossed the Alps and joined with Italian patriots to march against the French. Despite several early victories, Conradin's troops were ultimately defeated by the French army and forced to retreat.

Conradin was captured, put on trial by the French for treason, and at the age of sixteen, he was beheaded. His lover, Frederick of Baden, titular duke of Austria, voluntarily accompanied Conradin to the block. The remains of the two men rest in the monastery of Santa Maria del Carmine at Naples.

COWARD, Sir NOEL. (1899-1973), *British playwright, composer, and actor.* Noel Coward is best known for his light and intricate comedies of manners. Although primarily a playwright, Coward performed nearly every possible function in the theater, including acting, producing, directing, dancing, and singing. His work was greatly appreciated both in the United States and Britain, and he was knighted by Queen Elizabeth in 1970.

Coward's homosexuality was well known both within and outside of drama circles. He once met writer Edna Ferber when she was wearing a suit similar to his. "You look almost like a man," he told her lightheartedly. "So do you," she replied.

CRANE, HART. (1899-1932), *U.S. poet.* A leading poet of the American literary renaissance of the 1920s, Hart Crane was an experimental poet and an outspoken admirer of Walt Whitman. He is best known for his collection of poems titled *The Bridge,* in which the Brooklyn Bridge becomes a symbol of his belief in America's spiritual destiny. Homoerotic themes run through several of Crane's works, and he was especially partial to portrayals of virile sailors. In 1932, while on board a ship, Crane called "Good-bye, everybody," jumped overboard, and drowned.

CUKOR, GEORGE. (1899-1983), *U.S. film director.* Cukor's Hollywood career spanned more than fifty years and included such classics as *The Women, The Philadelphia Story,* the 1954 version of *A Star Is Born,* and *My Fair Lady,* which won him an Academy Award for Best Director in 1964. He was often labeled a "woman's director," because of his ability to draw bravura performances from some of the great actresses of the screen, including Katherine Hepburn, Greta Garbo, Judy Garland, and Norma Shearer. In an interview shortly before his death, he said of his homosexuality, "I didn't put on any big act. You know, a lot of people are so funny. They go out with girls and all that, and that's absolutely ridiculous. I didn't pretend."

DAVID. (1035?-960? B.C.), *Israeli king.* Born into a rural peasant family, David earned his place in history when he killed the giant Philistine warrior Goliath with his slingshot. This helped establish his position in the court of King Saul, where he became a military leader and also a close friend of Jonathan, the king's son. Jonathan and Saul died in the battle of Gilboa (1013 B.C.), and David was griefstruck. "My brother Jonathan," he wrote, "thy love to me was wonderful, surpassing the love of women."

After Saul's death, David became the king of Israel, beginning a line that lasted over four hundred years. The exact nature of his friendship with Jonathan is subject to speculation, but its intensity is not; it is recounted in the book of I Samuel of the Bible.

DEAN, JAMES. (1931-1955), *U.S. actor.* In his first two films, *Rebel Without a Cause* and *East of Eden*, James Dean became the idol of the post-war generation with his portrayals of a sensitive and tormented teenager searching desperately for love. This screen portrayal was not much different from the real-life James Dean, who identified himself as bisexual but whose main emotional and physical bonds were with other men.

Dean's third film — *Giant,* with Rock Hudson and Elizabeth Taylor — was his last, and before it was released he died in a high-speed car crash.

DELANY, SAMUEL. (1942-), *U.S. writer.* One of America's most popular and critically acclaimed writers of science fiction, Samuel Delany is also one of relatively few black writers in the genre. His writing style is highly original, having been developed as the result of his struggle to overcome dyslexia.

Delany was born in Harlem to a family of successful professional blacks. He married poet Marilyn Hacker — who was aware of his gayness — in 1961. In the early sixties, Delany plunged into the East Village scene, participating in "Happenings," experimenting with bisexuality, and discussing innovative approaches to literature. He documented these years in his highly candid memoirs, *The Motion of Light in Water.*

Michael Willhoite

Demosthenes

DEMOSTHENES. (384-322 B.C.), *Athenian orator.* The best known orator of the ancient world began his career with a speech against his guardian, who had attempted to steal his inheritance. His success in that case encouraged Demosthenes to pursue this career, and he is best remembered for his orations against Philip of Macedonia, which gave birth to the word *philippic.*

According to legend, Demosthenes was bothered by a stammer in his youth. To cure it, he practiced speaking on the beach with pebbles in his mouth, and to gain lung power, he rehearsed poetry while running uphill. Although married, Demosthenes was reported to have had several male lovers.

DEMUTH, CHARLES. (1883-1935), *U.S. painter.* The work of Charles Demuth was for many years virtually unknown except to specialists. His choice of subjects — flowers, gay baths, bars, and sailors — prevented his paintings from being received with much

enthusiasm at a time when the United States was puritanical in its artistic tastes. One of the many artists who emigrated to Europe in the pre-World War I era, he did much to contribute to the introduction of modernist styles and a greater sexual openness in art.

Little is known of the actual circumstances of Demuth's life; he wrote few letters and was generally quite secretive. He was born and raised in Lancaster, Pennsylvania and spent much of his adult life in Europe. How actively homosexual he was is open to debate, although his paintings clearly indicate that he was familiar with gay bars and baths. He exhibited at the gallery of Alfred Stieglitz, the influential Manhattan dealer, but because of his homosexuality Demuth was never truly accepted by Stieglitz's circle.

DIAGHILEV, SERGEI. (1872-1929), *Russian impresario.* Diaghilev began his career organizing art exhibitions in Russia, then switched his interests to ballet. His imperious and domineering personality soon earned him the title "Tsar of the Arts."

In 1909, he arranged a Parisian tour of Russian ballet. This brought him in touch with Vaslav Nijinsky, then still a teenager but already Russia's most promising ballet dancer. Nijinsky was captivated by Diaghilev's strong personality, referring to him as "a genius, a great discoverer of talents, and the only man I could compare to Leonardo da Vinci." The two men became lovers.

In 1911, Diaghilev was named director of the new Parisian company, the *Ballets Russes,* which flourished thanks to his ability to discover and bring together talented choreographers and musicians. For two years, Diaghilev's genius as an impresario combined with Nijinsky's dazzling talent to create performances that became the talk of Europe.

Diaghilev, however, was a difficult employer and a possessive lover. Nijinsky eventually began to chafe under these conditions, and a rift developed between the two men. Diaghilev continued as director of the *Ballets Russes* until his death three decades later. During his lifetime, he collaborated with such geniuses as Picasso, Stravinsky, and Cocteau.

DOLAN, TERRY. (1950-1986), *U.S. conservative activist.* John Terrence Dolan was one of several gay New Right activists in the early 1980s who suffered from the very homophobia they actively helped to stir up. Dolan was most prominent as the founder (in 1975) and head of the National Conservative Political Action Committee (NCPAC), which in its earliest years was in the forefront of the New Right movement. It pumped two million dollars into Ronald Reagan's 1980 campaign while sponsoring vicious — and often inaccurate — television ads against liberal senators that it targeted for defeat.

But Dolan's approach soon grew counterproductive, and even fellow conservatives questioned NCPAC's effectiveness. In 1982, Dolan put together a "hit list" of twenty senators; nineteen won re-election anyway.

Frustrated by NCPAC limitations, and by the militantly anti-gay posturing of his fellow conservatives, Dolan co-founded Concerned Americans for Individual Rights (CAIR) in 1981. CAIR was to be a gay Republican organization, combining a conservative economic philosophy, strong support for military spending, and a libertarian approach to gay rights. Dolan opposed gay civil rights legislation, for example — he considered it government intrusion — but felt that the government should not discriminate against gays in the military and in other jobs.

In 1982, Perry Young chronicled the growth of the New Right in his book *God's Bullies*; the book charged that Dolan was gay, and it included an account by a man who claimed to have had an affair with him. Dolan denied that the affair had ever taken place, but refused to discuss his sexual orientation, a position he often took in the years that followed. Dolan's death in 1986, at the age of thirty-six, was reported by the Washington *Post* to be the result of AIDS; his doctor denied that story.

DUQUESNOY, JÉRÔME. (1602-1654), *Flemish sculptor.* Although less famous than his brother François (whose works include Brussel's *Mannekin Pis*), Jérôme Duquesnoy was the official court sculptor in Flanders. While in that position, he was accused of sodomy with two church acolytes who had served as his models; he was found guilty, and was strangled, then burned at the stake.

Michael Willhoite

Amelia Earhart

EARHART, AMELIA. (1898-1937?), *U.S. aviator.* Earhart was the first woman to fly alone over the Atlantic, a feat which won her the nickname "Lady Lindy." This was soon followed by other aviation milestones: she was the first person to fly alone from the coast of California to Hawaii (actually a longer distance than from the U.S. to Europe), and the first to make a solo flight from Mexico City to the east coast of the U.S. In the summer of 1937, she and navigator Frederick Noonan were attempting to fly around the world when their plane disappeared under mysterious circumstances near the Marshall Islands in the South Pacific.

Speculation about Earhart's sexuality is based almost entirely on circumstantial evidence: her masculine dress and appearance, her fierce independence, and a letter in which she expressed reluctance to marry her future husband, publisher George Putnam.

Michael Willhoite

Edward II

EDWARD II. (1284-1327), *English king.* Although his father, Edward I, was famous for his wartime exploits, Edward II showed little interest in military affairs. He did, however, show interest in Piers Gaveston, the orphaned son of a French knight who became his companion when Edward was fourteen and Gaveston sixteen. Rumors about their relationship were soon circulating in the castle. In 1307, Edward I banished Gaveston from the kingdom and arranged for his son's marriage to Princess Isabel of France. But the king died soon afterwards, and as the new king, Edward II invited Gaveston back before proceeding with the marriage.

In the years that followed,

Edward's devotion to Gaveston did not go unnoticed by Isabel. She conspired with the country's powerful barons to have Gaveston banished once more. When he returned from that exile, at Edward's urging, Isabel helped the barons approach the French king for support in a rebellion. It succeeded, and the barons executed Gaveston in 1312.

The conflict between Edward and the barons continued over the next decade. Edward found a new lover, Hugh le Despenser, and his wife likewise began an affair, with the Earl of Mortimer. Isabel and Mortimer again sought French help for an uprising. In 1326, with support from many barons, they attacked and eventually defeated the troops of Edward II. Hugh le Despenser was captured, tortured, and executed; Edward II was persuaded to abdicate, and his son Edward III was crowned king. Edward II was then killed by having a red-hot poker thrust into his rectum, a method which satisfied his executioners that he was being punished for his sins, but that left no marks on his body.

ELLIS, HAVELOCK. (1859-1939), *British essayist and physician.* Ellis is best known for his ground-breaking work on sexuality. When his seven-volume *Studies in the Psychology of Sex* was published, it met, not surprisingly, with a great deal of controversy. Ellis was even brought to trial over it. The judge called claims for the book's scientific value "a pretense, adopted for the purpose of selling a filthy publication." Nevertheless, much of Ellis's work did eventually gain acceptance within the scientific community and beyond. His writings encouraged further study of human sexuality and helped pave the way for the open discussion of sexual problems.

EPSTEIN, BRIAN. (1934-1967), *British businessman.* The first manager of the Beatles, Epstein was homosexual, and was clearly in love with John Lennon. The extent to which Lennon returned that love physically is open to dispute; certainly, it was reciprocated less than Epstein would have wished.

Michael Willhoite

Desiderius Erasmus

ERASMUS, DESIDERIUS. (1466?-1536), *Dutch theologian and scholar.* Born in Rotterdam, the illegitimate son of an educated priest, Erasmus is often considered the greatest scholar of the Reformation. Among his achievements were definitive editions of many of the classics, including the Greek New Testament.

Shortly after joining the monastery in 1488, Erasmus became enamoured of Servatius Roger, who spurned his attentions. His most enduring relationship was a platonic one with William Blount, Fourth Lord Mountjoy.

FLYNN, ERROL. (1909-1959), *U.S. actor.* During his lifetime, Errol Flynn was surrounded by an aura of romantic mystery which he deliberately fostered. Little is known of his origins; he claimed on different occasions to have been born in Tasmania and in Ireland. After spending much of his youth in New Guinea where he prospected for gold, sailed a schooner, and wrote stories for

the *Sydney Bulletin,* Flynn went to Hollywood and achieved instant stardom in *Captain Blood.* A string of swashbuckling roles followed in films such as *The Adventures of Robin Hood, The Sea Hawk,* and *Gentleman Jim.* In 1942, he was tried for statutory rape, and despite his acquittal, his popularity dropped. Flynn was notorious for his romantic adventures and was considered to be a ladies' man; it was only after his death that his homosexuality became widely known outside of Hollywood circles.

FORSTER, E.M. (1879-1970), *British writer.* Although in his lifetime he was well known as an essayist and critic, Forster's fame rests primarily on the novels *Howard's End* and *A Passage to India.* Forster made sure that his novel of homosexual love, *Maurice,* was not published until 1971 — the year after his death — although he had finished it in 1914. The work was revolutionary in its treatment of homosexuality as an inherent trait of a person, rather than simply a behavior.

Forster broke with conventions of the nineteenth-century novel, favoring a freer, more straightforward style and discarding the intricate descriptions and elaborations which characterized works of the last century. Forster was intensely interested in and drawn to Mediterranean culture, which he considered more spontaneous and closer to nature than the culture of Britain and other countries of Northern Europe.

FOSTER, STEPHEN. (1826-1864), *U.S. composer.* Foster was probably the most popular American composer in the years before the Civil War. His better-known tunes include "De Camptown Races," "Beautiful Dreamer," and "Jeannie with the Light Brown Hair."

Foster's early family life was unsettled from its beginning and he spent most of his childhood with his older brother William. After marrying and fathering a daughter, Foster spent more and more time in New York City, away from his wife and family. He finally made the separation permanent in 1860. From that time until his death in 1864, his closest relationship was with a poet named George Cooper, fifteen years his junior. They collaborated on more than twenty of Foster's songs. It was Cooper who cared for Foster in the days after the accident that eventually claimed his life.

FOUCAULT, MICHEL. (1926-1984), *French philosopher.* Foucault is considered to be among the most important thinkers of the twentieth century; he is known particularly for his analyses of the concepts and codes by which societies operate. In his *History of Sexuality*, a three-volume examination of Western attitudes towards sexuality, he challenged the traditional belief that Victorian society was characterized by a repressive silence surrounding sexuality; in reality, he maintained that sexual issues were discussed then with a greater frequency than ever before. Foucault died in 1984 of an AIDS-related illness.

FRANK, ANNE. (1929-1945), German diarist. Anne Frank, who from 1942 to 1945 hid from the Nazis with the rest of her family in an Amsterdam attic, gained posthumous fame when her diary of that period was published. Until recently, only edited versions of the diary have been available, as many publishers found the original version too sexually explicit. The passages that were particularly problematic were those in which the young girl described what could be considered lesbian urges and fantasies. In January 1944, for example, she wrote, "I become ecstatic every time I see a naked figure of a woman, such as Venus, in my art history book. Sometimes I find it so wondrous and beautiful that I have to hold myself in, so that I do not begin to cry."

FRANK, BARNEY. (1940-), *U.S. politician.* For years, Frank established a reputation as one of Massachusetts' wittiest and most liberal politicians, first in the state legislature, then in the U.S. Congress. In 1987, Frank gave an interview to the Boston *Globe* in which he became the first member of the U.S. House of Representatives to come out completely voluntarily. It was a point he had been moving toward steadily for several years, as he had come out to an increasing number of friends and acquaintances.

The process had been hastened somewhat by Robert Bauman, a former representative who lost his seat in the House after being charged with soliciting sex from a sixteen-year-old boy. In his 1986 autobiography, Bauman had implied that Frank was gay.

Michael Willhoite

Frederick the Great

FREDERICK II (THE GREAT). (1712-1786), *Prussian king.* Born to the iron-willed military ruler Frederick William I, the young Frederick II often found himself at odds with his father. Unlike his father, the young Frederick was absorbed by the arts and literature, and developed an effeminate air. Most galling to the king was his son's passionate friendship with the 25-year-old Hans von Katte, a lieutenant in the

Prussian army. As his father grew increasingly abusive, Frederick made plans at the age of eighteen to flee to England with Katte. They were caught and imprisoned, and Frederick was forced to watch as his father had Katte beheaded.

Upon the death of his father ten years later, Frederick became king. His reign was marked by a number of reforms, including the abolition of torture and increased religious tolerance.

GENET, JEAN. (1910-1986), *French writer*. Genet spent most of his adolescence and young adulthood in prison for robbery. Although he didn't begin writing until the age of thirty-two, he was one of the most prolific French writers of the century. His works include poetry; the plays *The Balcony* and *The Maids*; and the novel *Our Lady of the Flowers*. From the beginning of his writing career, Genet's work was distinguished by a rigorous, pure, and highly original style. This is particularly remarkable in that for most of his life, he had been exposed only to slang and literature of poor quality.

Genet was aware even at a very young age of his attraction to boys. In fact, he recalled later, he was happy for the first time in his life when he was sent to reform school, because it gave him the chance to express his homosexual desires. During the Great Depression, he earned a living as a male prostitute, and he was involved in relationships with men throughout his life, most of them short-lived.

Genet was "a cat's cradle of contradictions," says his biographer, Edmund White. "He was a homosexual whose closest friends were women, a world celebrity who lived in crummy railway hotels, the author of a handful of the most sumptuously stylish novels of this century who, after the age of ten, received all of his education in reform schools." He died in a Paris hotel in 1986

after falling and hitting his head. His death followed that of Simone de Beauvoir, his old friend and ally, by just a few hours.

GIDE, ANDRÉ. (1869-1951), *French writer*. Among the most prolific and distinguished French writers of the twentieth century, Gide did much to further the cause of gay people. His works include novels, plays, and essays. He shocked his contemporaries in 1924 when he published his autobiographical *Si le grain ne meurt (If It Die)*, in which he openly noted his homosexual experiences.

The first of those had come at the age of twenty-three, with a fourteen-year-old Arab boy in Tunisia. Although he was married, Gide's relationship with his wife was probably purely platonic. At the age of forty-seven Gide began a relationship with Marc Allégret, then sixteen, who went on to become a well-known film producer. Gide also had a long-standing, non-sexual friendship with Oscar Wilde.

GILLES DE RAIS. (1404-1440), *French general*. Born into a noble French family, Gilles de Raiz grew up surrounded by the finest books, art, and music. At the age of twenty-two, he personally organized and funded a small army to help France in its fight against the English. His abilities in combat brought him fame, and he became a close friend and bodyguard to Joan of Arc.

Ending his military career, Gilles proceeded to set up his own castle in Brittany, rivaling even the palace of the French king in its pomp and splendor. When his massive fortune was depleted, an assistant persuaded him that through alchemy Gilles could create new wealth for himself, though doing so would require the sacrifice of human children, mostly boys, to appease the devil. In the years that followed, some two hundred peasant boys are believed to have been lured into his castle, where they were raped, tortured, and murdered. Gilles's high position protected him from the growing suspicions of the local population for a time, but his luck eventually ran out. In 1440 he was arrested by the Bishop of Nantes; he made a full confession under the threat of torture, and was promptly hanged.

GOODMAN, PAUL. (1911-1972), *U.S. writer.* A leading anarchist influence of our times, Goodman represented a voice of dissent in the gay liberation movement. While many insisted on the necessity of singlemindedness in the fight for gay rights, Goodman advocated alliances with other progressive causes. His philosophy called for self-awareness and encouragement of individualism on the part of the community.

His book *Growing Up Absurd* brought him fame in 1960, and he soon became known as "the Father Figure of the New Left." Goodman's ideological anarchism was reflected in his life. Although he made no secret of his homosexual desires, going so far as to fondle his male students, he was married twice and fathered three children.

GRIMKÉ, ANGELINA WELD. (1880-1958), *U.S. writer.* In 1868, former abolitionist leader Angelina Grimké learned about an Archibald Henry Grimké, a black man who was eloquently arguing and working against racism. Because he shared an uncommon name with her, she wrote to him, and they soon established that he was her nephew. Although Angelina and her sister Sarah had been prominent abolitionists, their brother John was a slaveholder. When his wife died, he had become involved with a slave, and Archibald Henry Grimké was their child. Yet only because of their common work did Angelina and Archibald learn of one another's existence.

Archibald named his only child after his aunt. The younger Angelina

Grimké was born in Boston; she became a poet and writer and was a part of the Harlem Renaissance along with black lesbian writers Georgia Johnson and Alice Dunbar-Nelson. She experienced perhaps her first love affair at the age of sixteen, when she wrote to her friend Mamie Burrill: "If you only knew how my heart overflows with love for you."

As an adult, her poems often included verses of love to other women:

My sweetheart walks down laughing ways
Mid dancing glancing sunkissed ways
And she is all in white...

HADRIAN. (76-138), *Roman emperor.* Orphaned at the age of ten, Publius Aelius Hadrianus was adopted by the future emperor Trajan, whose wife Ploina became especially fond of the boy and took responsibility for his education and personal development. In 98, Trajan became emperor and designated Hadrian as his heir. In 117, upon Trajan's death, Hadrian was crowned emperor.

Hadrian was better trained for his position than many of his successors, and is considered one of Rome's better emperors. He instituted welfare payments for poor children, reduced taxes, codified the laws, and enacted legislation against the mistreatment of slaves. In about the year 124, Hadrian met and fell in love with Antinous, a Greek youth of great beauty. For six years the two were virtually inseparable, and all records indicate that they had a satisfying and happy relationship. In 130, on a trip to Egypt, Antinous drowned himself in the Nile. The reasons for his apparent suicide are obscure. According to one popular account, an oracle had foreseen Hadrian's death, and Antinous decided to sacrifice himself in the hope that Hadrian would survive in his place. Hadrian was grief-stricken. He deified Antinous, but never fully adjusted to the loss. Hadrian deteriorated, both physically and mentally, until his own death eight years later.

Michael Willhoite

Dag Hammarskjold

HAMMARSKJÖLD, DAG. (1905-1961), *Swedish statesman.* Dag Hammarskjöld, whose father was the Swedish prime minister during World War I, gained national prominence first as secretary and then as chairman of the board of governors of the Bank of Sweden. In 1953, Hammarskjöld was elected secretary-general of the United Nations, and was re-elected to the office in 1957. During his term of office, he greatly enhanced the prestige and influence of the United Nations. He was killed in an airplane crash in Northern Rhodesia (now Zimbabwe) while flying there to negotiate a cease-fire between U.N. troops and Katanga forces.

Hammarskjöld never married, and, as a result, there was a great deal of speculation about his sexuality. The rumors were discussed publicly for the first time when Hammarskjöld became a candidate for the office of secretary-general; Hammarskjöld flatly denied them. It is undeniable, however, that throughout his life Hammarskjöld's closest emotional ties were with other

men. In *Markings,* a record of his spiritual life which was published after Hammarskjold's death, several passages seem to indicate that he experienced feelings for other men which went beyond what one would ordinarily expect in a heterosexual man. One such passage is particularly striking:

"I only understood much later, understood that his words had hurt so because my love had still a long way to go . . . Understood that he had reacted instinctively and justifiably in self-defense, and with a sure sense of what was the right path for me and for him."

HANSBERRY, LORRAINE. (1930-1965), *U.S. playwright.* With the production of *A Raisin In The Sun*, Lorraine Hansberry became the ⟩first black woman to have a drama produced on the Broadway stage. The play met with tremendous success and won the New York Drama Critics' Circle Award.

As a child, Hansberry lived with her family in a white neighborhood of Chicago and encountered open hostility in her walks to and from school. This experience had a profound impact on her writings.

In 1950, she moved to New York City and worked at several jobs, while at the same time she perfected her writing style. Hansberry became politically active and outspoken on behalf of civil rights and freedom of sexual expression. In a 1957 letter to *The Ladder*, an early lesbian periodical, she expressed her belief that "homosexual persecution and condemnation has at its roots not only social ignorance, but . . . anti-feminist dogma." In one of her last plays, *The Sign in Sidney Brustein's Window*, Hansberry presented a homosexual character with sympathy and insight, making him one of the best adjusted members of the cast. Her promising career was cut short by her death from cancer at the age of thirty-five. *To Be Young, Gifted and Black*, an adaptation of her writings prepared by her ex-husband Robert Nemiroff, was produced Off-Broadway in 1969. The lesbian aspect of Hansberry's life has been discussed by Adrienne Rich in *Freedomways* magazine, and elsewhere.

HARMODIUS. (532?-514 B.C.), *Athenian patriot.* In 527 B.C., after the death of their father, Hippias and Hipparchus jointly assumed the position of tyrant of Athens. They were less capable than their father, however, and public sentiment gradually turned against them. Their downfall came when Hipparchus sought the attention of the handsome Harmodius. Harmodius rebuffed him and Hipparchus, out of spite, publicly insulted Harmodius's sister.

This event triggered a long-simmering democratic uprising. It was led by Harmodius and his lover Aristogeiton, who conspired to assassinate the co-tyrants. The plan was only partially successful. Hipparchus was killed, but Hippias escaped and briefly put down the uprising after having the two lovers executed. Other patriots, however, continued the battle, and in 510 B.C., Hippias was driven from Athens. Meanwhile, Harmodius and Aristogeiton had achieved the status of folk heroes, creating a legend which later encouraged the elevated status of homosexuality in Athens.

HENRY, PRINCE OF PRUSSIA. (1726-1802), *Prussian general.* The younger brother of Frederick the Great, whose homosexual interests have also been documented, Henry is remembered chiefly as the prince who might have been the first American king. In 1786, many influential Americans were dissatisfied with the weakness of their new country under the Articles of Confederation. One solution they considered seriously was to install a liberal-minded European monarch as king. A group which included Alexander Hamilton and James Monroe expressed their support of Henry for such a position. However, by the time they could

communicate this to him and receive a reply, the Constitutional Convention had already convened in Philadelphia. A monarchy was no longer being considered.

Had events turned out otherwise, America's first king would soon have been embroiled in scandal. Henry had never made much effort to hide his interest in young men, and an exposé published in 1789 was explicit on the subject, referring to Henry's "passion for pederasty," and noting that "The aristocracy of the army knows that with Prince Henry, the Ganymedes shall always be in control."

HIGGINS, COLIN. (1941-1988), *U.S. film writer, producer, and director.* Colin Higgins, who died in 1988 as a result of AIDS, was one of the few openly gay producers and directors in Hollywood. Born in New Caledonia of an American father and an Australian mother, he enrolled at the U.C.L.A. film school in 1967, beginning his successful career as a filmmaker. His master's thesis at U.C.L.A. was a screenplay about a 20-year-old man who falls in love with a 79-year-old woman; it was produced as the film *Harold and Maude,* which launched his career as screenwriter and director. Among his other credits are *The Devil's Daughter, Silver Streak, Foul Play, 9 to 5,* and most recently *Out on a Limb,* based on Shirley MacLaine's best-selling autobiography.

HINSON, JON. (1942-), *U.S. congressman.* A conservative Republican from Mississippi, Hinson had good news and bad news in 1977. The good news was that he survived the fire that destroyed Washington's Cinema Follies theater while he sat in the audience. The bad news was that Cinema Follies was a gay porn theater, and his presence there soon became known.

Hinson's constituents nonetheless re-elected him the following year to another term in Congress. In 1981, his political luck ran out; he was arrested in the restroom of a House office building while soliciting sex with another man, and his career in Congress soon came to an end.

HIPPARCHUS. *(See Harmodius.)*

HIRSCHFELD, MAGNUS. (1868-1935), *German sexologist.* Hirschfeld began his career as a general practitioner, but the trial of Oscar Wilde and the suicide of a patient on the eve of his wedding sparked his long-standing interest in homosexuality and sexology. In 1897 Hirschfeld founded the Scientific-Humanitarian Committee, an early gay-advocacy organization, and drew up a petition to the Reichstag for the repeal of German laws against homosexual offenses. In 1900, in a landmark study, he prepared a questionnaire on a wide range of sex-related topics which was ultimately filled out by ten thousand men and women. After publishing a number of studies on sexual problems, Hirschfeld gained the reputation of being Germany's leading expert on homosexuality and its first avowed specialist in psychosexual studies. With the rise to power of the Nazis, Hirschfeld was forced to leave Germany. He eventually settled in Paris and died in Nice on his sixty-seventh birthday.

Besides being homosexual, Hirschfeld was also a transvestite, and many gay men of the time referred to him as "Auntie Magnesia." In spite of his exhaustive work, the fact that he was homosexual led many to question his objectivity. Consequently, it was some time before his works on the subject were accepted as authoritative.

HOOVER, J. EDGAR. (1895-1972), *U.S. criminologist.* The man who had secrets on everyone else in government was often rumored to have a secret of his own — but if so, he was careful never to let anyone get tangible proof of it. It is

well documented that Hoover and Clyde Tolson (1900-1975) were extremely close friends for forty-four years. Hoover's biographer, Richard Gid Powers, writes that "The relationship was so close, so enduring, and so affectionate that it took the place of marriage for both bachelors . . . An indication of the intimacy of the relationship is the collection of hundreds of candid photographs Hoover took of Tolson (who was strikingly handsome as a young man.)" Powers concludes that the relationship between the two men could accurately be described as "spousal."

HOUSMAN, A.E. (1859-1936), *British poet and educator.* Housman was born into a distinguished and close-knit Worcestershire family. He showed an early talent for scholarship and poetry and entered St. John's College, Oxford on a scholarship in 1877. Although he failed to graduate from Oxford, he went on to pursue an academic career, teaching at Trinity College at Cambridge and elsewhere. In 1896, at his own expense, Housman published five hundred copies of *A Shropshire Lad,* the work for which he is best known. This book consists of a loosely connected series of poems and is notable for its directness of wording and its reflections on life and death. Although the critics' reactions were mixed, the volume had an enormous influence on modern English poetry.

Housman's romantic experience was probably limited to one unsatisfying affair with Moses J. Jackson, a roommate at Oxford. Housman fell deeply in love with Jackson, who, although he reciprocated with friendship, was, at least initially, not interested in pursuing a sexual relationship with Housman. Apparently Housman did later persuade Jackson to engage in sexual relations of some kind. But when Jackson accepted a post at Sind College in India, the affair ended, as did Housman's sex life.

HUDSON, ROCK. (1925-1985), *U.S. actor.* Born Roy Scherer, Jr., in Winnetka, Illinois, Hudson served in the Navy during World War II before going to Hollywood in 1946 to look for work. There he was discovered by agent Henry Wilson. Through careful grooming and well-orchestrated publicity, Wilson transformed Hudson into a leading star on the Universal Studios lot. "He's wholesome," said *Look* magazine, when they chose Hudson as their Star of the Year in 1958. "He doesn't perspire. He has no pimples. He smells of milk. His whole appeal is cleanliness and respectability — this boy is pure." By the late 1950s, Hudson was one of Hollywood's most successful leading men, thanks to his performances in such popular films as *Magnificent Obsession, Giant* (for which he received an Oscar nomination in 1956), and *Pillow Talk,* the first of several light bedroom comedies co-starring Hudson's friend Doris Day.

Throughout his later career, Hudson repeatedly denied rumors that he was homosexual. However, in 1984, with the announcement he had AIDS, his sex life became a matter of open speculation and, finally, public certainty. The announcement also gave a public face to a disease that had, until then, been given scant coverage in the national media. Shortly after Hudson's death, *Time* magazine praised Hudson for his courage in publicly announcing his condition and said that it "may have been the best and most dramatic gesture in his long career."

HUGHES, LANGSTON. (1902-1967), *U.S. poet and writer.* Hughes has long held the place of premier black American writer and has had a profound influence on black culture, as well as on American literature. He has been an inspiration to black writers hoping to earn their living from writing alone.

Despite his upbringing in all-white neighborhoods, Hughes was a deeply

Langston Hughes

Michael Willhoite

black-identified writer. In his work, he incorporated both black themes and the rhythms of black music. He was extremely prolific, and his works include the collection of poetry, *Fine Clothes to the Jew*; a short story collection, *The Ways of White Folks*; and the novel *Not Without Laughter*.

In the summer of 1924 — in a move designed to help his career — Hughes had an affair with Alain Locke, the Howard University professor Hughes described as the "mid-wife" of the Harlem Renaissance. Locke, in return, arranged a great deal of valuable patronage for Hughes, including a "blank check" from the wealthy, eccentric Mrs. Charlotte Osgood. (*See also Alain Locke.*)

HUNTER, ALBERTA. (1895-1984), *U.S. vocalist.* Alberta Hunter was the last of America's great black blues stars, and she performed right up until the end of her life. She was also very open about her lesbianism in her later years.

The great love of Alberta's life was Lottie Tyler, whom she met in 1919 and maintained a relationship with for many years. Alberta also knew and worked with the great Louis Armstrong, and several other lesbian or bisexual vocalists, such as Billie Holliday, Bessie Smith, and Ethel Waters. After the heyday of the blues, Alberta retired for twenty years and became a nurse, but began her career again when she lost her job on account of her age. She once again became a sensation, earning several invitations to sing in the Carter White House, and was among the first performers in the "Kennedy Center Honors" awards program in 1978.

HYDE, EDWARD (LORD CORNBURY). (1661-1724), *British colonial governor.* Lord Cornbury, who became the colonial governor of New York and New Jersey in 1702, spent each afternoon walking about in public dressed as a woman. He explained that this was a tribute to his cousin, Queen Anne — an explanation which did not satisfy the townspeople, who complained to the queen about her cousin's behavior. She did not respond to these complaints, but in 1708 she had him recalled for his financial shenanigans, including the misuse of public funds and extortion of bribes from wealthy landowners. Although his cross-dressing is well documented, and gave rise to speculation that he was gay, there is no evidence that Cornbury was homosexual.

ISHERWOOD, CHRISTOPHER. (1904-1986), *U.S. writer, born in England.* Considered by many to be a virtual prophet of the gay rights movement, Isherwood is probably best known in literary circles for his novels set in the Berlin of the early 1930s. These novels, which inspired the musical comedy *Cabaret,* were based on his personal experiences while living in Berlin between 1929 and 1933. Having witnessed the decay of the Weimar Republic and the rise to power of the Nazis, Isherwood left Germany and in 1939 moved to the United States, choosing to settle in southern California where he spent much of the rest of his life. Upon his arrival in the United States Isherwood embraced pacifism and Vedanta Hinduism, becoming a follower of Swami Prabhavananda.

In addition to his Berlin novels, Isherwood wrote a number of works in which he explored the issue of homosexuality. In *A Single Man,* perhaps the best known and most highly regarded of these, he presents one day in the life of a lonely, middle-aged gay man.

From 1953 until his death, Isherwood lived with his lover, the artist Don Bachardy; both were involved in the gay rights movement and in gay circles of southern California.

JAMES I. (1566-1625), *English king.* James, the son of Mary Queen of Scots, was born in Edinburgh Castle and became the titular king of Scotland the year after his birth. Although he married at the age of twenty-three and had several children, there was frequent gossip of his many liaisons with male lovers, beginning with his cousin, Esmé Stuart, when James was thirteen. The rumors were to continue for the rest of his life.

The ambitious James allied himself with Queen Elizabeth of England, and succeeded her in 1603. Already, however, he was unpopular with many of his subjects, and as he took the throne the quip circulated among them that "Elizabeth was king, now James is queen." His twenty-two years as king were marked by the beginning of work on the King James Version of the Bible and by his constant feuds with Parliament, which he usually ended by dissolving that body.

James's series of male lovers continued while he was king. Among them was the handsome Robert Carr, who was made a Gentleman of the Bedchamber. When Carr later married, James wrote to him complaining of Carr's "withdrawing yourself from lying in my chamber, notwithstanding my many hundred times earnestly soliciting

Michael Willhoite

James I

When the young shepherd David appeared in the court, eager to help the new ruler, the Bible reports that "the soul of Jonathan was knit with the soul of David, and Jonathan loved him as his own soul."

Eventually, however, King Saul grew afraid that David was plotting to capture his throne, and he made plans to have David killed. When Jonathan learned of this plot, he was torn between his loyalty to his father and his love for David; he chose to help David hide, and later to escape.

Jonathan and Saul both perished in the Battle of Mt. Gilboa, in which the Israeli army was crushed by the Philistines. It was left to David, in the years to come, to reunite the kingdom. *(See also David.)*

you to the contrary." Of a later favorite, George Villiers, the Earl of Buckingham, James said: "You may be sure that I love the Earl of Buckingham more than anyone else. Christ had his John and I have my George."

JENKINS, WALTER. (1918-1985), *U.S. political aide.* A longtime political aide and close personal friend of Lyndon Johnson, Jenkins was forced to resign from his position as Special Assistant to the President after he was arrested in 1964 on charges of having committed homosexual acts in a YMCA two blocks from the White House. It was later revealed that Jenkins had been arrested once before, in 1959, on similar charges at the same YMCA. His resignation caused a scandal for Lyndon Johnson and was used by Barry Goldwater's presidential campaign to imply that the nation's security might have been breached under Johnson's administration.

JONATHAN. (1045?-1013 B.C.), *Israeli crown prince.* In 1028 B.C., Saul became the first king of Israel. His son Jonathan, first in line for the throne, was among his chief military aides.

JULIUS III. (1487-1555), *Pope.* Julius III's short five-year reign as pope was a relatively uneventful one, during which he devoted far more time to boys than to religion. While still a cardinal, Julius made no secret of his preferences. One of his teenage boyfriends, nicknamed the Prevostino, accompanied him to meetings; when other cardinals objected, he told them, "The Prevostino is worth more than the whole lot of you."

Upon his election as pope in 1550, Julius made cardinals out of the Prevostino and several other teenagers. His orgies were well known to his colleagues, and when the archbishop of Benevento wrote *In Praise of Sodomy,* it was dedicated to Julius III — to Julius's amusement.

KEMP, JACK. (1935-), *U.S. politician.* Conservative New York congressman Jack Kemp originally gained fame as a professional football player. In 1967, as athletic adviser to Ronald Reagan, then governor of California, Kemp's name became associated with a gay sex scandal which has hampered Kemp's political career ever since. Kemp and his boss were close friends and together bought a cabin on Lake Tahoe where homosexual parties allegedly occurred. Although Kemp insisted that he had never spent any time at the cabin and viewed it only as a good investment, rumors have nonetheless persisted that Kemp himself is gay.

As a presidential candidate in the 1988 primaries, Kemp continued to be dogged by rumors about his sexual orientation. Far from making him more sensitive to gay and lesbian issues, however, Kemp's experiences seem only to have hardened him in his narrow view of "family values."

KEYNES, JOHN MAYNARD. (1883-1946), *British economist.* Six years after the death of Keynes, who is often regarded as the greatest economist of the twentieth century, a biography of him managed to completely omit any mention of his bisexuality. But in reality, despite his 1926 marriage to ballerina Lydia Lopokova, Keynes was essentially homosexual.

Keynes's influence was enormous in a number of areas. In addition to his economics expertise, Keynes was a strong supporter of the arts, and a highly respected teacher. He pursued a

Michael Willhoite

John Maynard Keynes

brilliant career in the British government, and played an important role in the Bloomsbury group.

Although in many ways a member of the British establishment, Keynes's homosexuality made him something of an outsider. He carried on a long correspondence with Lytton Strachey, in which they openly discussed their homosexuality.

KING, BILLIE JEAN. (1943-), *U.S. athlete.* King was a four-time winner at the U.S. Open Championships between 1967 and 1974, and took the women's crown at Wimbledon four times from 1968 to 1975. In 1981, she shocked the sports world when, as the result of a "palimony" suit (it became "galimony" in the tabloids) brought against her, she publicly acknowledged a lesbian affair with her former hairdresser and secretary, Marilyn Barnett. However, King resisted being classified by the media as a lesbian. "If you have one gay experience, does that mean you're gay?" she asked one interviewer. "If you have one heterosexual experience, does that mean you're straight? Life doesn't work quite so cut and dried."

KING, WILLIAM RUFUS DE VANE. (1786-1853), *U.S. politician.* After graduating from college in 1803, King began a long political career that included serving in the North Carolina legislature, the U.S. House of Representatives, the U.S. legation to Russia, as minister to France, and as a U.S. senator from Alabama. A lifelong bachelor, King reportedly got the nickname "Miss Nancy" in Washington, where he and fellow politician James Buchanan were roommates for over twenty years.

After Buchanan lost the presidential nomination in 1852 to Franklin Pierce, party bosses offered the vice presidential spot to King, hoping to placate Buchanan supporters. Although he won the election, King never actually served as vice president. After taking the oath of office in Havana, Cuba, where he had gone to seek relief from tuberculosis, King died before he could return to Washington. *(See also James Buchanan.)*

Michael Willhoite

Horatio Herbert Kitchener

KITCHENER, HORATIO HERBERT. (1850-1916), *English general.*

Kitchener, the son of a British officer, was born in Ireland. In 1892 he became commander-in-chief of the Egyptian army, and by 1896 was a major-general in the British army. His role in the Boer War, in which he ruthlessly destroyed Boer farms and herded 120,000 women and children into concentration camps, secured his position as England's greatest military hero since Wellington. After serving consecutively as field marshal, consul general to Egypt, and war secretary, Kitchener was killed in 1916 when the ship in which he was conducting a secret mission to Russia struck a mine. His death was mourned throughout the British Empire.

Kitchener was said to have been both a woman-hater and an active homosexual. The most notable of his homosexual liaisons was with his military secretary, an affair which lasted many years.

KOPAY, DAVID. (1942-), *U.S. athlete.*

David Kopay seemed to have everything going for him — a professional athlete, he was intelligent, charming, and handsome. Then, in December 1975, he publicly announced that he was gay, sending shock waves through the world of professional athletics.

Raised in a devoutly Catholic household, Kopay entered a junior seminary which prepared boys for the priesthood. He left after eighteen months, and in 1961 he entered the University of Washington on a football scholarship. After a successful college football career, he signed on as a professional with the San Francisco Forty-Niners. Over the next ten years, he played for a number of teams, including the Detroit Lions, the Washington Redskins, the New Orleans Saints, and the Green Bay Packers.

After a serious depression, Kopay began psychotherapy. His doctor convinced him to get married, but the marriage eventually ended in divorce.

In 1975, after ten years as a professional football player, Kopay ended his athletic career and came out in a series on homosexuuality which appeared in the Washington *Star.* He elaborated on it in his autobiography, *The David Kopay Story.*

KRUPP, FRIEDRICH ALFRED. (1854-1902), *German industrialist.*

Krupp's father was "the cannon king," who made a fortune through innovative new uses of cast steel. Krupp expanded his father's empire, and became a major supplier of ships for the expanding German navy.

Part of his fortune Krupp invested in building an elaborate pleasure palace on the island of Capri, where he entertained Italian youths. When his wife learned what was going on, she went straight to the Kaiser — and was promptly committed to an insane asylum; the Krupp empire was too valuable to be destroyed by such stories. Eventually, however, the truth did come out, and Krupp committed suicide.

KUZMIN, MIKHAIL. (1875-1936), *Russian poet.* The first noted Russian author to make homosexuality a central theme in his work, Kuzmin scandalized the literary high circles of pre-Revolutionary Russia with an explicitly homoerotic autobiographical novel, *Wings* (published in 1906), and with a number of sonnets and poems that explored homosexual desire. Not long after the Revolution, the poet fell into disfavor with the ruling Stalinist regime. Kuzmin's lover was executed during a purge in the 1930s, and Kuzmin himself was apparently marked for deportation to a labor camp just before he died in Leningrad in 1936.

LAUGHTON, CHARLES. (1899-1962), *British actor.* One of the most critically acclaimed character actors in Hollywood history, Laughton appeared in over fifty motion pictures, giving memorable performances in such films as *The Mutiny On The Bounty, The Private Life of Henry VIII* (for which he won an Oscar), *The Hunchback of Notre Dame,* and *Witness for the Prosecution.* He married actress Elsa Lanchester in 1929; two years later, he revealed to her that he was homosexual. They remained married for thirty-three years: no longer lovers, but close friends.

Laughton's homosexuality is discussed at length in Charles Higham's biography of the actor and in Elsa Lanchester's own memoir, *Charles Laughton and I.*

Once as they were driving along the freeway, Laughton told actor Robert Mitchum, who starred in Laughton's *Night of the Hunter,* "I don't know if you know, and I don't know if you care, and I don't care if you know, but there is a strong streak of homosexuality in me." Mitchum cried out in response, "No shit. Stop the car!"

LAWRENCE, T.E. (LAWRENCE OF ARABIA). (1888-1935), *British soldier and writer.* Lawrence was one of the most colorful figures to emerge from World War I. His lifelong interest in Arabia began in his youth; he studied archaeology and the Near East at Oxford, and when the war broke out, he was working as an archaeologist. The British government sent him to Cairo, where he worked in the map department, and was later transferred to the military intelligence section. Lawrence was instrumental in the efforts to incite an Arab revolution against the Turks, and after the war he was hailed as a great military hero. He began work at that time on his memoirs, *The Seven Pillars of Wisdom,* published in 1926. In 1935, Lawrence was killed in an accident while riding a motorcycle which George Bernard Shaw had given him.

There is general agreement that Lawrence was a repressed homosexual. In his book, he writes about Arab homosexuality and refers to it as "pure" and "clean" — and even "sexless." There is no agreement as to whether he was ever sexually involved with anyone, though he certainly had passionate feelings for the handsome Arab youth Dahoum, whom he met in Syria. Dahoum, whom Lawrence called "Sheik Ahmed," died during the war, and Lawrence dedicated *The Seven Pillars of Wisdom* "to S.A."

LEONARDO DA VINCI. (1452-1519), *Italian artist, scientist, and inventor.* Often considered the greatest genius of all time, Leonardo da Vinci began demonstrating his remarkable promise at an early age. His career began as an artist, and he is still best remembered for such paintings as the *Mona Lisa* and *The Last Supper.* His genius went far beyond this, however. He developed a reputation in his own life as an architect and engineer, and his notebooks show that he was experimenting with scientific ideas far ahead of his time, includ-

Michael Willhoite

Leonardo da Vinci

ing a plan for a helicopter. His other interests included anatomy, mathematics, and meteorology.

At twenty-four, Da Vinci and four other Florentines were arrested for sodomy with a seventeen-year-old boy, and he was imprisoned for two months. He left Florence for the more liberal climate of Milan, where he acquired an apprentice, Andrea Salaino, a graceful and curly-haired youth whom he described as "a thieving, lying glutton"; nonetheless, they were inseparable for twenty-five years. Salaino was eventually succeeded by Francesco Melzi, who remained with Leonardo until Leonardo's death, and inherited many of his drawings and writings.

Centuries later, Freud wrote extensively about Da Vinci, and theorized that he was homosexual.

LIBERACE, WLADZIU VALENTINO. (1919-1987), *U.S. showman.* Liberace, his fans and critics would probably agree, was a reasonably talented pianist who decided to put showmanship ahead of music. His abbreviated versions of musical classics, combined with his extravagant presentations and glittery costumes, won him

legions of fans. Liberace was considerably less popular with the critics. He responded to one reviewer by saying, "What you said hurt me very much. I cried all the way to the bank."

Many of Liberace's fans were middle-aged women, and he walked a fine line between being a flamboyant and sometimes even effeminate showman, while at the same time keeping his homosexuality a secret. In the 1950s, at the height of his fame, he successfully sued a London tabloid that suggested he was gay. Years later, when he was sued for palimony by a young man, he was less successful in keeping the rumors at bay. But right up until his death from AIDS in 1987, Liberace and his family tried to cover up his gayness.

In the end, the truth didn't hurt his celebritydom. At the auction of his estate in 1988, nearly all of Liberace's possessions brought far more than their estimated value, as eager fans bid for a souvenir of the performer. His Nevada driver's license, expected to bring under $100, commanded a price of $4250.

Michael Willhoite

Alain Locke

LOCKE, ALAIN. (1886-1954), *U.S. writer.* Alain Locke was the first black American to become a Rhodes scholar.

After leaving Harvard in 1907 he studied at Oxford and the University of Berlin before returning to Harvard, where he earned his Ph.D. in philosophy in 1918. Locke became a professor of philosophy at Howard University in Washington, D.C., where he remained on the faculty for forty years. With his writings and criticism, he became a leader and chief interpreter of the Harlem Renaissance.

Locke also used his connections to secure patronage for young, male writers he felt deserved such assistance — often after they had showed their appreciation in the bedroom. Writers Countee Cullen and Langston Hughes were rewarded in this way. Others in Locke's circle of gay associates were black writers Richard Bruce Nugent and Claude McKay, and white literary critic Carl Van Vechten.

Locke was less generous to women writers, regardless of their talent. He was said to have dismissed women students on the first day of his class with an automatic "C". Even writer Zora Neale Hurston, whom Locke liked and recommended, described him as "a malicious, spiteful little snot."

LORDE, AUDRE. (1934-), *U.S. writer.* One of the most inspiring contemporary writers of both poetry and prose, Audre Lorde grew up poor in Harlem. Her work is both deeply personal and intensely political, always incorporating her radical view of the world. Far from adopting an "art for art's sake" stance, her poetry is always intimately connected to real-life experience, which often includes her lesbianism. In *Zami: A New Spelling of My Name*, which she describes as a biomythography, one of the passages in her dedication reads, "To the first woman I ever courted and left. She taught me that women who want without needing are expensive and sometimes wasteful, but women who need without wanting are

dangerous — they suck you in and pretend not to notice."

LOUIS XIII. (1601-1643), *French king.* Backward, reserved, and withdrawn, King Louis XIII nevertheless enjoyed a triumphant reign largely due to the efforts of master politican Cardinal Richelieu. One of Louis's early romantic attachments was with Baradas, a beautiful but simple-minded page, who was made First Gentleman of the Chamber. But Baradas, who engaged in affairs with other nobles, eventually found himself in the king's disfavor and was replaced.

In about 1637, for reasons that remain obscure, Richelieu introduced Louis to the handsome young Marquis de Cinq-Mars. Some historians believe Richelieu arranged, with Louis's permission, to have Cinq-Mars impregnate the king's long-neglected wife, Queen Anne, so as to produce an heir to the throne. For several years, Cinq-Mars was the king's favorite, but in 1641, angry because Richelieu would not give him an important military post, Cinq-Mars entered into a conspiracy with Louis' renegade brother, the Duke of Orleans. Faced with proof of this treach-

Michael Willhoite

Louis XIII

ery, Louis condemned his lover to death. The episode left Louis heartbroken, and less than a year later, the collapse of his reign was complete with the deaths of both Richelieu and Louis.

Michael Willhoite

Amy Lowell

LOWELL, AMY. (1874-1925), *U.S. poet.* Born in Brookline, Massachusetts, to a prominent New England family, Amy Lowell did little in her early adulthood to set herself apart from other well-off Boston women of her time. In 1912, however, two events radically changed Lowell's life: she discovered poetry, and she met Ada Dwyer Russell, a professional actress who was to provide the emotional support Lowell needed to write. Most of her poetry that concerns women describes them from a traditionally "male" perspective, such as this stanza from "Loon Point":

> But her power of enchantment is
> upon us,
> We bow to the spell that she
> weaves,
> Made up of the murmur of waves,
> And the manifold whisper of
> leaves.

Lowell was in London when war was declared in 1914. Late for an ap-

pointment and annoyed by the crowds in the street, she burst out, "Don't they know I'm Amy Lowell? And it was this month that my book of poems was coming out here! What attention will it get with this going on? What has happened to England? Why doesn't she simply stop the war?"

From the time she began to write, Lowell's life was filled with constant activity. She gave frequent speaking engagements in Europe and the United States and was involved in the Imagist movement, of which Ezra Pound was the leader. She exuded an independence and defiance of the norm which her contemporaries found unnerving, right down to her love of a good cigar. At her death, Lowell was one of the best known and most controversial figures in American poetry. She was awarded a posthumous Pulitzer Prize for her collection *What's O'Clock.*

LUDWIG II. (1845-1886), *Bavarian king.* Ludwig is best known for his insanity and his passion for beauty, which led him to build or alter a vast number of rococo palaces. His building program nearly resulted in the financial collapse of the Bavarian state. Ludwig was obsessed, moreover, with the work of the composer Richard Wagner; in addition to backing extravagant productions of Wagner's works, he paid the composer's debts and provided him with a large subsidy. Throughout his reign, Ludwig surrounded himself with young artistic favorites as well as soldiers and woodsmen.

Ludwig's behavior became increasingly eccentric and led him to neglect his duties as king. Eventually, he was forced to abdicate and was committed to the care of medical specialists. On June 16, 1886, Ludwig persuaded his doctor to take a walk with him on the shore of Starnberger Lake. Some hours later, the drowned bodies of the two men were found. The exact circumstances of their deaths have never been determined.

MARLOWE, CHRISTOPHER. (1564-1593), *English dramatist and poet.* Marlowe is said to have been the originator of truly effective English blank verse, and his influence can be detected in a number of Shakespearean works. He himself wrote several successful dramatic pieces, including *Edward II* with its explicitly homosexual theme, and *Dr. Faustus.*

Marlowe is famous for his homosexual tastes as well as his unrestrained lifestyle. This is perhaps best illustrated by his statement that "All they that love not tobacco and boys are fools." Marlowe was stabbed to death by a drinking companion, apparently in a quarrel over a boy.

Michael Willhoite

W. Somerset Maugham

MAUGHAM, W. SOMERSET. (1874-1965), *British writer.* Somerset Maugham's work is characterized by a clear, straightforward style in which keen psychological analyses are presented of people living in cosmopolitan settings. He was a prolific writer, best known for four novels, *Of Human Bondage, The Moon and Sixpence, Cakes and Ale,* and *The Razor's Edge.* A cynic, Maugham held to a resigned atheism and general skepticism regarding the extent of humanity's innate goodness and intelligence. Although he was involved sexually with both women and men at various times in his life, Maugham was primarily homosexual, a fact he ultimately admitted.

Maugham's inclinations were known to his friends during a substantial part of his life. On one occasion, a friend encouraged him to stay longer at a party. Maugham, who believed that early nights would keep him young, declined, saying that he "wanted to keep his youth." The friend retorted, "Then why didn't you bring him with you? I should be delighted to meet him."

McKUEN, ROD. (1933-), *U.S. poet.* Called by The New York *Times* "America's only native *chansonnier,* Rod McKuen has produced a vast body of work. His poems are noted for the simplicity of their images and style and by their accessibility. Although McKuen acknowledges having had affairs with men as well as with women, he hesitates to call himself gay. On one occasion, he said, "I have had sex with men; does that make me gay?"

MEAD, MARGARET. (1901-1978), *U.S. anthropologist.* Margaret Mead was born in Philadelphia in an academic and woman-oriented household. One of the closest relationships of her life began when she was a student at Barnard College — with her instructor, Ruth Fulton Benedict. Benedict's enthusiasm for anthropology rubbed off on Mead. After the publication of her famous *Coming of Age in Samoa,* Mead became permanently linked with the study of sex and guilt-free love.

One of Mead's closest friends, describing Mead's three marriages and involvements with women, said that she "fell in love with women's souls and men's bodies. She was spiritually homosexual, psychologically bisexual, and physically heterosexual." When Mead herself was asked what she thought of homosexuals, she replied, "They make the best companions in the world."

MELVILLE, HERMAN. (1819-1891), *U.S. novelist.* The creator of such American classics as *Moby Dick, Billy Budd,* and *White-Jacket,* Herman Melville was a writer who was intensely aware of the technical aspects of his art. Unlike American novelists before him, he made extensive use of symbolism, and greatly influenced literary trends to follow.

Although he married and fathered children, his closest emotional attraction seems to have been to fellow writer Nathaniel Hawthorne. The two men met in 1850 in Pittsfield, Massachusetts, and immediately formed an intense friendship. About the meeting, Melville wrote, "I feel that the Godhead is broken up like the bread at the Supper, and that we are the pieces." Their friendship continued until Hawthorne's death in 1864, after which Melville wrote "Monody," his elegy to Hawthorne.

> To have known him, to have loved him
> After loneness long;
> And then to be estranged in life,
> And neither in the wrong;
> And now for death to set his seal—
> Ease me, a little ease, my song!

MENOTTI, GIAN CARLO. *(See Samuel Barber.)*

MICHELANGELO BUONARROTI. (1475-1564), *Italian artist.* The painter of the Sistine Chapel ceiling, and also the creator of such timeless pieces of homoerotic sculpture as the statue *David,* Michelangelo possessed a complex and often difficult personality. His relationships with several of his male models, including the beautiful young Gherardo Perini, caused much gossip at the time. In his later years, Michelangelo added poetry to his list of achievements, and wrote several son-

Michelangelo Buonarotti

Michael Willhoite

nets to the young aristocrat Tommasso Cavalieri, who is believed to have been his great love.

Toward the end of Michelangelo's life, the liberal cultural climate of the Renaissance began to change, and Pope Paul IV ordered loincloths painted on the male nudes of "The Last Judgment." Worse, following his death, Michelangelo's poems and sonnets were published, but not before being altered to suggest that they were addressed to women. Not until 1960 were the original texts restored and published.

MILK, HARVEY. (1930-1978), *U.S. politician.* Harvey Milk grew up on Long Island, an average child and teenager in almost every respect. After serving in the Navy, he returned to Long Island, where he taught high school and met Joe Campbell, and the two settled into a marriage-type relationship.

As a young adult, Milk was a political conservative; he worked hard and spent his free time creating a stable home life. After moving to San Francisco, his conservatism gradually gave way to an ardent liberalism, and he began attending anti-war demonstrations and associating with flower children. He was elected in 1977 to the San Francisco Board of Supervisors after having made several unsuccessful attempts to gain a seat. When California state senator John Briggs sponsored an electoral initiative to ban gay people from teaching, Harvey Milk was at the forefront of the opposition. A few weeks after the California electorate rejected the Briggs Initiative, both Harvey Milk and Mayor George Moscone were shot and killed by former city supervisor Dan White, a rabid opponent of gay rights. A jury from which gay people were excluded convicted White of manslaughter, a charge which carried a maximum sentence of seven years and eight months, although the murder of public officials was subject to the death penalty in California. The leniency of the sentence enraged the gay community, and a riot followed in which 120 people were injured. White later committed suicide.

MILLAY, EDNA ST. VINCENT.

(1892-1950), *U.S. poet.* In 1912, with the publication of her poem "Renascence," Millay became an overnight literary celebrity when she was only twenty. Eleven years later, she was the first woman to receive the Pulitzer Prize. During the 1920s, her poetry was seen as the embodiment of romantic rebellion and bravado, as illustrated by the famous line "My candle burns at both ends," from her 1920 work *A Few Figs from Thistles.* Today, she is regarded as one of the greatest love poets of the English language.

Throughout her life, Millay — who was known to friends as "Vincent" — remained completely unabashed about her bisexuality. She once wrote, "For surely, one must be either undiscerning, or frightened, to love only one person, when the world is so full of gracious and noble spirits."

MILLER, MERLE. (1919-1986),

U.S. writer. Merle Miller was among the first prominent Americans to come out in the early days of the modern gay movement. In 1971, after almost fifty years in the closet, he openly discussed his gay identity in his book *On Being Different: What It Means to be a Homosexual.*

Miller's best-known books were portraits of recent presidents: *Plain Speaking* was based on several years of interviews with Harry Truman, and *Lyndon: An Oral Biography,* portrayed the life of Lyndon Johnson. Miller wrote over a dozen books in all, including a gay novel titled *What Happened.* When he died at the age of sixty-seven, he was survived by his companion of twenty-two years, David Elliott.

MISHIMA, YUKIO. (1925-1970),

Japanese writer. Virtually all of Mishima's many works reveal his preoccupation with the conflict between Westernization and traditional Japanese values, a conflict he finally resolved for himself in a public ritual suicide. In his first novel, *Confessions of a Mask,* he introduced the theme of homosexuality which recurs throughout his work. The novel met with both critical and commercial success, and Mishima began to devote his full energies to writing.

Mishima's life was filled with paradox. Although he raged continually against Japan's imitation of the West, he himself maintained an essentially Western lifestyle and possessed a wide knowledge of Western culture.

On November 25, 1970, Mishima, along with four companions, seized control of the commanding general's office at the military headquarters in downtown Tokyo. There, he gave a ten-minute speech in which he attacked the weakness of Japan's post-war constitution, and then, following the ritual *seppuku* suicide, disemboweled himself before the eyes of his audience and was decapitated by one of his followers.

MOLIÈRE. (1622-1673), *French dramatist.* Molière was born in Paris, the

son of an upholsterer to the king. He received a good education, and, after studying law for a short time, decided to pursue a dramatic career. He joined the Béjard family troupe and toured the provinces with them. The success of Molière's comedies established him as one of the most popular of French playwrights, a reputation he still enjoys today.

Throughout his life, Molière was surrounded by intrigue and controversy for both his writings and his personal life. There was a great deal of speculation that his wife was actually his own daughter, and his long-standing relationship with the young actor Michel Baron led to rumors of another kind. This relationship eventually resulted in the estrangement of Molière from his wife; he and Baron then lived together from 1670 until Molière's death in 1673.

Michael Willhoite

Florence Nightingale

NIGHTINGALE, FLORENCE. (1820-1910), *British nurse.* Called the "Lady of the Lamp" for her tireless work among sick and wounded British soldiers, Florence Nightingale was not only responsible for the reform of conditions in military hospitals, but was also the founder of trained nursing as a profession. After serving in Turkey during the Crimean War, she returned to England where she set herself to the tasks of improving conditions for the British soldier and of training nurses for the profession. From 1857 to the time of her death, she lived as an invalid, mainly in London, and from there carried on an enormous correspondence and received countless visitors. In 1907, the king conferred on her the Order of Merit, making her the first woman to be thus honored.

Though Nightingale was never married and lived in many ways a highly unconventional lifestyle for a woman of her time, her notions of sexual morality seemed on the surface to conform quite closely to conventional Victorian standards. Nevertheless, late in life she wrote, "I have lived and slept in the same bed with English countesses and Prussian farm women ... no woman has excited passions among women more than I have."

NIJINSKY, VASLAV. (1890-1950), *Russian dancer.* The child of Polish dancers, Nijinsky was already considered a phenomenon at the Imperial Ballet School when he met the great impresario, Sergei Diaghilev. Backward and uneducated, Nijinsky at first let his life and his career be formed by Diaghilev's strong personality; as Diaghilev's lover and protege, Nijinsky became one of the greatest dancers of this century.

For several years, the team of Diaghilev and Nijinsky produced spectacularly successful shows. Their success was amplified on some occasions, and threatened at other times, by Nijinsky's delight in adding unexpected sexual overtones to his performances, either in the choreography or in the costumes.

By the time he was twenty-three, Nijinsky was feeling suffocated by the highly possessive and misogynous personality of Diaghilev, who forbade his male dancers to associate with women. Separated from Diaghilev while on a South American tour, Nijinsky met and fell in love with Romola Markus, a Hungarian dancer, and they were married. When news of this reached Diaghilev, he promptly fired Nijinsky. Nijinsky continued to dance for several years, but by 1920 both his mental and physical health were in decay. He spent most of his last thirty years in institutions for the insane.

ORTON, JOE. (1933-1967), *British playwright.* Orton rocketed to fame in 1964 with his first play, *Entertaining Mr. Sloane,* a brilliant black comedy that crystallized Orton's own belief that people "are profoundly bad, but irresistibly funny." He followed it in 1965 with another success, *Loot,* which satirized police corruption, the Church of England, and English notions of justice.

In 1967, at the peak of his fame, Orton was beaten to death by his male lover of sixteen years, Kenneth Halliwell, a less successful writer who then immediately committed suicide. During the last year of his life, Orton kept a diary, which graphically detailed the disintegration of his relationship with Halliwell, as well as his rise to fame and his various homosexual encounters in London and Morocco.

PASOLINI, PIER PAOLO. (1922-1975), *Italian film director.* Among the most controversial of contemporary directors, Pasolini frequently clashed with government and church authorities over his graphic portrayals of sex and violence in such films as *The Canterbury Tales, The Decameron,* and *Salo — The 120 Days of Sodom.* An avowed Marxist with a deep but highly mystical belief in Christianity, he also frequently generated storms of public controversy with his numerous essays and articles espousing unorthodox political and religious reforms.

In 1975, Pasolini was murdered by a seventeen-year-old Roman boy, who first bludgeoned Pasolini with a two-by-four and then ran over him with a sports car. The boy later claimed that Pasolini had picked him up, driven him to a vacant lot, and tried to seduce him.

PEARS, PETER. (1910-1986), *British tenor.* Pears began his musical training at the age of five, later studied at Oxford, and in 1938 met composer Benjamin Britten, who was his lover for the next forty years. The 1945 premiere of Britten's opera *Peter Grimes,* in which Pears sang a leading role, brought world attention to both composer and tenor. Their successful personal and professional collaboration continued through the next three decades. When Britten died in 1976, it was said that Queen Elizabeth II, in a rare departure from custom, accorded Pears the same formal courtesies usually reserved only for the surviving mate of a heterosexual marriage. Pears was knighted by the queen in 1977 and died ten years after Britten.

PLATO. (427?-347 B.C.), *Athenian philosopher.* The most famous of Socrates' students, Plato founded his own school, known as the Academy, where he taught philosophy and mathematics. It became the first university in Europe, and provided a basis for Plato's vast influence through the ages.

In his youth, Plato was actively homosexual and had a number of male lovers. In the *Symposium,* to illustrate the highest kind of love, Plato drew his examples solely from homosexual love.

PROUST, MARCEL. (1871-1922), *French writer.* Proust is remembered today for his extensive psychological study of French society, his multi-volume novel *Remembrance of Things Past.* Born into a wealthy family, Proust made every attempt in his youth to associate himself with the most fashionable and intellectual circles of Paris. But he became increasingly reclusive as he grew older and, after the deaths of his parents, withdrew from society almost completely. His masterwork, on which he worked for seventeen years, is distinguished by the realistic portrayal of French high society.

Although Proust did much to demystify homosexuality in Western literature, his own attitudes regarding the subject were clearly ambivalent. He had relationships with a number of men, but he expressed negative ideas about homosexuality in his short piece, *A Race Accursed*. The Baron de Charlus, the principal homosexual character in his novels, was probably the most grotesque of the many characters he depicted

Nikolai Przhevalsky

Michael Willhoite

PRZHEVALSKY, NIKOLAI. (1839-1888), *Russian explorer.* Often called the Russian counterpart of David Livingston, Przhevalsky traveled through much of central and far eastern Asia and was a pioneer in mapping Siberia and Russia's far eastern territories. The extent of his explorations, as well as his route surveys and the plant and animal collections he brought back, opened up to European eyes a forbidding region previously shrouded in mystery.

At the time of his explorations, Przhevalsky generated perplexed comment among academic circles for his habit of choosing extremely handsome, often uneducated teenaged boys as assistants on his long journeys. He was also renowned for an isolated country estate, named Svoboda ("Freedom"), where women were forbidden to set foot.

RAINEY, MA (GERTRUDE PRIDGETT). (1886-1939), *U.S. vocalist.* Ma Rainey was the first great black professional blues vocalist, touring the southern and midwestern states from 1904 until she retired in 1933. At the height of her success in the 1920s, she was recording over ninety of her songs and travelling with her own troupe, which at times included black lesbian blues singer Bessie Smith.

Ma Rainey was arrested in 1925 during a police raid of an "indecent party," where she was apprehended, "clutching someone else's dress." Bessie Smith bailed her out the following morning. Later in her career, Ma wrote and recorded the openly lesbian "Prove it On Me Blues," a song in which one of the verses goes:

> They say I do it, ain't nobody
>   caught me,
> Sure got to prove it on me;
> Went out last night with a crowd of
>   my friends,
> They must've been women, 'cause
>   I don't like no men.

(See also Bessie Smith.)

RENAULT, MARY. (1905-1983), *British writer.* Renault — who was born Mary Challans — began her writing career while serving as a nurse during World War II. Though she was to become known for her historical novels, set in ancient Greece, her earliest books were all contemporary romances.

In the 1950s, Renault began exploring gay themes. Her first effort was *The Charioteer.* Written in 1953, it portrayed an injured young solder in World War II as he confronts the reality that he is homosexual. Many readers still believe this to be Renault's most eloquent work, but the honest treatment of a taboo subject didn't appeal to publishers of the time, and the book did not appear in the U.S. until six years later.

Perhaps because of that reaction, Renault chose a new approach: She set her novels in ancient Greece, where treatment of homosexual relationships was less threatening to editors of the time. With books such as *The Last of the Wine* and *The King Must Die,* she established her reputation as a pre-eminent writer of historical fiction.

One of the unanswered questions about Renault's life is why she chose to portray gay male relationships so often, and lesbian ones so rarely. She herself lived with a companion, Julie Mullard, for the last fifty years of her life.

RICHARD I (RICHARD THE LION-HEARTED). (1157-1199), *English king.* More warrior than ruler, Richard became king of England in 1189 but spent less than a year of his ten-year reign in England. A year after taking the throne, he left his kingdom in the hands of his brother John and embarked on the Third Crusade, hoping to liberate Jerusalem from the Moslem forces of Saladin. Instead, he met Saladin and the two established a surprisingly amicable relationship; they signed a treaty allowing access to Jerusalem by both sides.

On his return to England, Richard was taken prisoner as he passed through Austria. According to some accounts, it was the great love of his life, his troubadour Blondel, who helped him secure his freedom. A legend that circulated in the thirteenth century recounts how Blondel traveled from one castle to another singing the first lines of a song that he and Richard had composed together in happier times. When Richard sang back the answering refrain, Blondel knew with certainty that he had found the king.

Michael Willhoite

Arthur Rimbaud

RIMBAUD, ARTHUR. (1854-1891), *French poet.* Famous for his tempestuous affair with fellow poet Paul Verlaine, Rimbaud was a child prodigy, already showing brilliant intellectual gifts at age ten. By age fifteen, he had produced some of his finest poems. In 1871 he wrote the great symbolist poem *Le bateau ivre* and sent it to Verlaine, who was already an established poet. Verlaine invited Rimbaud to his home in Paris and, upon meeting him, immediately fell in love. The two men ran off together and traveled in France, England, and Belgium. Verlaine's alcoholism and Rimbaud's infidelity led to quarrels between them, which climaxed when Verlaine shot and seriously wounded Rimbaud.

At the age of nineteen, Rimbaud decided to abandon both poetry and France. He spent most of the rest of his life pursuing adventures in the East Indies, Cyprus, the Middle East, and Africa. He died in a Marseilles hospital after the amputation of one of his legs. His poems have proved to be immensely influential in the development of modern poetry throughout the Western world.

Michael Willhoite

Maximillien de Robespierre

ROBESPIERRE, MAXIMILIEN DE. (1758-1794), *French statesman.* Robespierre, a leading figure in the French revolution, was a young idealist who eventually became a ruthless fanatic and tyrant, eliminating almost all of his friends and colleagues. When the National Assembly was formed after the French Revolution, Robespierre was soon identified as being on the radical left. Largely through his association with the Jacobin Club, he gained influence in the government and was instrumental in accelerating the revolutionary tempo. In July, 1793, Robespierre began his famous Reign of Terror and began executing his political opponents. This only served to increase the number of his enemies, and Robespierre was eventually arrested and sent to the guillotine.

Although Robespierre may never have acted on his homosexual feelings, his strong attraction to members of his own sex is indisputable. His attachment to the handsome Saint-Just, known as "The Archangel of the Revolution," was the source of frequent rumors.

RÖHM, ERNST. (1887-1934), *German militarist.* After Germany's defeat in World War I, Röhm became associated with the ultranationalist, militaristic movement that was gaining strength in Germany. He was the guiding spirit in building up a secret army with connections throughout Germany, which later became known as the S.A., or Brown Shirts, and was the military arm of the Nazis. They made their first attempt at revolution in the Munich *Putsch* in which they tried and failed to overthrow the Bavarian government. Adolf Hitler, with whom Röhm by this time was closely associated, was put in prison. Röhm broke with Hitler shortly thereafter and spent several years in Berlin where he was active in homosexual circles.

In 1928 Röhm and Hitler were reconciled, but Röhm left for Bolivia not long afterwards. In 1930 Hitler invited Röhm to return to Germany to take command again of the Brown Shirts, and Röhm accepted. The relationship quickly grew tense, however, as Röhm soon filled many top posts with homosexuals.

By June 1934, Hitler had become convinced that Röhm was conspiring against him, and he had Röhm arrested at the Bavarian resort where Röhm was holding a conference of S.A. leaders. Röhm was given an opportunity to shoot himself. He refused, and was executed in his cell at Stadelheim Prison. The formal charges made against Röhm were for his homosexual activities, although Hitler had known about them for at least fifteen years and had always chosen to overlook them.

ROOSEVELT, ELEANOR. (1884-1962), *U.S. humanitarian and First Lady.* Often surrounded by controversy during her long lifetime, Eleanor Roosevelt continued that tradition after her death with the discovery of letters that revealed an intense love affair between her and reporter Lorena Hickok.

Roosevelt first entered the public eye as the wife of Franklin Delano

Roosevelt. During the earlier years of their marriage, from 1905 to 1918, she filled the traditional role that was expected of her, although she did not do so with much relish; she confided at one point to her eldest daughter that marital sex "is an ordeal to be borne."

Then she discovered the love affair between her husband and his secretary, Lucy Mercer. The discovery marked a major change in her life. Eleanor and Franklin remained married — his political career could not have survived a divorce. But their relationship changed from that of man and wife to that of colleagues, emotionally independent of one another.

During her husband's 1932 campaign for the presidency, the Associated Press assigned reporter Lorena Hickok to cover the Roosevelts. A relationship developed which, whatever its physical manifestations, was undoubtedly the major love affair of Eleanor Roosevelt's life. They exchanged sapphire rings, and when they were separated Eleanor once wrote to Hickok, "Your ring is a great comfort. I look at it and think she loves me or I wouldn't be wearing it." On another occasion, she wrote that "All day I've thought of you. Oh! I want to put my arms around you; I ache to hold you close."

ROREM, NED. (1923-), *U.S. composer.* Rorem has been called "the world's greatest composer of art song," and in a career spanning some forty years, he has written numerous symphonies, concertos, and operas, as well as the hundreds of songs and song cycles that have made his reputation. He has also authored eight books, including four volumes of diaries that unsparingly examine his own life — including his homosexuality — as well as the lives and works of other artists he has known.

Although completely open about his homosexuality, his attitude towards the subject is perhaps best summarized by his often-repeated remark that "Anyone can be gay — it's no accomplishment — but only I can be me."

RUSTIN, BAYARD. (1910-1987), *U.S. civil rights activist.* Bayard Rustin is best remembered for his role in organizing the giant 1963 civil rights march on Washington and for his continuing involvement in that cause. His tactical and organizational skills were vital to the success of the black civil rights movement of the sixties. His advocacy of gay civil rights, unfortunately, has often been overlooked.

In an interview with *The Washington Blade* in 1986, Rustin said he had informed his civil rights colleagues during the early 1960s that he was gay, and had not concealed his homosexuality since that time. He often spoke to gay organizations in the 1980s, and a common theme was his encouragement that young people come out. "Although it's going to make problems, those problems are not so dangerous as the problems of lying to yourself, to your friends, and missing many opportunities," he said.

SADE, COUNT DONATIEN ALPHONSE FRANÇOIS DE (MARQUIS DE SADE). (1740-1814), *French writer.* Although he was a count for most of his life, the man whose name provided the root for *sadism* is best known as the Marquis de Sade. His father forced him to marry Renée de Montreuil, a woman he greatly disliked. In reaction, Sade threw himself into a life of debauchery and gained fame for his ability to devise new and refined vices. With Mlle de Beauvoisin, a witty and hedonistic dancer and courtesan, he presided over orgies conducted at one of his wife's estates in Provence and was involved in one scandal after another.

Sade wrote a number of highly successful novels in which he contrasted the happy fortunes of the amoral Juliette with the tragic fate of her priggish sister Justine. In 1800 he published a pornographic novel, *Zoloe and her Two Acolytes,* in which the chief characters were clearly based on Napoleon and Josephine. As a result, he was put in prison and later sent to an insane asylum, where he died at the age of seventy-four. Although he had many affairs with women, his novels are filled with references to homosexual relations, and he even went so far as to preach the superiority of male attractions.

SAPPHO. (c.600 B.C.), *Greek poet.* The first person in the western world known to depict romantic love was the poet Sappho. Her beautiful poetry won praise both from her contemporaries and from later generations; Plato called her the "Tenth Muse." Most of her poetry, unfortunately, was destroyed centuries later by church authorities, and only a twentieth of her total output remains.

Sappho spent most of her life on the Greek island of Lesbos, where she ran a girls' school that taught poetry and writing. She drew lovers from both sexes, and had a child, but from her own time onward, Sappho was especially remembered for her romances with her students. Today, two words synonymous with love between women — sapphism and lesbian — are derived from her name and that of her island.

SCHULTE, STEVE. (1946-), *U.S. politician.* Steve Schulte was raised on a farm in Iowa and was a member of the Boy Scouts and 4-H. He left Iowa to study political science at Yale and in the late sixties became active in the movement against the Vietnam War. Later, he taught at an inner-city school in Newark, New Jersey, and ran a children's health project in Iowa.

Schulte then moved to California, where, among other activities, he posed nude for a series of photographs, a decision that was to cause him some embarrassment when he later became involved in politics. After serving for more than four years as executive director of the Los Angeles Gay and Lesbian Community Services Center (GLCSC), he announced his candidacy for a seat on the city council of West Hollywood, just after the creation of that city. When Valerie Terrigno, the first mayor of West Hollywood, was forced to leave office following allegations of embezzlement, Schulte became mayor and served in that capacity until June of 1987.

SHAKESPEARE, WILLIAM. (1564-1616), *English playwright.* Shakespeare was born in Stratford-on-Avon into a leading family of the town. Little is known of his actual life. He was married to Anne Hathaway in 1582 and had

Michael Willhoite

William Shakespeare

three children. The marriage turned out to be an unhappy one, and Shakespeare eventually left his wife.

Although there is no proof that Shakespeare was actively homosexual, homosexual themes and imagery abound in his work. This is especially true of the *Sonnets,* in which Shakespeare writes of his intense feelings for a handsome young man. There have been efforts on the part of scholars to show that the sonnets were not autobiographical or that they were in fact addressed to a woman, but there is little evidence to uphold either of these theories.

SMITH, BESSIE. (1898?-1937), *U.S. vocalist.* Regarded by many as the greatest blues singer in history, Smith was renowned for her violent temper, her bouts with alcoholism, and her lusty, pleasure-seeking lifestyle. She enjoyed sex with both men and women, and reportedly told one chorus girl in her show, after the girl publicly rebuffed her advances, "The hell with you, bitch. I got twelve women on this show and I can have one every night if I want it."

Smith's first recording, "Down-Hearted Blues," was made in 1924; to Columbia Records' surprise, it sold 780,000 discs in less than six months. She died following a car accident in 1937; according to a rumor at the time, she might have lived except that she was turned away from the first hospital where she was first taken because she was black.

SOCRATES. (469?-399 B.C.), *Athenian philosopher.* Although he received only a limited education in his youth, Socrates taught himself geometry, astronomy, and philosophy. At one point he claimed to have received a divine commission to expose ignorance and promote intellectual and moral improvement, and he eventually earned the reputation of being the wisest man in Greece. In 399 B.C., charges were brought against Socrates for "denying the gods recognized by the state" and for "corrupting the young." He was found guilty, and the death penalty was prescribed.

Socrates' passion for beautiful boys became proverbial after his death, as shown by the term "Socratic love," which referred euphemistically for many years to homosexuality. The most famous of his lovers was the Athenian statesman and general Alcibiades.

STEIN, GERTRUDE. (1864-1946), *U.S. writer.* Through her famous salon and her patronage of the arts in Paris during the early part of this century, Stein influenced and inspired many writers and artists, among them Pablo Picasso, Henri Matisse, Guillaume Apollinaire, Ernest Hemingway, and Jean Cocteau. Stein herself wrote stories, poems, novels, criticism, drama, and several memoirs, all in her distinctively repetitious, impressionistic style; she has often been labeled by critics a "cubist writer."

In 1907, while living with her brother Leo in Paris, Stein first met Alice B. Toklas, a young American visiting Europe from her home in San Francisco. Toklas soon became a lover, secretary, cook extraordinaire, and inseparable companion to Stein. Their enduring relationship — perhaps the best-known lesbian relationship in history — lasted for nearly forty years, until Stein's death from cancer in 1946.

STRACHEY, LYTTON. (1880-1932), *British biographer and critic.* Strachey adopted an irreverent attitude to the past and wrote biographies and biographical essays — such as his *Eminent Victorians* and *Queen Victoria* — that emphasized personality over achievement, and personal relationships over affairs of state. He is credited with revolutionizing the art of biography, by working from the position that a biographical subject should be treated not necessarily with respect, but instead with "warts and all." He was a leading figure in the Bloomsbury group, a circle of brilliant writers, artists, and intellectuals that included Virginia Woolf, E.M. Forster, and John Maynard Keynes.

Strachey's homosexuality was well known among his contemporaries, as was his ironic and often acerbic wit. Questioned by a tribunal investigating his stance as a conscientious objector in World War I, he was asked what he would do if he discovered his sister being raped by a foreign soldier. Strachey dryly replied, "Do my best to get between them."

STUDDS, GERRY E. (1937-), *U.S. politician*. Elected to Congress as an anti-war candidate in 1972, Gerry Studds was the first Democratic congressman to represent the Cape Cod district of Massachusetts in two generations. His 1972 victory came with a margin of only a fraction of a percentage point, but by staunchly protecting the interests of the local fishing industry, Studds was soon being returned to office by votes of landslide proportions, despite his controversial stance on foreign affairs.

In 1983, Studds was censured by Congress for having engaged in sexual activity with a seventeen-year-old House page ten years earlier. Rather than deny the incident, or plead that he was drunk, as others in similar circumstances had done in the past, Studds chose to publicly come out in a speech to the House. While not excusing his actions of a decade earlier, he discussed the difficulties of combining the pressures of a public life with his gayness. Studds won re-election sixteen months later by a comfortable margin, thus becoming the first openly gay person elected to the U.S. Congress.

SULLIVAN, Sir ARTHUR. (1842-1900), *British composer*. Sullivan is best known for his collaborative work with William S. Gilbert. Together, they created some of the best-loved musical comedies in the history of the theater, among which are *H.M.S. Pinafore, Pirates of Penzance, Iolanthe,* and *The Mikado.*

Sullivan made no secret of his homosexuality, and it seems to have been widely tolerated, in contrast to that of his contemporary, Oscar Wilde. Some scholars believe that the quarrel which led to the breakup of Gilbert and Sullivan were due, at least in part, to Gilbert's inability to accept his partner's sexual orientation.

Algernon Swinburne

SWINBURNE, ALGERNON. (1837-1909), *British poet*. Although he once was considered the liberator of a generation, Algernon Swinburne has been largely neglected by critics. In his time, he was well known for his innovative, unconventional approach to poetry.

Correspondence with friends indicates virtually beyond doubt that Swinburne was homosexual. On one occasion, when he was living alone on the Isle of Wight with a monkey, Swinburne is said to have met a young man whom he then invited home. Once there, Swinburne began to make advances on the young man. The monkey, overcome with jealousy, attacked his guest, who ran away.

SYMONDS, JOHN ADDINGTON. (1840-1893), *British essayist and critic*. An outspoken proponent of sexual freedom, Symonds reached that position by a nearly unimaginable route. His father, a strict doctor, taught Symonds that the love of men was evil. Despite that warning, Symonds became infatuated with one choirboy after another as a fellow at Magdalen College — and suffered several nervous breakdowns. He married and fathered four daughters, but his efforts to suppress his homosexuality were unsuccessful and finally Symonds arrived at a liberal understanding with his wife which allowed him the sexual freedom he craved.

The death of his father unleashed a flood of creative energy, which resulted in Symonds's many contributions to literature and history. Among them was one of the earliest attempts at a scientific investigation of homosexuality.

TCHAIKOVSKY, PETER I. (1840-1893), *Russian composer.* The composer of such legendary works as *The Nutcracker Suite* and *The 1812 Overture,* Tchaikovsky was known for his high-strung temperament. His homosexuality is well documented in his correspondence; in an 1876 letter to his brother he wrote that "I am aware that my inclinations are the greatest and most unconquerable obstacle to happiness; I must fight my nature with all my strength. I shall do everything possible to marry this year." The next year he did marry, but their union was doomed. His wife, frustrated by his lack of interest in her, finally took another lover; she later was institutionalized.

Tchaikovsky's many homosexual affairs included one with his student, Vladimir Shilovsky. Toward the end of his life, he became devoted to his nephew, Bobyk, to whom he dedicated his famous *Pathétique* Symphony.

TEASDALE, SARA. (1884-1933), *U.S. poet.* Although recently she has been somewhat neglected by critics, Sara Teasdale was probably the best-loved poet in the United States in the 1920s. From a conventional St. Louis background, she struggled all her life to express herself despite the Victorian and Puritan standards that dominated her upbringing.

Teasdale focused on issues of interest to women and explored questions of female passion in her verses. In *Sonnets to*

Duse, she addressed Eleanora Duse, a well-known actress at the time. For Teasdale, Duse represented a woman who, despite the constraints of her society, refused to hide her feelings. Teasdale herself found the struggle for self-expression significantly more difficult; throughout her life, she suffered from nervous conditions and was admitted to sanitariums on several occasions. During the last few years of her life she grew particularly despondent, and finally ended her life with an overdose of sleeping pills.

Although Teasdale married, her strongest feelings were reserved for other women. In 1926 she met Margaret Conklin, a woman several years her junior, and the two developed an extremely intense relationship which was to last until Teasdale's death. Whether or not their feelings were expressed physically remains uncertain; nonetheless, it is undeniable that the women were deeply devoted to each other.

THOMPSON, DOROTHY. (1893-1961), *U.S. journalist.* Thompson was a journalist who wrote with passion about the issues of the day. In 1939, *Time* magazine called her one of the most influential women in the United States. Her career began in New York where she wrote articles for various magazines and newspapers. In 1920 she went to Europe, where she lived for several years, working as a foreign correspondent. In 1925 she was assigned to Berlin for two newspapers, thus becoming the first woman to be a foreign correspondent for a major news bureau. In 1931 she interviewed Adolf Hitler for *Cosmopolitan,* but was later ordered by the führer to leave. Thompson returned to the United States as a celebrity. From 1936 to 1958 she wrote a highly successful and influential newspaper column, which she used as a platform for her ideas on various issues.

Although she was married three times, Thompson had several affairs with women, about which she felt decidedly ambivalent. After her divorce from Josef Bard, her first husband, she blamed him for "throwing me back into . . . an adolescent homosexuality. . ." In 1932, when Thompson and her second husband, novelist Sinclair Lewis, were in Austria, she met Christa Winsloe, with whom she fell deeply in love. Thompson and Winsloe lived together as a couple for a time, until Winsloe went to France in 1935.

TILDEN, WILLIAM II. (1893-1953), *U.S. athlete.* During the 1920s, "Big Bill" Tilden became the best known tennis player in history. From his first Wimbledon victory in 1920, to his last, in 1930, he drew huge crowds as he toured Europe and the U.S.

During his years as an active player, Tilden seems to have put his greatest energy into his tennis game, while suppressing his sexuality. But in later years, that began to change. He took on a succession of young men as proteges, apparently in a confused search for companionship. In 1946, Tilden was arrested for making advances to a fourteen-year-old boy and served seven months in prison. Three years later, he was arrested again under similar charges, and again spent time in prison.

During his earlier career, Tilden had been known for his outspokenness. On at least one occasion he had been quick to stand up against what he saw as unfair discrimination: when a Hispanic player was barred from playing on a tennis court in Los Angeles, Tilden protested and the ban was lifted. But when his own life took a turn for the worse, Tilden found that his friends deserted him and he was no longer welcome at tournaments. He died a few years later.

TOLSON, CLYDE. *(See J. Edgar Hoover.)*

TURING, ALAN M. (1912-1954), *British mathematician.* Turing, who played an instrumental role in the defeat of Hitler, met his own destruction six years later when he was charged with twelve counts of "gross indecency."

Turing was a prodigy obsessed with the concepts that paved the way for the modern computer. At the age of thirty, he joined the British intelligence project at Bletchley Castle and masterminded the cracking of the Enigma, the German secret code. Thanks to his genius, the Allies obtained access to Hitler's most secret communications, thus significantly shortening the war.

After his first love, Christopher Morcom, died of tuberculosis, Turing spent much of the rest of his life seeking to replace him. One of his later lovers was Arnold Murray, a working-class boy whom Turing reported to the police when he suspected him of burglary. Turing naively revealed his sexual relationship with the boy and found himself on trial. The classified status of his wartime activities made it impossible to use this information to save him, and he was forced to choose between prison and "organotherapy," hormone treatments which caused him to grow breasts and develop a chemical depression. Turing died in 1954 of cyanide poisoning, an apparent suicide.

ULRICHS, KARL HEINRICH. (1825-1895), *German lawyer and early gay rights advocate.* Karl Heinrich Ulrichs was the first person in modern history to publicly acknowledge his homosexuality when he announced at a convention of jurists that he was an "Urning." Two years before, he had written an article in defense of a young Frankfurt lawyer who had been caught with a boy in a park and sent to prison. Other articles and pamphlets in favor of homosexual rights were to follow. Not surprisingly, he was violently opposed by members of both the legal and medical establishments. Ultimately, he was forced to leave Germany and settle in Italy where he spent the last years of his life.

Although Ulrichs failed in his efforts to gain legitimacy and respectability for homosexual men, his work paved the way for others who came after him. German sexologist Magnus Hirschfeld, for example, acknowledged his debt to Ulrichs and called him a pioneer in the study of homosexuality.

VALENTINO, RUDOLPH. (1895-1926), *Italian-U.S. actor.* A landscape gardener by training, Valentino went to Hollywood in 1917, and landed various bit parts in films before achieving instant stardom in the lead role of *The Four Horsemen of the Apocalypse* in 1921. He soon became a national phenomenon, with women fainting in the aisles during screenings of his films. Because of his screen image as a lithe love god with foppish manners, he was often lambasted in the national press as the "Pink Powder Puff," and his influence on popular culture at the time was lamented by journalists. "When will we be rid of all these effeminate youths," complained one columnist, "powdered, bejeweled, and bedizened, in the image of Rudy — that painted pansy?" Nonetheless, his sudden death from a perforated ulcer, at the age of thirty-one, provoked a national wave of hysteria in 1926.

Although he was married twice (once to lesbian set designer Natasha Rambova), Valentino wrote explicitly of at least one homosexual experience in his private journal.

VISCONTI, LUCHINO. (1906-1976), *Italian film director.* Visconti's film style ranged from the stark, trend-setting neo-realism of *Ossessione,* to the garish operatics of *The Damned,* to the haunting lyricism of *Death in Venice.* An aristocrat by birth (he once proudly proclaimed, "I myself belong to the times of Mann, Proust, Mahler"), he was obsessed by form and dignity in his work, and was exceedingly circumspect in his personal life. In his seventies, when asked by some younger friends if he wanted to go to a gay bar, he indignantly replied, "A gay bar? When I was young, homosexuality was a forbidden fruit, a fruit to be gathered with care, not what it is today — hundreds of homosexuals showing off, dancing together in a gay bar. What do you want to go there for?"

VIVIEN, RENÉE. (1877-1909), *French writer.* With Natalie Barney, Renée Vivien laid the groundwork for a new lesbian consciousness. They hoped to reclaim the powerful female figures of myth by retelling their stories from a new, non-patriarchal perspective.

Born in London of Scottish and American ancestry, Vivien (originally Pauline Mary Tarn) was the more literary of the two women. She wrote nine volumes of poetry, two volumes of short stories, and two novels. In one of her short story collections, *The Woman of the Wolf,* she tells the story of chaste women who choose to die rather than yield to the cravings of men. She also translated Sappho's poetry in *The Women of Kithara.*

Throughout her life, Vivien was obsessed with death. She suffered from ill health, and may well have been anorexic, alcoholic, or both. She committed suicide at the age of thirty-two.

WADDELL, THOMAS. (1938-1987), *U.S. athlete.* Dr. Tom Waddell devoted much of his life to dispelling myths about gay people. During his lifetime he was an Olympic decathlon competitor, a Vietnam protester, and a medical director in the Middle East. He was also the founder and driving force behind the Gay Games, originally known as the Gay Olympics, which were first held in 1982.

In that year, however, Waddell ran into opposition from the U.S. Olympic Committee. Although it had never objected to activities ranging from the Police Olympics to the Crab-Cooking Olympics, the USOC objected to anything called the Gay Olympics. It filed suit against the group, on the grounds that Congress had granted the Committee exclusive rights to use the word "Olympics." At the same time, they filed a personal suit against Waddell. The resulting ligation slowly worked its way through the court system, and in 1987, in a five-to-four ruling, the Supreme Court decided against Waddell and the Gay Games. Waddell died a few weeks later of complications associated with AIDS.

WALPOLE, HORACE. (1717-1797), *British writer.* Walpole, a member of the House of Commons, is best remembered for popularizing the Gothic style in both literature and architecture. In 1754, he began altering his villa on the Thames, called Strawberry Hill, creating from it a unique Gothic castle that greatly influenced subsequent architecture. He also introduced a new type of novel, the gothic, from which are descended both the gothic novel and the detective novel of modern times.

Walpole's extensive correspondence documents, among other things, his strong attraction to his cousin, the military general Seymour Conway. Conway was heterosexual, however, and Walpole's love went unrequited.

WARHOL, ANDY. (1927-1987), *U.S. artist.* Born Andrew Warhola in McKeesport, Pennsylvania, the son of Czech immigrants, Andy Warhol had three nervous breakdowns by the age of ten. As a young man, he left Pennsylvania for New York, and worked his way up from illustrator and commercial artist to become one of the most influential pop artists of our times. Fascinated with the rich and famous, he gained entry to their circles by doing portraits of such celebrities as Elizabeth Taylor and Mick Jagger.

Always cultivating a highly ambiguous sexual image, Warhol was told early in his career that he was "too swish" to be a major artist. Although he never actually identified himself with the gay movement, Warhol made no secret of his homosexuality. In 1986 he donated a painting to the Philadelphia gay and lesbian art show, perhaps revealing some sympathy for the cause; not surprisingly, the work did not portray a gay or lesbian theme.

WASHINGTON, GEORGE. (1732-1799), *U.S. president.* Known as "the father of his country," Washington was the first president of the United States and had a long and distinguished career in the military and the government. In 1774 Washington was chosen as a delegate from Virginia to the First Continental Congress. When the actions at Lexington and Concord brought on the American Revolution, Washington was unanimously elected commander-in-chief of the armed forces of the United Colonies and served in that capacity throughout the war.

In 1783, Washington retired from the army and spent a few years in private life. He was elected as a delegate to the Constitutional Convention of 1787, where he used his influence to secure the adoption of the Constitution. Washington took office as president of the United States on April 30, 1789, after being elected unanimously. As president, he was largely responsible for the respect the new nation gained at home and abroad. In 1796 Washington decided against a third term of office and retired to Mount Vernon, his estate in Virginia.

Throughout his life, Washington showed little interest in women. As a young unmarried man, he told friends that there was only one woman that he would ever consider marrying and that she was already married to his friend George William Fairfax. He did eventually marry Martha Dandridge Custis after being persuaded that it was unseemly for a public figure to remain unmarried. Nevertheless, his closest attachments were always to men, particularly Alexander Hamilton.

Throughout the Revolution, Hamilton served as Washington's aide-decamp, personal secretary, and closest companion. During Washington's term of office, Treasury Secretary Hamilton was the guiding force of the administration and was the author of Washington's famous Farewell Address. Due to the fact that Hamilton also had a history of intense friendships with men, there has been speculation — but no hard evidence — that the relationship went further than that.

WHALE, JAMES. (1896-1957), *U.S. film director.* Whale is best remembered for the quartet of successful horror classics he directed in the 1930s: *Frankenstein, The Bride of Frankenstein, The Old Dark House,* and *The Invisible Man.* To each, he brought sophistication, a fluid camera style, and unmistakable wit. He was a perfectionist and a bit of an eccentric in an industry more comfortable with compromise and predictability; he was also quite openly gay and, according to some sources, often entertained guests at his home by reading extracts from his own explicitly homoerotic diary. For many years he and Hollywood producer David Lewis were lovers.

Four years after a bitter artistic dispute with Universal Studios, Whale retired. After a disastrous attempt at a comeback in 1949 and a series of debilitating strokes, he committed suicide in 1957.

WHITMAN, WALT. (1819-1892), *U.S. poet.* Best known for his ambitious collection of poems, *Leaves of Grass,* Whitman has had an enormous influence on the development of modern poetry, as well as on the modern gay movement. Although his own homosexuality has been the subject of great debate, his verses actually leave little room for doubt on the subject. The most clearly homosexual of his poems are in-

Michael Willhoite

Walt Whitman

cluded in the *Calamus* section of *Leaves of Grass,* in which he dealt with the "institution of the dear love of comrades." In the poem "When I Heard at the Close of Day," the poet describes his truly happiest moment as being when "the one I loved most lay sleeping by me under the same cover in the cool night . . . And his arm lay lightly around my breast — and that night I was happy."

Whitman apparently formed a number of close attachments with men in his life, but only one is clearly documented. This was with Peter Doyle, a trolley-car conductor to whom Whitman wrote a long series of letters between 1868 and 1880. In these letters Whitman expressed intense feelings for Doyle, and closed with such phrases as "Many, many loving kisses to you."

At one point, the English poet and sexologist, John Addington Symonds, with whom Whitman carried on a longstanding correspondence, inquired point-blank about Whitman's sexual orientation. In his response, Whitman hotly denied having any homosexual tendencies. Those scholars who have rejected the idea that Whitman was homosexual have depended largely on this letter to back up their argument. Whitman's homosexuality is now almost universally accepted among scholars.

WILDE, DOLLY. (1899-1941), *British wit.* The niece of playwright Oscar Wilde, Dolly shared many traits with her famous uncle, including an extravagant wit, a literary talent expressed in brilliant conversation — and a taste for members of the same sex. "I am more Oscar-like than he was like himself," she once declared. According to contemporaries, she even looked like her uncle. "Her face," wrote Bettine Bergery, "is exactly like Aubrey Beardsley's drawing of Oscar Wilde." Dolly became renowned as part of Natalie Barney's circle in Paris in the 1930s, and for more than ten years she maintained a tumultuous, on-again, off-again love affair with Barney; their unhappy relationship drove Dolly to two suicide attempts. She became renowned as an acidic wit and brilliant conversationalist. Eventually, she abandoned Paris and returned to London, where she died in obscurity of cancer at the age of forty-one. Summing up her short and tragic life, Gertrude Stein eulogized, "Well, she certainly hadn't a fair run for her money."

WILDE, OSCAR. (1854-1900), *Irish dramatist and wit.* The legendary Irish playwright (*The Importance of Being Earnest*) and novelist (*The Portrait of Dorian Gray*) achieved fame more for his wit and flamboyance than for his writing. Even at college, he talked of "art for art's sake," decorated his room with peacock feathers, wore his hair long, and adopted the affectations which later made him a caricaturist's delight. In 1882, he boarded a ship to begin a tour in the United States, announcing to customs upon his arrival that "I have nothing to declare except my genius."

Wilde married in 1884 and fathered several children. But within a few years, his homosexual nature could no longer be suppressed. He became in-

Oscar Wilde

volved first with Robert Ross — later to serve as Wilde's literary executor — then with the young Lord Alfred Douglas. Douglas's father was furious that his son should be associated with such a man, and made charges which led to Wilde's arrest, conviction, and imprisonment on charges of sodomy. Five years later, an alcoholic and a physical wreck, Wilde died.

WILDER, THORNTON. (1897-1975), *U.S. novelist and playwright.* With the publication of *The Bridge of San Luis Rey* in 1927, Thornton Wilder achieved overnight success. He was awarded the Pulitzer Prize for the novel, and a number of other successful novels and plays followed, including the Pulitzer Prize-winning *Our Town, The Skin of Our Teeth*, and *Theophilus North*. Wilder's work broke with the realism of the 1920s, and is noted for its blending of urbane sophistication and American folksiness.

Wilder never married, and many have suggested that he was homosexual. At one point, Gore Vidal teased Wilder about a hiking trip he had taken in 1928 through France and Germany with champion heavyweight boxer Gene Tunney. Wilder himself, however, was always reticent about his sexuality and about his private life in general.

WILLIAM II (WILLIAM RUFUS). (1056?-1100), *English king.* William Rufus was the first king of England known to be accused of homosexuality. Although he was nominally a Christian, William actually practiced pagan rites which incorporated sex and sex-magic. As a result, he was constantly in conflict with the Archbishop of Canterbury, and eventually Pope Urban threatened to excommunicate the king. Among the accusations directed at the monarch was that of "the crime not spoken of between Christians."

William was killed by an arrow in the back while on a hunting expedition. Some historians believe this to have been an assassination orchestrated by his brother, who immediately seized the throne as Henry I. Another theory was that the arrow came from his lover's bow as a part of an ancient ritual in which a man was killed by his homosexual lover.

WILLIAMS, TENNESSEE. (1911-1983), *U.S. playwright.* Born Thomas Lanier Williams in Columbus, Mississippi, Williams achieved his first success with the production of *The Glass Menagerie* in 1945 and followed it two years later with his most acclaimed play, *A Streetcar Named Desire,* in 1947; *Streetcar* won both the Pulitzer Prize and the Critics' Circle Award for that year. His later plays included *Summer and Smoke, Cat on a Hot Tin Roof,* and *Suddenly Last Summer,* which aroused considerable controversy for its treatment of such subjects as lobotomy, homosexuality, and cannibalism. After the early 1960s, critics were generally disappointed with his work, and he never again wrote anything to compare with his earlier critical triumphs. Williams also authored numerous short stories and poems, as well as two novels, including *The Roman Spring of Mrs. Stone.*

Williams had been open about his homosexuality for years, but the 1975 publication of his explicitly candid *Memoirs* — in which he discussed his career, his love affairs, and his one-night stands — brought his sexuality to the attention of the general public, and created even more controversy for an already controversial author. The book was an instant national bestseller.

WITTGENSTEIN, LUDWIG. (1889-1951), *Austrian philosopher.* Among the most original philosophical thinkers of the early twentieth century was Ludwig Wittgenstein; it is said that he was so brilliant he nearly drove Bertrand Russell out of the field. Although he attended Cambridge and spent much of his time in England, Wittgenstein was born in Vienna, to a wealthy Jewish family.

In his youth, the handsome Wittgenstein often cruised Vienna for what one biographer calls "rough young men [who] were ready to cater to him sexually"; he later lived with a lover in England. His homosexuality probably had little influence on his philosophical thinking, and his family and estate did their best to keep it secret. "There are certain stories which it would be foul to relate or tell about somebody even if they were true," complained an executor of his estate after a biographer touched on this aspect of Wittgenstein's life.

WOLLSTONECRAFT, MARY. (1759-1797), *British writer.* An early advocate of educational and social equality for women, Wollstonecraft led an unorthodox and controversial life. In 1774, Mary met Frances "Fanny" Blood, two years older than she, and they began an intense affair. Mary wrote to her sister, "The roses will bloom when there's peace in the breast, and the prospect of living with Fanny gladdens my heart: — You know not how I love her." They did live together for a time, but Fanny married Hugh Skeys in 1784, ending Mary's dream of living together permanently. Although Fanny died in child-birth in 1785, Mary never forgot her love.

Mary published two books with feminist themes, *Thoughts on the Education of Daughters* and *A Vindication of the Rights of Women,* before leaving London in 1792 to observe firsthand the French Revolution then in progress. During her two years in France, she delivered her first illegitimate child and named her after Fanny Blood. Returning to England in 1794, she became even more involved in radical politics, coming to know Thomas Paine and William Blake. She died eleven days after the birth of her second child, a girl whom she also named Mary. This second Mary later became famous in her own right as the wife of poet Percy Shelley and the author of *Frankenstein.*

Virginia Woolf

WOOLF, VIRGINIA. (1882-1941), *British writer.* A leading figure of the Bloomsbury group and one of the most original writers of the twentieth century, Woolf created such landmark works as *Mrs. Dalloway, Jacob's Room,* and *The Waves.*

Although the direction of Virginia Woolf's sexual orientation remains open to debate, it seems that the greatest love of her life was Vita Sackville-West. The two women may never actually have had a physical relationship, but Virginia Woolf's deep feelings of esteem and affection for Sackville-West are undeniable. In fact, it was in honor of Sackville-West that she wrote the novel *Orlando,* in which the main character starts out as a man and becomes a woman.

Throughout her life, Woolf suffered bouts of insanity. In 1941, she committed suicide by drowning herself.

Alexander Woollcott

WOOLLCOTT, ALEXANDER. (1887-1943), *U.S. journalist and critic.* An acerbic theater critic, journalist, and radio commentator from the 1920s to the early 1940s, Woollcott was variously described by other prominent figures as "a butterfly in heat," "a New Jersey Nero who mistakes his pinafore for a toga," and "a fat duchess holding out her dirty rings to be kissed." He was renowned (and sometimes despised) for his often scathing reviews and for his devastating wit, as when he wrote of pianist and writer Oscar Levant, "There's nothing wrong with Oscar Levant — nothing that a miracle couldn't fix."

Woollcott, who enjoyed dressing as a woman in college and who handed out calling cards introducing himself as "Alexandra Woollcott," was apparently tormented much of his life by confused sexual feelings. Even after he had achieved fame, he once sobbingly confessed to playwright Anita Loos that all of his life he had wanted to be a woman. Whether he was ever actively homosexual, however, remains a matter of speculation.

YOURCENAR, MARGUERITE. (1903-1987), *French writer.* Yourcenar was born in Belgium and was a French national, but lived much of her life in the United States. In 1981 she received France's highest intellectual honor when she was named to the Academie Francaise — the first woman ever honored in that manner.

Yourcenar was a translator, critic, and scholar, but she is best known for her novels. The most famous of these is *Memoirs of Hadrian*, published in 1951. In this fictional memoir, she portrays a passionate romance between the Roman emperor Hadrian and his lover Antinous.

Marguerite Yourcenar

In her author's note to *Hadrian*, Yourcenar wrote that she should have dedicated the novel to Grace Frick, her lifetime companion, but "even the longest dedication is too short and too commonplace to honor a friendship so uncommon . . . [with someone] who leaves us ideally free, but who nevertheless obliges us to be fully what we are."

INDEX

Other books of interest from
ALYSON PUBLICATIONS

☐ **THE GAY BOOK OF LISTS,** by Leigh Rutledge, $7.00. Leigh Rutledge has compiled a fascinating, informative and highly entertaining collection of lists that range from the historical (6 gay or bisexual popes) to the political (17 outspoken anti-gay politicians) and the outrageous (16 famous men, all reputedly very well-hung).

☐ **OUT OF ALL TIME,** by Terry Boughner, $7.00. Terry Boughner scans the centuries from ancient Egypt to modern America to find scores of the past's most interesting gay and lesbian personalities. He brings you the part of history they left out in textbooks. Imaginatively illustrated by Washington *Blade* artist Michael Willhoite.

☐ **UNNATURAL QUOTATIONS,** by Leigh Rutledge, $8.00. The author of *The Gay Book of Lists* has been back digging through his files and has put together this entertaining collection of quotations by or about gay people. Well-illustrated and indexed for handy reference, *Unnatural Quotations* is another must for your bookshelf.

☐ **THE TWO OF US,** by Larry Uhrig, $7.00. The author draws on his years of counseling with gay people to give some down-to-earth advice about what makes a relationship work. He gives special emphasis to the religious aspects of gay unions.

☐ **THE LAVENDER COUCH,** by Marny Hall, $8.00. Here is a guide to the questions that should be considered by lesbians or gay men considering therapy or already in it: How do you choose a good therapist? What kind of therapy is right for you? When is it time to leave therapy?

☐ **QUATREFOIL,** by James Barr, introduction by Samuel M. Steward, $8.00. Originally published in 1950, this book marks a milestone in gay writing: it introduced two of the first non-stereotyped gay characters to appear in American fiction. For today's reader, it remains an engrossing love story, while giving a vivid picture of gay life a generation ago.

☐ **REFLECTIONS OF A ROCK LOBSTER: A story about growing up gay,** by Aaron Fricke, $6.00. When Aaron Fricke took a male date to the senior prom, no one was surprised: he'd gone to court to be able to do so, and the case had made national news. Here Aaron tells his story, and shows what gay pride can mean in a small New England town.

☐ **COMING OUT RIGHT, A handbook for the gay male,** by Wes Muchmore and William Hanson, $6.00. The first steps into the gay world — whether it's a first relationship, a first trip to a gay bar, or coming out at work — can be full of unknowns. This book will make it easier. Here is advice on all aspects of gay life for both the inexperienced and the experienced.

☐ **UNBROKEN TIES: Lesbian Ex-Lovers,** by Carol Becker, Ph.D., $8.00. Lesbian relationships with ex-lovers are complex and unusual ways of building alternative families and social networks. Carol Becker's interviews with numerous pairs of ex-lovers tell the trauma of breaking-up, the stages of recovery, and the differing ways of maintaining close emotional connections with former lovers.

☐ **BETTER ANGEL,** by Richard Meeker, $6.00. For readers fifty years ago, *Better Angel* was one of the few positive images available of gay life. Today, it remains a touching, well-written story of a young man's gay awakening in the years between the World Wars.

☐ **WE CAN ALWAYS CALL THEM BULGARIANS: The Emergence of Lesbians and Gay Men on the American Stage,** by Kaier Curtin, $10.00. Despite police raids and censorship laws, many plays with gay or lesbian roles met with success on Broadway during the first half of this century. Here, Kaier Curtin documents the reactions of theatergoers, critics, clergymen, politicians and law officers to the appearance of these characters. Illustrated with photos from actual performances.

☐ **REVELATIONS: A collection of gay male coming out stories,** edited by Wayne Curtis, $8.00. Twenty-two men, ranging in age from their teens to their seventies, tell their own coming out stories. No book has ever presented such a varied and personal look at coming out as a gay man in modern America.

☐ **ONE TEENAGER IN TEN: Writings by gay and lesbian youth,** edited by Ann Heron, $4.00. One teenager in ten is gay; here, twenty-six young people tell their stories: of coming to terms with being different, of the decision how — and whether — to tell friends and parents, and what the consequences were.

These titles are available at many bookstores, or by mail.

— — — — — — — — — — — — — — — — — — — —

Enclosed is $_____ for the following books. (Add $1.00 postage when ordering just one book; if you order two or more, we'll pay the postage.)

1. _____   2. _____

3. _____   4. _____

5. _____   6. _____

name: _____ address:_____

city:_____state:_____zip:_____

ALYSON PUBLICATIONS
Dept. B-19, 40 Plympton St., Boston, Mass. 02118

After Dec. 31, 1991, please write for current catalog.